Praise for *West of Eden*

"As a gray army of undertakers gather in Sacramento to bury California's great dreams of equality and justice, this wonderful book, with its faith in the continuity of our state's radical-communitarian ethic, replants the seedbeds of defiant imagination and hopeful resistance."
—Mike Davis, author of *City of Quartz* and *Magical Urbanism*

"Utopias—we can't live without them, nor within them, for long. In *West of Eden* we see California, an earthly utopia, and the 1960s, a utopian moment, in full flower. Brave souls creating a heavenly host of communal spaces on the edge of America, hoping to break free of a world apital, sexism, oligarchy, race. An amazing place and time that, for all its f s, c..uged the world—and which finally gets its due in this marvelous collection."
—Richard Walker, UC Berkeley, author of *The Country in the City*

"There are a lot of versions of the 1960s, and this is one that isn't stale or familiar, a book by a lot of good writers and original thinkers about how some much older ideas about the commons and the community were tinkered with, enlarged upon, turned into experiments that sometimes succeeded, sometimes failed, but left legacies that mattered. It's also a book about California's tendency to go experimental, idealistic, and eclectic, a fit successor to the classic *California's Utopian Colonies* that looked at some of the great nineteenth-century experiments."
—Rebecca Solnit, author of *Storming the Gates of Paradise*

"The counterculture—from the North Beach Parnassus to the underground press—and 'the Movement'—from Marxists to anarchists—all of it depended on a magnificent base, and here it is described, magnificently: the Oakland breakfast program, the Alcatraz occupation, the Mime troupe, and pot farms, the communes, the collectives, the co-ops of California during the 1960s. On the lam? A bad trip? Burnt out? Cracking up? AWOL? Dropping out? Requiring metamorphosis? These could provide rural and urban alternatives to old W patriarchy, speed-up, or death in the jungle. With roots in previous deca of struggle by trade unions, ethnic enclaves, religious breakaways, and nineteenth-century dreams, and with branches in the lore of our own contemporary foodways, child-rearing practices, decision-making and meeting protocols, sexual politics, and DIY culture, the California communards cleared the path. Both veterans and young folk, grey-hairs and newbies, will find beautiful memoire, authentic experience, and brilliant analysis in the pages of *West of Eden*

arta Manifesto

The Retort imprint publishes books and pamphlets in the spirit of resistance to capital and empire, emerging from the collaborative activity of the Retort group of antinomian writers, artists, and artisans.

RETORT

West of Eden

Communes and Utopia in Northern California

West of Eden
Communes and Utopia in Northern California

Edited by
Iain Boal, Janferie Stone, Michael
Watts, and Cal Winslow

RETORT

ISBN: 978-1-60486-427-4
Library of Congress Control Number: 2011927960

Cover design by Lisa Thompson (www.duckdogdesign.com)
Cover illustration by Mona Caron (www.monacaron.com)
Retort logo by Lori Fagerholm (www.lorifagerholm.blogspot.com)
Layout by Jonathan Rowland

10 9 8 7 6 5 4 3 2 1

PM Press
PO Box 23912
Oakland, CA 94623
www.pmpress.org
Printed in the USA on recycled paper, by the Employee Owners of Thomson-Shore in Dexter, Michigan.
www.thomsonshore.com

Contents

For Jeff Lustig

Bay Area denizen,
radical communitarian,
and dean of California Studies

Acknowledgments

The editors would like to extend their thanks, first and foremost, to the *West of Eden* contributors, who have given generously of their time and energy in this collective effort; to the dozens of communards, cooperators, and intransigent utopians who gathered at various events—conferences, workshops, and convivia—in Berkeley and Mendocino, to excavate and discuss the history of commoning in California; and to all those who shared their experiences over the microphone or around the tables at Arch Street, Gibney Lane, Jughandle Farm, the Caspar headlands and Albion Ridge. Their communal memories gave form and their enthusiasm fuel to a project both lengthy and heterogeneous, a many-hued patchwork of memoir and documentation, testimony and analysis.

Among the many people who helped, unstintingly, in the weaving of *West of Eden*—informing, enriching, nourishing what the book became—we wish to acknowledge in particular the assistance of Zo Abell, Russell Bartley, Sylvia Erickson Bartley, Gillian Cartwright Boal, Jim Boydstun, Michaela Brennan, Summer Brenner, Charles Briggs, James Brook, Chris Carlsson and *Shaping San Francisco*, Edward Castillo, Lincoln Cushing and *Docs Populi*, Massimo De Angelis, Erin Elder, Tom Farber, Jack Forbes, Carmen Goodyear, John Gillis, Shirley Guevera, Bill Heil, Margo Hinkel and the pioneers of Project Artaud, Dawn Hofberg-Schlosser, Helen Jacobs, Billy X Jennings, Dave Jenson, Judith Keyssar, Sara Kirkpatrick, Walter Kirkpatrick, Jeff Kitzes, Art Kopecky the chronicler of New Buffalo and keeper of the communal flame, Sasha Lilley, Peter Linebaugh, Andrea Luna, Malcolm Margolin, Claude Marks and the Freedom Archives, Joseph Matthews, Marina McDougall, Bruce and Rosalind Moore, Richard Moore, Vijaya Nagarajan, Micah Perks, Joan Peterson, Megan Shaw Prelinger, Rick Prelinger, Mary Beth Pudup, Retort and its sustaining web of friendships, Walter Schneider, Carl Schoen, Steve Seid and the Pacific Film Archive,

Faith Simon, Penny Stinson, Terry Stone, Lee Swenson, Jim Tarbell, Judy Tarbell, Davis Teselle, Jason Wallach, Annie Waters, Dick Whetstone, Margie Whetstone, Diana Wiedemann, Andrea Wilder, Loyes Wilkinson, Mac Wilkinson, Tom Wodetzki, Eddie Yuen, and the late H.K. Yuen's Social Movement Archive and Frog in the Well Project.

A special word of thanks are due to Mona Caron and Lisa Thompson for their artistic and graphic skills with the cover design; the *détournement* of Holbein's woodcut—the frontispiece to *Utopia*—might have made even Sir Thomas More smile. Zoe Friedman-Cohen assiduously researched the illustrations, for which we are indebted to the Bancroft Library and staff, and to Tom Copi, William Gedney, Michelle Vignes, the Graduate Theological Union in Berkeley, Stephen Shames, the Stanford University Library (Special Collections), and Ramón Sender.

We are grateful to the Mendocino Institute and the Institute of International Studies, UC Berkeley for hosting the inaugural workshop and conferences; to Berkeley's Townsend Center for the Humanities for material support; and to the now dismantled Department of Community Studies, UC Santa Cruz, which was born on the floodtide of the 1960s and for forty years worked to keep the idea of the commons alive.

Finally, we are gratified that *West of Eden* is being published by PM Press, and encouraged by their unflagging support. The tireless editorial skills of Gregory Nipper, Jonathan Rowland, and Romy Ruukel brought order to an unruly manuscript, and Ramsey Kanaan is that *rarissima avis*, a publisher who combines comradely and practical good sense, a sharp wit, and fierce commitment to a better world.

IB, JJS, CW, MW
September 2011
Berkeley, San Francisco, Mendocino

Prologue
Iain Boal

West of Eden is the fruit of an extensive project conceived and organized by a quartet—two historians, a geographer, and an anthropologist by trade—all of whom have also by affinity been involved in the communal life of one sort or another.

The "Communes Project," as it was first called, began in 2003 as a collaboration between the Institute of International Studies at the University of California, Berkeley and the Mendocino Institute based near Fort Bragg on the coast of Northern California. The project focused from its inception on the extraordinary efflorescence of secular communal ventures initiated in the mid to late 1960s and flourishing into the 1970s across the Bay Area and its hinterland.

There is of course a long and rich tradition of communitarian living in the new world, and in California in particular. There was no singular point of origin for the remarkable burst of communal energy. There were simultaneous experiments in metropolitan and rural settings across a swath of different environments, and encompassing a variety of ethnic and racial communities. Although the phenomenon was ubiquitous, it is incontestable that the Bay Area provided one of the most generative settings in which a range of communal movements came to fruition—if "movements" is a term that can be justified, and we believe it can.

We were aware that the chronicling of this movement has barely been approached—with distinguished exceptions who are mostly represented in this volume. In particular, the deep history of utopian communities owes a large debt to the sociological labors of Timothy Miller, whose books on nineteenth- and twentieth-century communes are an essential resource for students of the subject, and whose survey of Californian communalism opens Part 1 of *West of Eden*. The striking dearth of new work on the topic requires explanation in itself; it must surely be related to the knowing smile, the weary condescension that greets the word "commune," and to the general anathematizing of the '60s examined in Michael Watts's retrospect in the concluding "Legacies" section.

To complement Miller's historical overview, we found Michael Doyle's book *Imagine Nation: The American Counterculture of the 1960s and '70s* (edited with Peter Braunstein) to be an indispensible *vade mecum* in this project, pointing to the legacies of that time. For tens of thousands of Americans, the experiencing of a life in common, one that consciously rejected dominant modes of consumption and representation, even if later disavowed, proved to be formative and surprisingly enduring. Is it an exaggeration to say that the antisystemic politics and organizing style evident in Seattle a full generation later had their roots in the collective antinomian struggles of the '60s?

West of Eden aims to synthesize the elements that composed the Communes Project: ethnographic fieldwork of a sort, depending sometimes on flashbacks, usefully supplemented by FOIA documents based on unobtrusive FBI note-takers; a memorable Mayday workshop at Jughandle Farm in Mendocino; an undergraduate course entitled Experiments in Community; two conferences in Berkeley focusing on the country communes of Albion Ridge, Mendocino, as a type of case study, and the second focusing specifically on the phenomenon of urban communalism. We recognized early in the research that the key theoretical task was to think the rural and urban together. The project was initially framed between the poles of a "city vs. country" opposition, and it has proved a useful heuristic. But this framing immediately raises the question whether Morning Star and Wheeler's Ranch—the two most important communes in San Francisco's immediate hinterland—constituted in some way an intermediate "third space." In reality, the complex relations between the city and the country with respect to the network of communitarian nodes contradict any facile cliché based on dichotomizing the urban and the rural.

The other key terms of the project turn out to be no less complex and are freighted with a long, convoluted history. The lexical cluster that the contributors to *West of Eden* set resonating in productive ways—*commune, communal, communard, community, communication, commons, commoning*—are all highly charged terms and much contested. Consider the ur-commune—the Paris Commune of 1871—that lasted only seventy-three days, and was instantly the object of bourgeois hatred and scorn. Understandably. On March 18, the French government, which had fled to Versailles, sent in troops who then refused to fire on the jeering crowds; instead, they turned their weapons on the officers, shooting their commander. The Commune had begun. Factories became co-ops; education was declared free and universal; priests and nuns were evicted from schools; day nurseries were opened next to places of work. George Sand wrote to Flaubert, "[Your Commune's] chosen leaders, administrators, inspirers—are they all brigands and cretins? ...It is an orgy of self-styled renovators, who possess not an idea, not a principle." And Flaubert (no more your average bourgeois than Sand), wrote to her, "I hate democracy... Always formulas! Always gods! ...The only reasonable thing is a government of mandarins... The people is an eternal infant."

Flaubert need not have worried. The Commune was crushed by a bloody massacre of thirty thousand citizens of Paris. It was a slaughter that, if you were to believe the wall-text at the "Utopia" exhibit in the New York Public Library some years ago, the communards brought on themselves. The take-home message to the visitor was loud and clear: Thinking of realizing utopia? Forget it...they usually end in a bloodbath. The Kronstadt Soviet, the Spanish Republic, Jonestown, the Manson family, helter skelter.

The curators at the New York Public Library exhibit were, of course, by no means the only defamers of utopia. For utterly different reasons, Karl Marx snorted, "I do not write cookbooks for the kitchens of the future." In the United States, antiutopianism is linked to fear and contempt of anything that smacks of commoning, of communism. Orwell's version of it was hardly separable from anticommunism, which no doubt accounts for his popularity in Cold War America.

The relationship of utopian literature to the social experiments of the '60s is a fascinating and unstudied topic. It would be revealing to survey the bookshelves of California communes. Utopias are notoriously liable to a negative reading, even in the home of positivity. The young Philip K. Dick lit out for dystopian territory, perhaps because, as a Cold War teenager growing up in Berkeley in the 1940s, he registered the fact that on the Edenic hillside campus from which he soon dropped out, the weapons of apocalypse were being imagined and designed. Another wartime denizen of Berkeley, Ursula Le Guin, daughter of the Kroeber household on Arch Street, navigated the genre with brilliant ambiguity in *The Dispossessed*. Her anarchist utopia joins *News from Nowhere* and *Bolo-Bolo* as beacons in a mostly dismal dreamscape. The historian of urban dystopias, Mike

Davis, once said that Ernest Callenbach's *Ecotopia*, set and written in Berkeley, was the scariest book he ever read; a green—read: white—utopia, with Oakland and its ferment of Black Power nowhere on the map. Robyn Spencer's essay in Part II of this volume is an important historical corrective, exploring the Panthers' communal ethos and practices, which went much further than simply breakfast programs.

To present-day cooperators drawn to the communal life, the word "commune" itself is sufficiently embarrassing that almost nobody will own the name. They prefer the anodyne term "intentional community." "Community," after all, offends no one. In fact, it is the maximum shibboleth of the culture, with a positive valence across the entire political spectrum. A journalist on National Public Radio once introduced a sound-bite from a spokesman for the "organized crime community." Only that lonely misanthrope and quondam Berkeley mathematics professor, Ted Kaczynski, has come out publicly out against "community" as such. He continues to live a solitary existence.

Another recurrent issue, one that haunts the pages of *West of Eden*, can be expressed thus: what is it to claim that commune x, or cooperative project y, was a "success"? Or, alternatively, that it was a "failure"? It is striking how little one can gauge the true significance of some communal endeavor, either for the participants or for the wider society, by knowing only its lifespan. The sharing of a house in common that might have lasted but one summer often had effects that continue to resonate forty years on in the lived experience of those involved, far beyond its brief moment. To take one notorious local example, how should the collapse of the Berkeley Co-op in the late 1980s be interpreted? Can it partly be explained as a case of corporate rip-off? Was the now universal practice of the "unit pricing" of groceries simply appropriated by the capitalist food system? Or does it rather represent a quiet triumph for those canny Finnish cooperators who founded the Berkeley Co-op in the 1930s and invented this obviously rational thing? Is it not truly a victory when unit-pricing, like the weekend, or contraception, is no longer tagged as "radical" but belongs to all, and is generalized across the globe?

Another thorny question involves the issue of periodization. This is of course a perennial problem for historians, but especially when it comes to the 1960s. Decadalism is distinctly uncooperative in this case. It has led to statements such as, "The '60s didn't begin till 1964, and went on well into the '70s." Fair enough; indeed, you could go further and push the '60s back, so to speak, into the '50s, especially if you look past the clichés to what was happening in San Francisco during that supposedly conformist decade. Fredric Jameson's 1984 essay "Periodizing the Sixties" remains an essential starting point for those attempting to chronicle and comprehend the tangled complexities of the historical moment of *West of Eden*.

There is further the difficult matter of the old race/gender/class triad. The dimensions of race and class, perhaps more than gender, are typically occluded in discussions of communalism, partly because communes, especially the rural communes, were overwhelmingly white and so-called middle class. The issue of Native America and its vexed relation to the counterculture has already been alluded to. The chapters by Robyn Spencer on the communalism of the Black Panthers and by Janferie Stone on the collective arrangements during the Native American occupation of Alcatraz begin to fill a historiographical void. As to class, the issues of livelihood, of money, of resources and the need for sharing of goods and property, were surely on the minds of the Panthers. And they were never far from the minds of many rusticating communards. Were they outside capital? Hardly. Not a few communes foundered precisely because some members of the beloved community, especially when it came to care of children, could call on "outside capital." The demands of the cash nexus, the regime of private property (such as ground rent) and the reign of the commodity constituted a force-field that soon enough produced the elephant on the Northern Californian common—"green gold."

The researches into the lives of the communards of Albion Ridge presented in *West of Eden* offer an illuminating account of one central, specifically rural, aspect of the counterculture of the '60s and '70s. The history of this movement has not been told, even though the legacy of Californian communes of that period permeates the wider culture in ways that are mostly unacknowledged and urgently demand documentation and analysis. The great commoning experiment was a major thread in the development of the U.S. Left, and its aftermath can be detected in many facets of contemporary American life—for example, in foodways, in the protocols of group meetings and decision-making, in sexual politics and child-rearing, in the practices of civic life and local politics, in a very widespread green sensibility, and in a general valorization of "community."

*

Our focus on California in no way denies the very widespread phenomenon of communalism in the '60s and '70s. It insists, however, on the Bay Area and the Mendocino coast as one of the richest sites of commoning and communal life since the inception of the long postwar capitalist boom. *West of Eden* tells this story—this tragicomedy, some would say—in four acts; the opening and closing sections flank the two central, contrapuntal parts that reflect the spatial logic of the history we aim to tell.

Part I opens with Timothy Miller's overview of the counterculture and communes in California, including historical antecedents both of communal movements in the widest sense, as well as the more immediate context of the remarkable burst of '60s communalism in city and country. Miller, the dean of communal studies in the United States, begins his survey with the observation that "a historical account of communes in California should begin with American Indian communities, or perhaps the Spanish missions." He focuses, however, on "communes founded in California mainly by non-Hispanic, non-Indian people since the mid-nineteenth century," including Fountain Grove by the Brotherhood of the New Life, the Icarians of Cloverdale, the socialists at Kaweah in the High Sierra, and Llano de Rio in Antelope Valley, Southern California, the single largest of all California communes—with 1,100 members at one point—before moving on to the '60 and '70s.

The second essay in Part I focuses on the flowering of the counterculture in San Francisco. Michael Doyle, a communard-historian, recalls first hearing of the Diggers "when they were lionized by the news media during 1967's Summer of Love, by which time the group's freewheeling experiment in the institutionalization of *communitas* was in high gear. ...The operative term for [their] various enterprises was 'free,' a word that in the Digger lexicon was used as noun, verb, and modifier indicating a plan of action. The collective maintained that the desired goal of maximal personal freedom would be realized only when the goods and services essential to social life were provided gratis to all." Doyle's excavation of the Diggers and the Free Family is exemplary of the work of retrieval urgently needed, in particular oral histories of the generation now passing.

The third essay considers the origins of '60s communalism in the context of the development of postwar radicalism and bohemian life in the Bay Area. The editors asked the doyen of California studies, Jeff Lustig, to frame his analysis in light of the following question: "What were the conditions of possibility of the events of the '60s in the San Francisco Bay Area?" Lustig suggests that the answer lies partly in the proximity of two great commons in the East Bay and San Francisco, respectively: the campus of a large public university, and the Golden Gate Park and its panhandle, the latter a site of a successful legal struggle by Ron Davis and his Mime Troupe to stage political theatre in the open air.

Lustig's suggestive hypothesis about the Bay Area as generative node of communalist experiment is followed by the account of a young East Coast runaway who ended up in a California commune, but one far from the Golden Gate. Jesse Drew, who later settled in San Francisco and became a pioneer in the independent media scene, tells the story of his journey to, and life at, the Black Bear commune in Trinity County near the Oregon border. Drew describes the continental network of communes through which he passed en route to Black Bear in terms of "autonomous" or "outlaw" zones, and remembers that "far from evoking a feeling of isolation and desolation, [they] encouraged a great feeling of liberation and self-reliance for many of us. It was the clearest example that the new vision many of us had for a new way of living actually worked. The remoteness of our existence created the perfect laboratory environment to explore and develop alternatives to an oppressive and shallow status quo, from social governance to technology to food production."

In comparison to the grand blueprints of nineteenth-century New World utopian communities, charted in Dolores Hayden's classic *Seven American Utopias*, the communes of the 1960s and '70s were for the most part improvised, ad hoc affairs. Almost all communal housing was adapted from existing structures and refunctioned to new collective projects—either Victorians or empty industrial buildings in the urban context or abandoned farmhouses beyond the city. Hippie architecture is a byword for the bodged and the half-built, but Simon Sadler's essay on the dialectics of hippie enlightenment excavates some radically fresh ideas about the form and materials of human shelter. Of course, the iconic utopian form associated with the rusticating counterculture is Buckminster Fuller's geodesic dome, a Cold War modernist object which has not weathered well (it leaks in sixty-four places), but did express commitment to a new world—albeit in tension with a nostalgia for the traditional and the indigenous.

Part II, "The City," focuses on the urban pole of the counterculture and its communal practices. One notable feature of the scene in

San Francisco was the burgeoning of the "underground" press, which both reflected and in part constituted the countercultural milieu. If the posters and anarchist comics—above all the indelible style and tone of R. Crumb—endure as the hallmark of the period, the graphic arts were carried on a flood of literary productions, mostly ephemeral, though some found their niche in the form of the "free weekly." The tone, the styles and the sheer weirdness of the Bay Area scene are distilled in the fading pages of newspapers such as the *Express Times* and the *Berkeley Barb*, which were countercultural organs in the struggle to create communal spaces in which to live, work, and perform.

One such space was Project Artaud, which began technically as a squat in an immense, disused factory in San Francisco under Potrero Hill. The struggle of the artists and artisans of the Artaud building to legalize their status lasted twenty years, and the residents became pioneers of the urban live/work movement, not to mention unwilling experts in zoning law. Project Artaud also became a model for city managers across the United States, as they devised schemes in the aftermath of deindustrialization for urban regeneration and renewal. In the late '60s, fights between government bureaucracies and the new commoners over violation of building regulations were so ubiquitous that we came to call the general phenomenon "code wars."

On another front, two path-breaking chapters consider the intersection of communalism and revolutionary politics in "third world" movements focused in the Bay Area: the "Red Power" movement and the Black Panthers. Beginning on November 20, 1969, a group of Native Americans from a number of different tribes occupied the island of Alcatraz in San Francisco Bay, and proposed an education center, ecology center, and cultural center. During the occupation, which ended in June 1971, the Indian Termination Policy, designed to end federal recognition of tribes, was rescinded by President Richard Nixon, and the new policy of self-determination was established, in part as a result of the publicity and awareness created by the occupiers.

Robyn Spencer, a social historian of post–World War II protest movements, digs deeply into the history of the Black Panthers to reveal the party and its activities from below—in particular efforts at collective housing and the creation of autonomous spaces and institutions—beginning with free breakfast programs, free clinics, and an independent newspaper. In the face of demonization by the state and the licensed media, the Oakland-based Panthers were at least fortunate in having access to the Bay Area's independent radio station, KPFA, whose importance to the local counterculture would be hard to overestimate. Pacifica Radio had its beginnings in the late 1940s as an intervention by anarcho-syndicalist war resisters aiming to present individual voices of conscience, dedicated to radical dialogics in a mediascape dominated by commerce and Cold War propaganda. Over the course of the '60s, KPFA morphed into a "community" radio station seen as an instrument serving the various liberation movements. KPFA's loose programming format—the result of a conscious decision by the founders of Pacifica to reject the Fordist, wall-to-wall commercialism of AM radio, in the belief that the politics was in the form as much as in the content—was unwittingly congruent with the relaxed style of the counterculture.

Felicity Scott's chapter complements the history of Project Artaud in San Francisco and delves into the dramatic case of two notable—and notorious—Bay Area communes, Morning Star and Wheeler's Ranch, located in the immediate hinterland of Sonoma County. Scott, a historian of art and architecture, traces the consequences of attempting "an exodus from official systems of managing land and the built environment—from property rights and trespass laws to building codes as well as health and safety regulations." It turns out that the firefighter's axe and the bulldozer are waiting for those who choose the commoning life and who challenge too directly the codes of capital's spatial order. One of the central figures in the San Francisco counterculture, particularly the music scene, was Ramón Sender, who has become a guardian of the flame and historian of Morning Star and Wheeler's. His own trajectory reveals a direct link between the utopian communities of the nineteenth century— the Mennonites and the Bruderhof—and the communalism of the '60s. Another communard turned remembrancer, Art Kopecky, whose memories and reflections have greatly enriched the *West of Eden* project, exemplified the "hippie" diaspora into the interior. He left the Bay Area to join the New Buffalo community in the southwest, and his diaries provide a vivid portrait of daily life "down on the commune."

In Part III, the focus shifts to the Mendocino coast. Cal Winslow, historian of working-class upheaval, primitive rebels, and Redwood ecologies, examines the chain of communes on Albion Ridge and their relation to the back-to-the-land movement. He describes the efforts to create more than the sum of the communes—a nation, some proposed. This included a community center, a food co-op, eventually a school, plus a host of social and cultural activities—hence the Albion nation. It became a politicized community as communards joined in the "code wars," the "whale wars," the rural ecology movement, the campaign against offshore oil drilling, Redwood Summer and a tradition of activism that endures to this day. In addition, he raises important questions considering the nature and efficacy of utopian thinking. In this section, four communards, three of them women, give accounts of their own paths to Albion. This is of particular interest given the flowering of a rural feminism that stands in contrast to images of male-driven movements and macho gurus. The publication *Country Women*, produced in Mendocino Country, was read nationally.

In the chapter that follows, "Our Bodies, Our Communal Selves," the anthropologist Janferie Stone, herself a veteran communard, describes the scene in an existential sense: "The communal movement must be posed against our sense of the world as a terminally dangerous place. Our dreams were reft by images of nuclear holocaust; we were the generation who had practiced hiding under our desks in the Cuban Missile Crisis. We had bomb shelter visions of a world that, if poisoned, might begin anew. Humanity, nuclearly cleansed, tutored by destruction, might do better in such a future. With the bodies of young men on line for the morass of Vietnam and American cities setting fire breaks against racial conflagration, we were bodies, almost without volition, moving away from the flames of a societal alienation that intensified. Our eyes opened through the mind-bends of drugs from marijuana to LSD, we saw the world as disintegrating. We thought that in a community of scale we could pick up the pieces, we could create if not a new society then an *On the Beach* fulfillment of each day that we had yet to live. We could take care of ourselves."

In Part IV, the concluding section, we consider the legacies of communalism that in a great variety of forms permeate the wider culture. The echo of the commune, if you listen for it, can be heard virtually everywhere in contemporary California, and far beyond. These legacies, it should be noted here at the outset, are profoundly ambiguous. Consider two or three of the most notorious slogans of the epoch. Take the slogan "free love"—it was no doubt subversive of the Cold War patriarchal order, while also congruent with the libertarian *Playboy* philosophy/phantasy. But it certainly did not impress some second-wave feminists; "Guru," said one ex-communard, "is short for sexual predator."

"Free land," likewise—the other half of the motto of Black Bear Ranch (the commune on the far northern edge of California, the focus of Jesse Drew's essay)—is an attempted critique of capitalist property relations of exclusion and enclosure. But it has deep historical connection to Jacksonian dispossession and the Westering Anglo empire. To the expropriated grandchildren and great-grandchildren of the Miwok and Modoc, it would be hard for "free land" not to trigger the memory of recent genocide. It is all the more bitter to some that the rusticating hippies spent a lot of time playing Indian, in all sincerity romancing "the red man" and intending to honor the ancestral inhabitants of Alta California. These ironies multiply in Ray Raphael's description of the pacifist hippie turning into the libertarian gun-toting marijuana farmer.

"Do your own thing" was the mantra on the lips of the passengers in Ken Kesey's bus when it erupted from the La Honda commune deep in the redwoods between Palo Alto and the Pacific. The message came blasting from the Merry Pranksters' PA system across the heartland—a suggestive slogan for drive-by shouting and no doubt meant to disturb mindless conformism in the unhip, Fordist suburbs. But could any proverb be a better motto for yuppies in training or for late capitalist narcissism? And so, the editors of this volume have tried to be mindful of the cunning of history.

One of the more complex, contradictory legacies of the '60s in California is to be found in the culture of Silicon Valley, which drew deeply from the communal wells of the Bay Area counterculture, refracted through the utopian globalism of the *Whole Earth Catalog*, bible of the rusticating hippies and back-to-the-landers who imagined an alternative green world powered by appropriate technics, available for purchase by mail order. The historian Fred Turner, in an illuminating study of digital utopianism, has shown how this unlikely trajectory has depended on the transvaluation of the computer from a Cold War accessory to omnicide and "soul murder" into a convivial tool of personal liberation, from an icon of disembodiment and dehumanization into the means to new forms of equality and transformation. Lee Worden, in his essay on counter/cyber culture, peers behind the Friday dresscode and the dissimulation of hierarchy spawned within the military-industrial-academic complex, where hierarchies have been replaced by flattened structures, long-term employment by short-term, project-based contracting, and professional positions by complex, networked forms of sociability; the current state of the art can be found at Google headquarters. Worden, a systems biologist and student of cybernetics, reviews the material and historical links between the counterculture and the emergent cyberculture as well as the forms of commoning that lie in the hidden roots of the Silicon Valley hacker community.

Ray Raphael's chapter explores the transforming of the rural counterculture and the adaptation of hippie values to the criminalized business of marijuana production as it came to dominate the economy of Northern California.

Lastly, Michael Watts, geographer and founder of political ecology, takes stock of the extraordinary historical conjuncture represented by the late '60s and concludes that 1968 did represent, as Marshall Berman put it, a sort of tragedy born of militant activism, prefiguring the slide into encounter culture, paranoia, and helter skelter. But in his retrospect of that moment, "Caught of the Hop of History," Watts brings into focus the political struggle to unite two logics of different provenance, one Marxist, the other libertarian. The efforts at unification may have failed—in the crucible of the counterculture, emancipatory struggles, and domestic resistance to the Vietnam War—yet a number of 1960s innovations "enlarged the field of the possible."

During the course of the *West of Eden* project, we were often reminded of the fundamental importance of war, and resistance to war, to any full understanding of what came to be called the '60s. It is often forgotten that communes in both the country and the city were refugia, spaces of safety, networks of solidarity, for those in hiding from the state. We are once more living in a time of war and a period of crises of legitimacy for the institutions of capitalist modernity. We may be entering another period when the possibility of serious change, at the level of society itself, is not dismissed as a utopian illusion. In the words of one participant in those heady days, the experience "has forever made me optimistic about history. Having lived through it, I can't ever say, 'It will never happen.'"

We are struck by the desire of today's young people not only to get out from under the long shadow of the '60s, but at the same time to learn about this history and even to discuss the possibilities of renewing communalism and cooperative projects of many different kinds. While we found in the course of research that almost none of the children of communes were keen to repeat the experiment of their own upbringing, or anything much like it, they appreciate being part of a kinship group larger than the modal nuclear family, and very grateful to be in a rich, far-flung network of siblings.

Ultimately, the communes of the Bay Area were only one aspect of a general spontaneous flowering of the practice of "commoning" in myriad forms. Indeed, talk of "commons" has lately become widespread, despite (or perhaps because of) neoliberal structural adjustment that has privatized or done away with much of what remained of the California commons. Commons has also become a key term among the peer-to-peer Internet community that is fighting for free and open access against the enclosure of the Internet by corporate claims to intellectual property. There are many direct links to the counterculture that was a spawning ground for much that is associated with the virtual life and its horizontalist ideology, explored in Lee Worden's chapter. Nevertheless, there are problems with modeling the commons in virtual, immaterial terms, and the lessons of *West of Eden* suggest that commons and commoning should be approached from below, both historically and with an eye to their future. Rights of common involve, first and before all, the earth and its productions—the fields, the gardens, the pastures, the woods and forests, the streams and rivers, the quarries and the orchards, and the gathering and the dwelling places. These mostly were, and must be again, not "resources" but the very ground of our lives. Above all, commoning is a social relation.

If this cautionary observation seems to give priority to the rural moment of the city/country dialectic as somehow more "basic," it contains a truth that the rusticating back-to-the-landers grasped, however naively at times: the cities of the future will have to minimize their parasitism on the hinterland. Experiments in cooperative living and urban farming that burgeoned in the '60s are beginning to flourish once again, prefiguring a social and ecological order... West of Eden.

Part I. Context

"For tens of thousands of Americans the experiencing of a life in common, one that consciously rejected dominant modes of consumption and representation, even if later disavowed, proved to be formative. And surprisingly enduring."

California Communes: A Venerable Tradition

Timothy Miller

Communal living has been an ongoing, if little-noticed, theme in California for over a century and a half. One could push the story back farther: the record could begin with American Indian communities, or perhaps the Spanish missions, both of which had elements of intentional community about them. But most of us would understand an intentional community as a group whose members deliberately separate themselves from the dominant society rather than simply a group of people who live near each other. Below, I will survey some communes founded in California mainly by non-Hispanic, non-Indian people since the mid-nineteenth century.

Probably the earliest commune thus defined was that of the Mormons who settled in San Bernardino in 1852, a hundred families strong. They had a strong communal existence for two years or so, after which the cooperative features of the settlement declined until 1857, when Brigham Young called them back to the Salt Lake Valley.

The first relatively long-lived California community was founded in 1875. Fountain Grove was the final community of the Brotherhood of the New Life, founded by the Spiritualist and sometime-Swedenborgian mystic Thomas Lake Harris. The Brotherhood prospered with a dairy farm and then extensive vineyards, boosted by the fortune of one of its members. Sensational and shamefully inaccurate stories in the press about sexual misconduct and abusive treatment of followers in the early 1890s led Harris to leave his comfortable community, although some members remained and continued to operate the winery for years thereafter. The buildings were eventually demolished, save one: the round barn in the northern suburbs of Santa Rosa that one can glimpse off east of Highway 101.

The year 1881 saw the birth of Icaria Speranza near Cloverdale. The Icarian movement derived from the French novel *Voyage en Icarie*, by Etienne Cabet, and was one of at least two communes in California that set out to enact fictional utopian scenarios. Cabet's followers purchased land in Texas and started to move there in 1848. Though that location proved disastrous, the group then managed to purchase Nauvoo, Illinois, recently abandoned by the Mormons. Eventually, internal dissension split the movement, and one of the Icarian bodies purchased land on the Russian River. For five years, they lived out the communal Icarian dream, making wine that they sold in their cooperative store in Cloverdale. The community lasted until 1886, when it went bankrupt.

One of the most ambitious projects of all was the Kaweah Cooperative Commonwealth, founded in 1885 near Visalia. Kaweah was the brainchild of Burnette G. Haskell and James J. Martin, socialist labor leaders in San Francisco who were inspired by a wave of communal fervor that swept through socialist circles in the latter years of the nineteenth century. They acquired land in a creative way: all forty-five colonists filed claims on adjoining tracts of homestead land at once. The colony was in full swing by 1886, and the colonists had completed the prodigious task of opening a road to their domain through the mountainous terrain of the Kaweah River valley by 1890. However, in that year the colony was destroyed by the federal government, which preempted colony land for Sequoia National Park. The government refused to compensate the colonists, claiming that their land claims were invalid. A final repudiation of the audacious socialists came when the largest tree in the world, which the colonists had named the Karl Marx tree, was renamed the General Sherman tree.

In 1893, Erastus Kelsey of Oakland and Kate Lockwood Nevins, a populist organizer, opened a commune on Winters Island, located in Suisun Bay near the confluence of the San Joaquin and Sacramento Rivers. Perhaps two dozen communards took up residence there, but the colony, alas, never got well established economically as the panic of 1893 swept the country. The resulting depression devastated the prices the colonists got for their onions and other crops, and things fell apart in the second half of the decade.

The following year, 1894, saw the creation of Altruria that like Icaria Speranza was based on a utopian novel, in this case William Dean Howells's book *A Traveller from Alturia*. The popular tale captivated the imagination of Edward Biron Payne, a young Unitarian minister, who along with half a dozen families and a few singles founded Altruria on Mark West Creek north of Santa Rosa. The pioneers built several houses and started work on a hotel and community center. Things seemed to go well, but the hotel was never finished, and within a few months the community was insolvent. Altruria was effectively finished in the summer of 1895.

The last California communal experiment of the century was established at Point Loma, near San Diego, in 1897. Following the death of founder Helena Blavatsky in 1891, the Theosophical Society fragmented, and Katherine Tingley emerged as the leader of one of the factions. At Point Loma, she built the most substantial community, in terms of its built environment, in California history. Supported by wealthy patrons including the sporting goods magnate Albert Spalding, the community featured dramatic, mystical architecture. After Tingley's death in 1929, however, the community declined. The property was sold in 1942 and is now occupied by the Point Loma Nazarene College, which operates in buildings erected for the pursuit of a radically different religion than the conservative Christianity of its current occupants. Other Theosophical communities were to follow later, including the Temple of the People near Pismo Beach; Krotona, in Hollywood and later Ojai; and the Summit Lighthouse, later known as the Church Universal and Triumphant, which was located at Malibu before it moved to Montana.

In the early twentieth century, the communal rage was small back-to-the-land farms. The first and probably best-known of them was the Little Landers project, the first of whose colonies was opened at San Ysidro under the enthusiastic leadership of William E. Smythe in 1909. Smythe believed that a family could eke out a living from the intensive cultivation of one acre, and by 1912, the colony had 116 families farming their acre plots and enjoying an active communal social and cultural life. By 1916, several other Little Landers colonies had opened elsewhere in California. Some settlers, unable to make farming on an acre pay, eventually left but the devastation of the original colony by a flood in 1916 was the biggest factor in the decline of the movement. A Little Landers museum operates today in the former community center of the Tujunga colony, however. In 1912, a similar project called Los Angeles Fellowship Farms was established by Kate D. Buck, a dentist. Fifty or sixty people settled on small plots near La Puente, but most found that they could not make a living on an acre, and the project slowly disintegrated.

Llano del Rio, founded in the Antelope Valley northeast of Los Angeles in 1914, was one of the most notable communal experiments in California history. Job Harriman, a prominent socialist attorney who became disillusioned with the prospects for socialism after losing a race for mayor of Los Angeles, turned his attention to creating the biggest commune in California history. By the summer of 1917, Llano del Rio had reached the astonishing population of 1,100 members and its atmosphere was sizzling. But it lacked the water rights it would need for enduring success, so the community moved to an abandoned lumber-company town in Louisiana in 1918, where it survived as Newllano until 1938.

At one point, the California state government sponsored two intentional communities. With appropriations of well over a million dollars, Durham and Delhi were opened in the late 1910s near Chico and Merced, respectively. Durham, particularly, had solid initial success, but both colonies fell victim to the rural depression of the early 1920s.

Holy City was one of the most eccentric of these early California communes. William Riker had been promoting his "Perfect Christian Divine Way," the most notable feature of which was white supremacy, for several years when he purchased land in the Santa Cruz Mountains in 1918. Around thirty followers joined Riker at the site, located roughly halfway between Santa Cruz and San Jose. They built a tourist-stop business there, with attractions ranging from a soda-pop factory to a zoo. The colony finally withered, not least because of Riker's arrest for sedition when he openly admitted his admiration for Adolf Hitler during World War II.

Yet another community that deserves mention is the Colony, located inland from Arcata, in which a group of Christian believers left Seattle and settled at their new location in 1940, quietly building a community that gradually became well accepted by its neighbors. A new generation of spiritual seekers rejuvenated the Colony in the 1970s, and it survives today with around a dozen members who reject human-created doctrines and ceremonies in favor of a lived faith, operating an organic farm and a plumbing business. The Colony is one of the longest-lived and most stable communes in California's history.

These brief vignettes of early communes could go on and on: California hosted the so-called "Polish Brook Farm" of Helena Modjeska at Anaheim; the raw-food vegan colony called Joyful near Bakersfield; the socialist colony called the Army of Industry at Auburn; Pisgah Grande, a religious colony near Simi Valley; the Thelemic Magic community of

Pasadena, inspired by the ceremonial magician Aleister Crowley; Trabuco College, a Vedanta commune at which Aldous Huxley lived for a time; Tuolumne Cooperative Farms, a Quaker-inspired colony near Modesto; and the Ma-Na-Har Cooperative Community at Oakhurst, also founded by Quakers. The list is extensive.

But let us move on toward the present and examine some of the plethora of communes of the 1960s era and after. There is no exact beginning to the new communalism of that period; rather, the communes were simply part of the larger emerging Zeitgeist. In the 1950s, hints of the cultural future began to emerge with publications such as Allen Ginsberg's *Howl* in 1956, the obscenity trial that followed, and the appearance of such shocking new magazines as Paul Krassner's *The Realist*. In 1959, Ken Kesey volunteered to be a subject in controlled experiments with psychoactive drugs, and soon an alternative community grew up around his home on Perry Lane in Palo Alto, where the daring new substances were freely available. Kesey moved on to a small house in La Honda, and an intentional, or perhaps unintentional, community began to emerge there. The Merry Pranksters, whose formative role in the emerging counterculture was anchored by the famous psychedelic cross-country bus trip in 1964, let us know that something new was happening.

Other parts of the new communal scene had already appeared by the time Kesey and the Pranksters became nationally known: Gorda Mountain, on the Big Sur coast, pointed the way to the open-land communes that would proliferate a few years later. In 1962, Amelia Newell, in the tiny town of Gorda, opened her land to anyone who wanted to stay here, and it became a popular bohemian stopping-off place between Los Angeles and San Francisco. Its population grew slowly, reaching a peak of perhaps two hundred during the summer of 1967, but Gorda's neighbors despised the place and managed to get it closed down in 1968.

Another piece of the mosaic of efforts emerged at about the same time as Gorda Mountain: Bob Hanson, who had grown up in the Lake Tahoe area and traveled to Ceylon to study yoga in the 1940s and had taken up Hinduism there, returned in the late 1950s to establish his own religious organization. By now known as Master Subramuniya, he bought an old brewery building in Virginia City, Nevada, and in 1962 established an intentional community for his religious movement, known as the Himalayan Academy, which helped shape the emerging new culture.

Meanwhile, outside of California, Timothy Leary and Richard Alpert had left Harvard University in 1962 amid enormous controversy over their research on LSD, and soon established the communal International Foundation for Internal Freedom in two houses in Newton, Massachusetts. The scene there resembled that of the Pranksters at La Honda, with strange music, weirdly dressed people, and psychedelically fueled behavior. Soon devotees Peggy, Tommy, and Billy Hitchcock, heirs to a huge fortune, offered Leary and company the use of their family estate at Millbrook, New York, a property of several thousand acres and many buildings, including a sixty-four-room mansion. There, a core group of twenty-five to thirty people and many visitors lived communally until about 1967, when outside pressure on the Hitchcocks had become unbearable and the place was shut down. A new communal experience, indeed.

Other experiments also pointed the way toward the communes that spread like wildfire after 1966 took place over the next couple of years. The open-land commune called Tolstoy Farm was opened in 1963, and influenced what was to come in California over the next few years. Very importantly, Drop City was founded in southern Colorado in 1965, a colony of bohemian artists who saw themselves as creating a whole new civilization, rejecting paid employment and making their art inseparable from their lives. In housing themselves, they created some of the most memorable communal architecture: geodesic-style domes colorfully covered with car tops retrieved from junkyards. Drop City was a major inspiration for the communes founded over the next few years.

Just as Drop City was getting underway, another influential commune begun to take shape in California as well. In 1965, Hugh Romney and friends were offered the free use of a farmhouse and thirty acres overlooking the San Fernando Valley if they would tend the owner's swine. From that beginning emerged the Hog Farm, which burst into national prominence as the "Please Force" at Woodstock. The Hog Farm is alive and well today, with a main enclave in Berkeley and a second location, Black Oak Ranch, near Laytonville, where Romney, now known as Wavy Gravy, runs his clown camp.

Not much later, the Diggers began contributing to the cultural scene in a way that would influence and promote communes. Living on society's leftovers and espousing a belief that everything should be free, the Diggers took a variety of people into their several communal households. Others emulated the Digger example, and for a time, informal urban communes and crashpads proliferated. Some of the scenes were chaotic, but others functioned well and introduced thousands to a new way of living.

As the Haight-Ashbury began to develop into the country's premier countercultural enclave, another landmark commune of the new era took form fifty miles to the north. Lou Gottlieb, the bassist for the popular folk-singing group the Limeliters, purchased a thirty-two acre farm in Sonoma County near Occidental. His friend Ramón Sender moved to the property in the spring of 1966, and others soon followed. No one was turned away, and the population grew steadily for a year. When the Summer of Love arrived in 1967, hundreds were living at Morning Star Ranch. Gottlieb became passionately dedicated to the precept of open land, and at one point deeded Morning Star to God. But the gospel of open land did not sit well with the Sonoma County authorities, and conflicts soon flared. Before the commune's end, county bulldozers had leveled the hand-built structures of Morning Star four times. Still, a number of dedicated souls did not give up the dream: some moved to Wheeler's Ranch nearby; others relocated to New Mexico, where they started a new Morning Star near the great communal mecca of Taos, which had blossomed after the founding of New Buffalo in 1967. Even today, when Morning Star survives mainly as an email list and an annual reunion, many of those who were there regard their Morning Star days as a peak life experience.

In 1967, Don McCoy rented the large house at Olompali Ranch, near Novato, and invited a circle of his close friends to move in. McCoy's ample checkbook paid all the bills, and for a year or so, a most mellow scene flourished, although a series of disasters led to Olompali's closing in 1969. But by then, communes were being founded at a torrid rate. In 1968, some Haight-Ashbury refugees started Table Mountain Ranch near Albion, in Mendocino County, where it continues to flourish today. Black Bear Ranch was founded about the same time in a remote location in northwest California, ten miles from any neighbor, a site chosen as a base for the revolution many thought was coming; it also continues today.

The 2007 edition of the *Communities Directory*, the most compre-hensive source available on the subject, lists over seventy active com-munities in California, and the related ic.org website, which is updated regularly, recently had an astounding 250 California listings. One could debate the status of some of those communities, which are small or in some cases exist solely as concepts that have not yet been actualized. Nevertheless, scores of intentional communities are active in California today, as they are in the rest of the nation and indeed the world. Ananda Village, founded in 1968 near Nevada City as a spiritual community by Donald Walters, or Swami Kriyananda, has a population in the hundreds. Harbin Hot Springs, a communally organized spa and resort near Middletown, has over a hundred resident members. The Magic community in Palo Alto, active in environmental work, recently listed thirty-one members. A number of religious communities also operate throughout the state, related to the Zen Centers of San Francisco and Los Angeles, various Christian churches, and several other religions ranging from the Church of Scientology to the Emissaries of Divine Light.

In the secular realm, two types of community represent the cutting edge today. One is the ecovillage movement, which seeks to create small, sustainable enclaves where people may live lightly on the earth, getting away from the prodigious consumption of resources that characterizes mainstream American life. Most of the ecovillage projects are rural, but an interesting variation is located right in the center of Los Angeles, where the principles of sustainable living are being woven into an intensely urban fabric. It will be most interesting to see how the Los Angeles Ecovillage plays out.

The fastest-growing type of community is probably cohousing. Like the ecovillage movement, cohousing seeks to use resources efficiently while creating a real sense of community that counters the alienation of so much of American life. In cohousing, people have private homes but share many facilities and typically eat several meals a week together. There are dozens of cohousing projects today in California, with more on the way.

Returning to the communes of the 1960s era, I have one last matter to address: the reason for the timing of these communities. Where did this enormous surge of communal energy come from? When I began taking a serious look at the history of the 1960s communes, the standard wisdom was they had either sprung from nowhere, like Athena from the head of Zeus, and thus were simply historical anomalies, or that they had developed in reaction to the degeneration of the counterculture—that is, as the Haight-Ashbury and other similar enclaves devolved from centers of peace and love to crime-ridden hangouts for intravenous drug users, the idealistic remnant fled the city to pursue new and communal ways of living somewhere out on the land. As it happens, both of those explanations fall wide of the mark. The communes of the 1960s era were not unconnected to history, but had clear ties to communities that came before.

The Diggers consciously named themselves after a countercultural movement of an earlier era; the Twin Oaks community in Virginia named its buildings after earlier communes—Llano, Harmony, Degania, Kaweah. Peruse the issues of *The Modern Utopian*, the magazine of the hip communes, and you will see abundant writings on communes of earlier times—of the Oneida Community, the large group-marriage commune in New York State in the nineteenth century, and the Hutterites, the Anabaptist communal farmers of the northern plains, to name but two examples. A Digger I interviewed several years ago told me that in his communal household in San Francisco, members read and discussed such works of American communal history as the *History of American Socialisms*, a survey of nineteenth-century communes written by the communal leader John Humphrey Noyes.

Did Drop City come out of nowhere? Hardly. Two of the founders had grown up in New York City as red-diaper babies, and the language of cooperation was in their red blood. The third founder was of Kansas Mennonite background, and the theme of cooperative interaction had been in his environment from birth. Lou Gottlieb, the impresario of Morning Star Ranch, had earlier been a Communist, as had Richard Marley, a red-diaper baby and cofounder of Black Bear Ranch. Piper Williams of Tolstoy Farm knew about the Catholic Worker movement, which had been operating both urban and rural communes since the 1930s. Stories of socialist, or cooperative, or communal, or at least politically progressive backgrounds are legion among the people who populated the 1960s communes.

The case of Ramón Sender, the first resident at Morning Star Ranch, is instructive. His father was an anarchist and sometime Communist in his native Spain. At age sixteen, the younger Sender met a great-granddaughter of John Humphrey Noyes, the leader of the Oneida Community in the nineteenth century. Together they visited the Oneida Mansion House, the three-hundred-room community home where her grandparents were still living. In 1957 they visited and then joined the Bruderhof, a Hutterite-like community that has endured for nearly a century, most recently in the eastern United States. For Ramón Sender, community did not come out of nowhere.

Moreover, many communes of earlier vintage were still active when the 1960s rolled around. Theosophists were still at the Temple of the People, and the Colony was alive and well in Northern California. When a new generation became interested in communal living, there were usually existing communities to visit. And visit they did, sometimes overwhelming the rather sedate older communities.

Thus it is not surprising to learn that many of the ideals and practices of the 1960s communes had solid historical precedents. Was vegetarianism, for example, something new? On the contrary, the Fruitlands Community of A. Bronson Alcott and Charles Lane, founded in 1843, avoided not only animal products in food and clothing, but the use of animals for farm work, and for good measure also forbade cotton clothing as a product of slavery. Was Lou Gottlieb doing something unprecedented when he deeded Morning Star Ranch to God? No: in the 1860s, Peter Armstrong, leader of the Celestia commune in Pennsylvania, did exactly the same thing. A yearning for a return to the land, for personal fulfillment, for simple living, for warm interpersonal relationships— those are the building blocks of intentional communities in all ages.

The problems of the communal enterprise, too, are familiar. The 1960s communes, especially the ones with open membership, had problems with deadbeats, loafers, and crazies. But what else is new? The Shakers had a long tradition of taking in "Winter Shakers," people who would come in the fall professing interest in joining and living comfortably in a colony through the winter, only to leave again when it warmed up.

As we historians like to observe, nothing comes from nowhere. Our past helps inform and define our future. California has a rich communal heritage, and it well deserves celebration.

For further reading

On California's earlier communal past, the standard survey is Robert Hine, *California's Utopian Colonies* (San Marino: Huntington Library, 1953). For an overview of the more recent past, see my *The '60s Communes: Hippies and Beyond* (Syracuse: Syracuse University Press, 1999).

Conviviality and Perspicacity: Evaluating 1960s Communitarianism

Michael William Doyle

The title of this essay, "Conviviality and Perspicacity," refers to two ways of framing and comprehending 1960s communitarianism. Before defining these two keywords, let me first as an aside explain my deliberate use of the term *communitarianism* in a book that's expressly about *communalism*. Both are linked to words such as *common, communion, communication, communism,* and *community,* and denote sharing and mutual obligation. Together they convey the essence of an approach to social life and property that sees the group and not the individual as the fundamental unit of society, a stance that forever puts it at odds with mainstream Americanism. But whereas all communes are communitarian by nature, communitarianism as a system of thought embraces many other social practices besides the commune.

As for *conviviality,* it of course connotes sociability, liveliness, festivity, élan, *gemutlichkeit*—where the sharing of good food and drink fosters fellow-feeling, happiness, boisterous joy in the presence of one's boon companions. I will forever associate this word with the 1960s counterculture because I first encountered it in the inaugural issue of the *Whole Earth Catalog,* which designated one of its sections "Tools for Conviviality." The discourse stream that flows from this trope channels both memories and analyses into a narrative about how communes, collectives, and other forms of cooperation promoted an effective antidote to anomie, the free-floating sense of alienation and breakdown in moral order that permeated America at midcentury. They also are presented as having countered the deleterious effects of radical individualism, which was then (as now) culturally ascendant across the social spectrum. The problem with viewing communitarian enterprises exclusively through the lens of conviviality is that we see tend to see "happiness" when what we were looking at was that quintessentially American endowment "the pursuit of happiness." Our nation's founding declaration did not guarantee the attainment of happiness, only that its citizens should be free from capricious governmental interference in the active search for it. Scholars and griots of 1960s communitarianism must take care not to conflate process with product. We must take care, in other words, not to read happiness back into a past that, when it was being experienced as the present, was fraught with other states of mind and emotion besides bonhomie. A misremembered past offers an illusory refuge for those unwilling to dwell fully in an unsettling present. An unsentimentalized history, on the other hand, may offer us a means to quell the fever of an overheated present.

My title's other keyword, *perspicacity*, is not the antonym of conviviality. The dictionary defines it as "acuteness of perception, the quality of discernment, intelligence manifested by being astute, the capacity to assess situations or circumstances shrewdly and to draw sound conclusions."[1] It thus should be considered an optimum complement to conviviality when casting a backward glance at our subject. My point here is to call for a disinterested assessment of 1960s communitarianism, for a constructive critique that seeks to learn what we can from these undertakings as a guide to propagating communal efforts today, while also deepening our understanding of human nature as it was expressed institutionally during an earlier time of collective duress. In so doing, however, we should be careful not prefer perspicacity to conviviality in our approach to that historical subject. An arid analysis that has drained away the impulse to hedonism, installed reason on the throne of feeling, subordinated embodied pleasure to discarnate intellectualizing will obliterate what led thousands of mostly young people in this country to yoke their lives together in peaceable pursuits and emit a defiant light against the Cold War's thermonuclear penumbra.[2]

How does one reconcile the unfettered imagination so essential to the utopian project with the practical limits of what can be accomplished

---

1   http://dictionary.reference.com, accessed February 21, 2006.

2   In 1970, the *New York Times* in a front-page story reported that it had identified "nearly 2,000 communes in 34 states." Bill Kovach, "Communes Spread as the Young Reject Old Values," (December 17, 1970), 1, 84.

in the here and now? How might one determine if the boundary between the possible and the impossible can—and should—be breached? What is the most effective and expeditious way to transform one's culture into a more perfect society? These are the questions that attracted me to study the Diggers, that loose group of what would now probably be considered performance artists who broke away from the San Francisco Mime Troupe in the fall of 1966.[3] Nearly all of the founding core hailed from the urban east and occupied a generational middle ground between the beats and the hippies. Their collective raison d'être was not principally to shock the bourgeoisie, as their training in avant-garde theater had prepared them to do. Instead, they sought to apply theatrical techniques in nontheatrical settings where, by ludic stealth, they would be used to galvanize the lotus-eating hippies of the Haight-Ashbury district into revolutionary action through spectacular happenings called simply "events." The Diggers were lionized by the news media during 1967's "Summer of Love," by which time the group's freewheeling experiment in the institutionalization of *communitas* was in high gear. Their ambitious if short-lived program consisted of operating free stores (which parodied the district's burgeoning hip boutiques and threatened to put the thrift stores out of business), a free daily outdoor food service, several communal "crash pads," a no-cost print news medium called simply "The Communications Company," a free health clinic (that paved the way for the Haight-Ashbury Free Medical Clinic), and a free transportation system throughout the Bay Area, among other schemes. The operative term for these various enterprises was "free," a word that in the Digger lexicon was used as noun, verb, and modifier indicating a plan of action. The collective maintained that the desired goal of maximal personal freedom would be realized only when the goods and services essential to social life were provided gratis to all.

How to provide such things was where the notion of play came in. For their midafternoon food-sharing ceremony in the Golden Gate Park Panhandle, the Diggers might spend the morning scavenging overripe vegetables from greengrocers, stealing bread from untended bakery

3   Michael William Doyle, "The Haight-Ashbury Diggers and the Cultural Politics of Utopia, 1965–1968." Unpublished PhD thesis, Cornell University, 1997. Some of the material in this section has been adapted from a review I published of Peter Coyote's memoir *Sleeping Where I Fall: A Chronicle* (Washington, DC: Counterpoint Press, 1998) in *Utopian Studies* 12, no. 2 (2001): 287–90.

delivery trucks, or stewing venison from a donated, fresh, road-killed deer. No one knew where the ingredients of each day's feast would come from. The act of hustling and preparing this meal constituted "guerrilla theater," an idea Peter Berg borrowed from Mime Troupe founder R.G. Davis and then altered to suit the purposes of actors who performed without stage, script, or even an audience per se. In the Diggers' dramaturgy, one attempted to persuade an unsuspecting public, initially consisting of youthful flower children and their "straight" defenders, to temporarily suspend their reflexive disbelief in communitarian property relations. The Diggers hoped to demonstrate that it was possible to "create the condition you described," in this case meaning that when a community's members voluntarily contributed according to their means and received according to their basic needs, there would be enough to go around. (Theft on behalf of public redistribution was justified by way of Rousseau's axiom that sometimes one needed to force others to be free.)

Of course, the Diggers faced no shortage of obstacles in keeping this production going, especially in maintaining its playful nature as the Haight's population swelled with thousands of scene-making hedonists, vagrants, teenaged runaways, and petty criminals who were inclined to take without giving in return and who consequently drove out those who practiced reciprocity. In this changed climate, hard drugs such as methamphetamine and heroin began to supplant nonaddictive psychotropic substances for spiritual and recreational use by the denizens of the Haight, and the Diggers were not immune. As the vision of San Francisco as "Psychedelphia" subsided, some of the Diggers' inner circle relentlessly pursued the outer limits of authenticity, which they defined, in Peter Coyote's words, as "honoring one's inner directives and dreams by living in accord with them, no matter the consequences."[4] For these members of the collective this involved combining heroin fixes with a lethal fixation on the Hell's Angels motorcycle club, legendary desperados for whom impulse control was an oxymoron. Coyote at least proved to be a phoenix: as he narrates in his memoir *Sleeping Where I Fall*, he managed to kick his addiction and recover from hepatitis at a ranch and sometime commune in rural Marin county. A number of his compatriots weren't as fortunate and succumbed to the outlaws' undertow.

---

4   Coyote, *Sleeping Where I Fall: A Chronicle* (New York: Basic Books, 1999) 64.

As the Diggers participated in the mass exodus of hip counterculturists from their urban enclaves into rural America, they evolved into a fluid social network known as the Free Family. This social formation reportedly consisted of several hundred people, including those who had been active in Digger activities in the Haight, and many more who had associated with its veteran members only afterward. The Free Family's communes were located up the Pacific coast as far as Puget Sound. Living by their wits, scrounging around, exploiting the economy of scale (up to thirty people at a time lived in the Red House commune in Marin county, which had but a single bathroom), they pooled their meager income from odd jobs, welfare checks, and food stamps, regarding these last two sources of revenue as government grants for research and development on sustainable lifestyles. "We reasoned," Coyote states, "that as more people became impoverished, disenfranchised, and betrayed by the corporate state, our numbers would swell; then we would be prepared with the operative alternatives produced by our social research."[5] Every dollar they extracted from the "butter" side of the Great Society's ledger, they maintained, would be deducted from the Vietnam-bound "guns" allocation.

Largely through hustling an affluent set of supporters, admirers, and wannabes, a dozen or so members of the Free Family raised some $50,000 to purchase Black Bear Ranch, a former gold-mining operation in Northern California's Siskiyou Mountains. There, on eighty acres at the end of a treacherous nine-mile dirt road, they conducted one of the most radical experiments in communal living of its day, and this was an era when, with apologies to the late Barry Goldwater, extremism in the pursuit of liberty was considered no vice. At various times they tried abolishing private property, even to the ownership of one's personal clothing, along with bans on exclusive sexual relationships, although without the regulation and monitoring practiced by John Humphrey Noyes's nineteenth-century Oneida community. Gradually, pragmatic survival trumped the ideology of perpetual revolution and the community stabilized. It persists today with a small population of first and second-generation members in permanent residence and a larger number of former communards who regularly sojourn there as time and weather permit.

---

5   Coyote, *Sleeping Where I Fall*, 295.

Besides a penchant for the hard kicks of heroin, another cue the Digger/Free Family took from the beat generation was their mobile celebration of the open road. Preferring 1940s vintage three-quarter-ton trucks to the school buses adaptively reused by Ken Kesey's Merry Pranksters and Stephen Gaskin's devotees, Coyote and his confederates caravanned across the country on more than one occasion. As he explains it, "The idea was to travel to far-flung locales and use our neutrality as newcomers to create meetings, détentes, and political alliances among people who should know each other but did not. It was apparent that the counterculture was growing; every state had pockets of people living as we did, creating relationships and new communities within their regions...so it seemed organic and evolutionary to begin weaving these places together, expanding the base of our economy and spreading the cultural word."[6]

The last of these excursions ended with part of the group taking up residence at a farm owned by Coyote's family of origin in eastern Pennsylvania near the Delaware Water Gap. Summoned east by the sudden death of his father Morris Cohon, a wealthy investor, Coyote assumed the role of dutiful son to his grieving mother, even dropping back in to mainstream society for a stint as Wall Street broker in a vain attempt to save the family firm from bankruptcy. His final communal effort proved no more successful. Coyote's assessment is characteristically blunt on this score: "While we developed refined vocabularies to discuss free economies, bioregional borders...intercommune trade, media manipulation, political subversion, and drug-related mental states, we possessed almost no tools for discussing interpersonal conflicts and personal problems or resolving the sometimes claustrophobic stresses and strains of communal existence."[7]

In the succinct summation of Freeman House, another of the former Diggers whom I later interviewed at his home in Petrolia, California recalled, "We were creating a culture instead of creating a life."[8] Their prescription for a utopian future foundered on the demands of a quotidian present.

My initial exposure to the Diggers occurred when I was a teenager living in Minnesota. I read about them in *Life* and *Look* magazine coverage of the Summer of Love and, sitting there in the public library, I

---

6   Ibid., 215–16.
7   Ibid., 291.
8   Ibid., 295.

ached to be a part of the scene that was unfolding in the Haight. By the following summer I had discovered the underground press and thereby learned about the Yippies. They described themselves as Diggers who were intent on staging a "Festival of Life" in Chicago during the 1968 Democratic Convention. A friend and I—he was one of the few longhairs in our town of twenty-eight thousand—hopped a train during the third week of August to Union Station and quickly found our way to Lincoln Park. There and then, I came of age. In the course of one long weekend, I crossed the line from innocence to experience. There was on the one hand, the *communitas* of thousands of mostly young people grooving in the park, snake-dancing, playing and listening to music, sharing food and joints. And on the other, the Chicago Police Department, backed up by the 101st Airborne, spoiling for a fight. As a fifteen-year-old who was more curious than serious about political activism, I got radicalized by witnessing the brutality unleashed in the ensuing "police riot" (as the Walker Commission Report was later to call it). That event effectively ended my childhood and launched me into the counterculture. The cumulative events of 1968 polarized a lot of people that same way. They also awakened in me a sense that we were alive in history, that what was taking place was epoch-making. I began to save the ephemera—underground newspapers, broadsides, buttons, armbands, bumper stickers—that documented this historical moment, although I was not yet aware of why it was important to do so.

After graduating from high school in 1971, I took to the road, hitchhiking across the United States and Canada several times on trips that lasted for weeks or months. I conceived of these excursions as pilgrimages for they often had spiritual sites as their destinations. My first such trip took place in summer 1972. Equipped with a Timberline backpack, and sporting hair to my waist, my mother offered to drive me out to the nearest interstate highway onramp provided that I allow her to take a snapshot of me before we set out. (She later told me it was to help the authorities better be able to identify my remains when, she feared, they were discovered in a ditch out in the middle of nowhere.) I visited a number of older religious communities, such as the Self Realization Fellowship's kriya yoga ashram established in the 1920s in Encinitas, California, and New Melleray Abbey in Iowa founded by Trappist monks from Mount Melleray, Ireland, back in the mid-nineteenth century. I spent a week living in a tent and cutting manzanita brush while on retreat at the Ananda Village outside Nevada City in the Sierra Nevadas, all the while observing the vow of silence. I also spent time in new intentional communities, such as the Abode of the Message, opened in 1975 by Sufis in Mount Lebanon, New York, which these so-called "whirling dervishes" had purchased directly from one of the last surviving Shaker groups. Mt. Lebanon had been the second community Mother Ann Lee, the charismatic founder of the Society of Brethren, had established in the late eighteenth century. And the Shakers who had transferred ownership to the Sufis told them that this transaction fulfilled a prophecy that when they were no longer numerous enough to maintain the property, another group who believed in ecstatic dancing as a form of communing with the godhead would appear to take it off their hands.

These pilgrimages quickened in me the urge to settle down in a community of like-minded souls who wanted to devote themselves to the ongoing promotion of spiritual growth through mutuality. By the spring of 1975, I had begun my search for a small farm to buy in the upper Mississippi River valley. During high school I had worked for spending money on area dairy farms in Minnesota and Wisconsin and thereby developed a deep and abiding love of the land. This part of the Midwest had been surrounded but not sheathed by glaciers during the last ice age, and the meltwaters that coursed over the region as the glaciers finally retreated some thirty thousand years earlier had carved five-hundred-foot crevices called "coulees" through the limestone and sandstone landscape. The valleys filled with windblown silt loam and the sides of the bluffs came to be cloaked with thick stands of hardwoods. Over the twentieth century, much of the rural population had moved into urban areas and the farms they abandoned were consolidated as farmers increased their holdings, which new agricultural technology permitted them to till more efficiently and profitably. This process made old farmhouses widely available, sometimes for sale along with small acreage. From 1973–74, I had lived alone on such a farm outside Waumandee, Wisconsin, where the neighboring owner allowed me to live rent-free in an old house with as much firewood as I wanted to cut and split for heating it. All I had to do in exchange was to feed the herd of beef cattle that wintered in the nearby barnyard. That year was a time of intense solitude for me during which I worked on my poetry and studied yoga and Buddhist philosophy.

Gradually I sought the company of my fellows in Winona, Minnesota, thirty miles distant. There the burgeoning new-wave food co-op movement caught my attention and before long I had worked myself into a position of responsibility as the first paid manager of Famine Foods Co-op. The pay was a dollar an hour—"people's wages." Many of the people I met through this enterprise were eager to go "back to the land." I knew my limitations, that my practical skills were relatively limited, certainly not up to the task of rural self-sufficiency. On the other hand, I wanted to live with other congenial souls. So by that fall, together with five married couples, with whom I had grown to be close friends, and their five children, we pooled our resources and purchased the ideal farm property that I had located: 180 acres with a four bedroom home, a commodious barn and other outbuildings, and with a springhead below the house that was the source of a creek that wound two miles down the valley to join a larger stream which ultimately emptied into the Mississippi.

Thus was Yaeger Valley Community Farm established as an experiment in communal living between people who self-consciously maintained a spiritual relationship with one another. We did this through a variety of means that evolved over the next six years. Time permits me to mention just one. We held regular meetings exclusively for Farm members, during which we practiced what were called "Relating Exercises," a technique developed by Charles Berner (later Yogeshwar Muni), and learned by one of our community at the Santana Dharma Center, near St. Helena, California. Pairing off, we would sit on the floor facing each other with knees touching and gently holding each other's hands. Then looking directly in your partner's eyes, you would ask a series of ten paired questions, not interrupting while your partner answered each one as truthfully and completely as possible. Here are a few examples:

1a) *Tell me a problem you are currently having in life.*
1b) *Tell me what I need to know in order to understand that problem completely.*

2a) *Tell me how you want to be loved.*
2b) *Tell me how you want to love others.*

8a) *Tell me how you want to be communicated with.*
8b) *Tell me how you want to communicate with others.*

9a) *Tell me how you could be helped.*

9b) *Tell me how you could help others.*

After all twenty questions had been worked through, the interlocutor and listener roles would be reversed and the questions repeated. These sessions were monitored by one person using a stopwatch to ensure that everyone had had equal time for talking and listening and also to prevent them from lasting all night. Relating Exercises were extremely effective in promoting group solidarity and alleviating interpersonal conflicts that might otherwise have sundered the bonds of our community. Although we eventually did come to part ways after ten years in 1985, it was noteworthy that our communal farm was dissolved by mutual consent and without acrimony. Our spiritual commitment to one another was reflected in how shared assets were disbursed: all members were reimbursed every cent of their capital investment. We broke even in the end.

So, you may well be wondering, what does *my* communal experience have to do with the Diggers, or, for that matter, with communes and utopia in Northern California? Well, for one thing, we modeled ourselves in part on their concept of "creating the condition you described." We discussed and visualized the world we wished to inhabit and then took concrete actions toward manifesting it, behaving as though we lived in that transformed world in the hopes of persuading others that it was a desirable and achievable goal. We were also inspired by the totalizing vision laid out in the Free City plan that the Diggers had articulated as their final act in Summer 1968: one that embraced all aspects of social life including housing, food, energy, transportation, communications, education, heath care, and artistic expression. To give examples from just the last two in that list, the Diggers were the first countercultural group to revive observance of the solstice and equinox as times for communal rites. For the ten years I lived communally I organized free performing arts festivals on those pagan holidays to showcase the work of local musicians, poets, dancers, filmmakers, and actors, and in the process knit together people from our region's hip community that were spread out over a thirty-mile radius. The women of our farm formed a lay midwifery collective, which helped provide women throughout the upper Mississippi River valley with home childbirths. (My wife, Eleanor Johnson, who was part of this undertaking, ironically first learned about the rudiments of obstetrics and gynecology by working with the underground abortion service called JANE in Chicago in the dark ages before *Roe v. Wade*.)

Our rural commune, like those of the Free Family's, also was networked with urban communes, collectives, and food co-ops. We helped start and operate an organic flour mill which distributed grain products through the food co-op system of the Midwest including seven states. When it was time in late September to harvest and process our crop of sweet sorghum, people from the Twin Cities' co-ops came down to our farm like the Cuban *brigadistas* to help us out; they were paid in five-gallon cans of nature's most nutritious sweetener. We opened a wholesale co-op warehouse and trucked produce from several organic farms and orchards to food co-ops in the Twin Cities and returned with preorders for storefront co-ops and buying clubs throughout our area.

It is perhaps in this respect that we differed from the Diggers' project of everything free. The material conditions that the Diggers skillfully exploited, including the bountiful surplus of the Golden State's produce and economy were simply not available to us. By the mid-1970s, when our community farm was organized, we were subject to stagflation and the oil shocks of the OPEC embargo. We could not see our way through to a viable alternative to the cash economy. The system of cooperation, which was rooted in the radical agrarian movement of the 1920s and '30s, was available and by placing the ownership of the means of distribution or production in the hands of consumers or farmers respectively, we embraced it as an alternative economy that combined the best features of socialism and small-scale capitalism.

In one other crucial aspect, our communal group differed from Diggers. We learned from their inability to develop a structure for resolving interpersonal conflicts by adopting the one earlier described that helped us cohere and stabilize. It would be tempting to hold this up as making us more "successful" than the Diggers. But let's face it, few have heard of Yaeger Valley Community Farm, while everyone knows of the Diggers. This observation, on the other hand, provides me with an occasion to interrogate the very notion of success as it applies to intentional communities, and here I would commend to you anthropologist Jon Wagner's seven criteria for evaluating their overall effectiveness.[9]

Criterion 1: An intentional community succeeds to the extent that it accomplishes its own goals. One possible justification for passing

---

9   Jon Wagner, "Success in Intentional Communities: The Problem of Evaluation," *Communal Societies* 5 (1985): 91–98.

judgments of "success" and "failure" on intentional communities lies in the very fact of their intentionality, which presumably could entitle us to ask whether the intentions have been fulfilled. By such reasoning, however, the most legitimate criteria for judging success would be the community's own goals, and the people best qualified to state and assess these goals would be the community's members. It does, after all, seem odd to think of evaluating the success of an intentional community according to ideals alien to the participants themselves.

Criterion 2: An intentional community is successful to the extent that it approaches objective social perfection. The most enduring concern of utopian theorists, anti-utopians, communitarians, legislators, humanists, and the interested public has been whether intentional communities can and do provide a genuinely superior social life for their participants. The suggestion of such value-laden criterion may be discomforting to many contemporary intellectuals schooled in relativism, but in practice it is quite common for scholars to address, in some indirect manner, the question of social merit.

Criterion 3: An intentional community is successful in proportion to the length of time it exists. Longevity is one of the most straightforward and easily measured criteria for community success.

Criterion 4: An intentional community is successful in proportion to its size. The term size is offered here in a broad sense, and it could be further defined in terms of population, wealth, power, or perhaps other factors.

Criterion 5: An intentional community is successful to the extent that it is socially cohesive. It seems reasonable to try and evaluate intentional communities according to some criterion that is qualitative (as opposed to such qualitative measures as longevity and population size), but based on empirical rather than moral criteria. The notion of social cohesiveness is admittedly an imprecise one, but it does have a long history in sociology.

Criterion 6: An intentional community is successful insofar as it has an important influence on society. From a broad perspective one might argue that a community is successful insofar as it contributes ultimately to the enterprise of human cultural development.

Criterion 7: An intentional community is successful to the extent that it provides for the personal growth of its individual members. It seems that anyone truly committed to human welfare cannot fail to consider the effect of a community in promoting or stifling the full "realization" (the self-actualization, mental health, etc.) of its members.

Wagner's criteria thus help us to rid ourselves of the idea that success or failure can be adequately assessed on the sole basis of how long a commune or collective lasted or how big it was. The Diggers attained lasting significance through the continuing influence on collective action and communal experimentation. For me, Yaeger Valley Community Farm's success lies in its fostering of social cohesiveness and personal growth among its members.

This chapter has touched on two of the themes of the present book, communalism in the city and in the country. I'd like to close by briefly discussing the third theme: legacies. As the demographic bulge of baby boomer communitarians eases into the grey zone, commentators have predicted that their generation will leave a distinctive mark on the way Americans contend with the aging process. In particular, such institutions that cater to the elderly as the nursing home, the assisted living facility, and the hospice have already begun to respond to the anticipated needs of those who once cautioned against trusting anyone over the age of thirty and "hoping to die before they got old." Stephen Gaskin has envisioned a hip retirement community patterned on the Farm in Summertown, Tennessee.[10] Emeriti faculty from UC Davis have constructed Glacier Circle, a cohousing project of octogenarians that was described by the *New York Times* as a "self-styled, potluck utopia" where "'the social consciousness of the 1960's can get re-expressed.'" One gerontologist who specializes in cohousing anticipates that "baby boomers are going to want to recreate the peak experiences of their lives. Whether a commune or a college dorm, the common denominator [for them] was community."[11] Will these sites become gated communities for the priv-

---

10 Don Lattin, "Twilight of Hippiedom; Commune Founder Dreams of Retirement Pasture for Ex-hippies," *San Francisco Chronicle* (March 2, 2003), A27, A30.

11 Patricia Leigh Brown, "Growing Old Together, in a New Kind of Commune," *New York Times* (February 27, 2006).

ileged, a psychedelicized Sun City for balding longhairs, self-imposed death camps where suicide is induced in slo-mo by Soma?

Of special interest to those who study contemporary trends in communality is discussed in yet another recent *New York Times* article: "Inviting Anarchy into My Home." The author, Liz Seymour, a self-described fifty-two-year-old divorced mother, narrates how four years ago she converted her three-bedroom Colonial Revival home in Greensboro, North Carolina, into an anarchist commune for seven, including herself and an adopted teenaged son, Justin. Theirs is a "collective, run by consensus and fueled by punk music, curse-studded conversation, and food scavenged from dumpsters." "Amid the chaos of my own life," she recalled, "I wondered if this approach to living might have something in it for me. Unconventional as it was, I figured it couldn't be any worse than struggling to pay the mortgage and being Justin's mother on my own." What she discovered is that "it is possible to live not just comfortably, but well, on $500 a month." The range of skills, services, and tools found among their extended household or procured by barter from those in the larger community saves them thousands of dollars a year. In this connection she noted, "If there is a historical model for the way we live, it is not the communes of the 60's or the utopian experiments of the 19th century, but the two-million-year prehistory of our hunting-and-gathering ancestors. Looked at through that lens, the life of our miniature tribe feels a lot like the way people were meant to live." "Where I live now," she concluded, "is not utopia. What it is, though, is fun. It is fun to hear people laughing on the porch; it is fun to dance in the kitchen; it is fun to go out on a Wednesday evening Dumpster run. As messy as it is, to my mind it is a lot more interesting than utopia could ever be."[12]

Pertinent to the topic of alternative ways of growing older in community is the fifty-year age span of their collective. It brings to mind Stewart Brand's idea from the early 1970s of designing combined institutions for the elderly and orphaned children deemed unadoptable, both populations that had much potentially to contribute to one another and were marginalized by the dominant society. It is no coincidence that one of the latest books by Theodore Roszak, who authored that groundbreaking study *The Making of a Counter Culture* some four decades ago, is entitled *Longevity Revolution: As Boomers Become Elders*. Jonathan Berman's doc-

---

12 Liz Seymour, "Inviting Anarchy into My Home," *New York Times*, March 9, 2006.

umentary film *Commune* released in 2005 poignantly portrays the care lavished on one of the founding members of northern California's Black Bear Ranch by his biological and communal family as he succumbs ever so gradually to mortal illness. If the many various communitarian projects of the Sixties era were about finding better ways to live forever young, perhaps one ironic legacy will be in fashioning more dignified ways to age gracefully and die. Their passing will not go unremarked by those of subsequent generations who have succeeded them in the resurgent intentional community movement.[13]

Such, anyway, are my peregrinations on evaluating 1960s communitarianism, suffused, I hope, with the twin imperatives of not overemphasizing conviviality and not overlooking perspicacity. Today, as we meet figuratively somewhere "West of Eden," with our backs to the garden gate that must be guarded by an angel with a flaming sword, may what we learn from our collective past help us chart a new course away from the postutopian and across this beguiling ocean of possibilities we behold before us.

---

13 The Fellowship for Intentional Community, established in 1948, serves as a clearinghouse for information on the contemporary communal movement: http://www.ic.org. Its online directory lists over 1,100 communal settlements, ecovillages, and cohousing developments that have been built or are in the planning stages, which is double the number that had been reported by the communities themselves in the 1990s. See also Andrew Jacobs, "Extreme Makeover, Commune Edition," *New York Times* (June 11, 2006). For parallel developments in the United Kingdom, see Charlotte Philby, "Easy Living: The Truth about Modern Communes," *The Independent* (July 10, 2010).

The Counterculture as Commons: The Ecology of Community in the Bay Area

Jeff Lustig

California has produced bumper crops of social experiments since early statehood. The solitaires of the Gold Rush had hardly exhausted their claims when organized groups showed up over the Sierra—religious, agriculturalist, Fourierist, and socialist, as Timothy Miller describes in his survey. I discovered this vein of state life when I was eight or so, hiking with a cousin through the brush atop Point Loma in San Diego, when the trees parted and we suddenly found ourselves in ancient Greece, we thought, complete with temples, columns, and amphitheater. It was the ruins of Katherine Tingley's recently shuttered Universal Brotherhood and Theosophical Society seminary. (By 1914 it had already established glass-domed a Raja-Yoga school, textile factory, joinery, bakery, publishing house, and fruit and vegetable gardens.)[1] California has always been a place where if you just parted the shrubbery or went around the bend, you'd stumble on a covey of utopians.

The 1960s and 1970s witnessed a surge of social experiments in California unrivaled in the rest of the country. Suddenly, young people dismayed by the suburban revision of the American Dream and fearful of nuclear ruin found it natural to build communes, join communes, work, and live in communes, and migrate when the spirit took them from one cooperative encampment to another. Where other generations founded new religious sects and political parties, the culture

---

1   Emmett Greenwalt, *The Point Loma Community in California, 1897–1942, A Theosophical Experiment* (Berkeley: University of California Press, 1955), 137.

rebels of the '60s built what Marx once called "duodecimo editions of the New Jerusalem."[2]

The period went Ralph Waldo Emerson one better. "We are all a little wild here with numberless projects of social reform," he wrote his friend Thomas Carlyle in 1840. It was hard to run into someone who didn't have "the draft of a new community in his waistcoat pocket."[3] By the early 1970s, it was hard to run into someone in Northern California who didn't have the draft of a new community in their lives.

It was a curious turn for people brought up in a culture of individualism and fables of the self-made man. The etymological root of the word community is the Latin *munus*, meaning to give or discharge the duties of office (and joined to *com*, "mutual service.") The idea at its heart is obligation—to others, to a shared purpose, or sometimes to a larger religious or political ideal. But curious or not for a people raised to think mainly of private rights, the desire to throw in one's lot with others and put the obligations of friendship at the center rather than the margins of social life was apparent not only in rural places like Black Bear and Morning Star and Table Mountain, but in urban communes and collectives like Kerista Village, Briarpatch and Sutter Street Commune in San Francisco, Harrad West and McGee's Farm in Berkeley, and with groups like the Diggers, who handed out free food in Golden Gate Park. It was also apparent in cooperatives like the Project Artaud theater group, the Cheese Board, Taxi Unlimited, and Uprisings Bakery in Berkeley, and the Free Print Shop in San Francisco, which in its newspaper, *Kaliflower* (named for the Hindu goddess Kali), exchanged information from almost three hundred communes by the time it closed down in 1972.[4]

The desire to join ones life with others' was also apparent with groups that shared some communal practices but were not full-fledged collectives—the Mime Troupe, the Free Universities of Berkeley and Palo Alto, the Black Bart Center, the Green Gulch Zen Center, and widespread free clinics and food conspiracies throughout the region. The hunches

---

2   Karl Marx and Friedrich Engels, *The Communist Manifesto*, 1848, Section III.

3   Dolores Hayden, *The Architecture of Communitarian Socialism, 1790–1975* (Cambridge, MA: MIT Press, 1976), 9.

4   Patricia Keats, "Kaliflower and the Free Print Shop," California Historical Society, 1998. Available at http://www.diggers.org/chs_article.htm. A number of these communes and cooperatives are noted in Robert V. Hine, *California Utopianism: Contemplations of Eden* (San Francisco: Boyd and Fraser Publishing, 1981), 63–70. Hine reported more than sixty communal houses in the San Francisco Bay Area by 1978 (69).

that people were not fated to live a dog-eat-dog existence, that they could accomplish more in a cooperative world, and that working with others was more rewarding than trying to impress them with the baubles of conspicuous consumption were widely shared by the young who grew up in the Bay Area or were drawn there by news of its rebels and revels.

Cities have been suspect places for millennia, the Bible ascribing their founding to Cain, who fled East of Eden after murdering his brother to build the first one. But out of the cities have also come those who sought alternatives to competition and fratricide as the basis for a common life together, setting out "West of Eden," as it were. Such were the commune-builders who emerged from the Bay Area's counterculture. And it was no coincidence that the centers of collective activity from which they set out on both sides of the Bay—the Haight-Ashbury in San Francisco and Telegraph Avenue in Berkeley—were adjacent to the two great commonses of the region: Golden Gate Park and the UC Berkeley campus. Utopia had a geography, and these visionaries, unlike California's in the nineteenth century, were homegrown. The grounds for their emergence had been worked for years, the one a vast garden space, the other a knowledge commons, both infused with the boisterous and creative energies of the times, and both increasingly politicized by local struggles, street theater, and growing antiwar rallies.[5]

II. Tributaries

What were the sources of this communal impulse in the Bay Area? What led people alienated from American life and politics to attempt a common life together? They had not, like the communards of the nineteenth century, all read a Charles Fourier or Robert Owen. Nor were they inspired by memories of California's own Kaweah Colony, Icaria Speranza near Cloverdale, or the African-American Allensworth, about which they knew comparatively little. Most were not aware that California had fielded more utopian experiments than any other state in the union, their number peaking at the time of World War I.[6] The surge of collective activ-

---

5   UC Berkeley may be considered a great commons not only because of its well-designed open spaces and plazas, and because of its federal land-grant origins, but also because a university is at its essence a knowledge commons, where the wealth of the past is open to all members and the intellectual wealth of the present freely shared.

6   Robert V. Hine, *California's Utopian Colonies* (San Marino: Huntington Library, 1953), 6, 168.

ity was due rather, I propose, to a unique geocultural terrain and to the mix of influences that came together in it. These influences worked to establish a special outlook and context of possibility, a context in which more personal motives unfolded. I count five of the larger impulses which, flowing together, bred the right ecology for producing so many cities on a hill.

1. *The best minds of my generation.* The most powerful of the immediate influences on disaffected youth from the suburbs of the early 1960s was exerted by the beatniks of San Francisco's North Beach. The gravitational pull they exercised is hard to gauge from this distance, the cultural shockwaves set off by a few artists, poets, and painters being far out of proportion to any single work by any of them. But Stew Albert was right when he declared them "the creators of the '60s oversoul." They "provided the image and imagination to elevate spirits."[7]

The beats blew the lid off the midcentury faith that postwar American life was the culmination of Progress. Discontented youth who suspected otherwise and agreed with Henry Miller that the American Dream had become an air-conditioned nightmare were regularly told there were no alternatives. They would wind up clambering up the ladder of private success too, stepping on the fingers of those one rung beneath them and burdened by a treadmill race to keep up with the Joneses. In the darker image of Ginsberg's famous poem "Howl," the reign of Moloch, the "sphinx of cement and aluminium" had already been secured: "Moloch whose buildings are judgment! Moloch the vast stone of war! ...Moloch whose breast is a cannibal dynamo! ...Moloch whose love is endless oil and stone!"

The beatniks showed it was all a lie. When they opened up a liberated zone in San Francisco, they showed American youth it was possible—pundits, parents, and the Chamber of Commerce notwithstanding—to chuck the whole hunkered-down existence, the Moloch who consumed real children and buried the real questions about life's ends beneath relentless ads about its supposed means.

Those who migrated to the communes of California followed their lead. Spiritual descendants of Walt Whitman, they were seekers and wanderers, not apostles of a new faith nor devotees of the esca-

---

7   Albert, "A Difficult Decade to Read," (review of Charters, *The Portable Sixties*) *Los Angeles Times Book Review*, February 16, 2003.

lator god, progress. The North Beach bohemians had set the example by ditching the rat race and deciding to live a full life *now*, today, not after the house was paid off or the career ended. They showed that dropping out was possible. They evoked in the new communards the spirit of disaffiliation that, for historian Robert Hine, distinguished the most committed of America's old communes and colonies.[8] It was a spirit also shared by the '60s New Left. Real social change had to come from "outside the system," it held, not from compromised parties and one-step-at-a-time reforms.

Especially attractive for those in isolated homes of the new America was the fact that the beats were a group, a band of brothers and occasional sister. The way they lived in North Beach, and Venice in L.A., and Berkeley, the way they traveled (as with Ken Kesey and the Merry Pranksters aboard the bus "Further"), the way they got stoned, penned their poetry and jammed at clubs all showed their solidarity. Those "who sat up smoking in the supernatural darkness of cold-water flats floating across the tops of cities contemplating jazz," as Ginsberg told it, were members of a group, a cabal, a "lost battalion of platonic conversationalists jumping down the stoops off fire escapes off windowsills...yacketayakking screaming vomiting whispering facts and memories and anecdotes."

The event that announced their presence epitomized this camaraderie. The poetry reading at the Six Gallery in 1955 included pieces by Allen Ginsberg (chanting "Howl"), Jack Kerouac, Gary Snyder, Philip Lamantia, Michael McClure, and Kenneth Rexroth. Nor was it a coincidence that both organizers of the reading, Rexroth and Lawrence Ferlinghetti, founder of City Lights Books near North Beach and publisher of "Howl," were advocates of the European tradition of communitarian anarchism.

2. *The civil rights movement.* The civil rights struggle in the South was a second influence on the Bay Area at the time, reports about it arriving with returning civil rights workers and soon supplemented by the lessons of local sit-ins at places like the Sheraton Palace hotel and on Cadillac Row in San Francisco. An editorial collective of the Student Nonviolent Coordinating Committee (SNCC) published *The Movement*,

---

8   Hine, *Utopian Colonies*, 6, 165: "For any utopian, religious or secular, [normal] politics provided no springboard for reform; by his withdrawal from society he tacitly admitted the impossibility of reformation by conventional legislative means."

its national newspaper, out of a church basement near the old armory building in San Francisco's Mission District. The civil rights movement was informed by the traditions of Black churches and possessed distinctly communitarian elements, especially the stream of Black Christianity descended from the old, interracial Social Gospel movement. For the social gospelers egotism and the pursuit of self-interest were sins, not economic virtues, and a blessed life was one that acknowledged mutualism and duties to others. This was the background that led King to place "the beloved community" at the center of the struggle.[9]

The principle of nonviolence strengthened their communitarianism. Having rejected armed struggle and being deprived initially of official sanction (the Southern Democrats being mostly segregationists), any of the movement's successes were dependent on building broad social support. The main proselytizers of this movement were community organizers, a rarity in political struggle. In the Bay Area, a network of pacifist groups protesting the nation's proliferation of nuclear weapons reinforced this communitarianism—the American Friends Service Committee, Fellowship of Reconciliation, and the Catholic Worker Movement in Oakland.

It is impossible to overestimate the importance of the civil rights movement for the politics of the '60s. Without its examples, lessons, and practice of putting one's "body on the line"—committing one's whole self in political acts—it is hard to imagine the later student, antiwar, or commune movements. The civil rights workers also inspired the early community organizing projects of Students for a Democratic Society (SDS), including a brief attempt in Oakland the summer of 1965, before SDS turned to its anti–Vietnam War organizing.

Berkeley's Free Speech Movement in the fall of 1964 began as an offshoot of the civil rights struggle. It started when UC campus authorities barred activists who had just returned from the South (Mario Savio and Jack Weinberg among them) from raising money for and handing out information about the struggle. Not surprisingly, the idea of community was also a central concern of the FSM's. A statement in January 1965, explaining the mass arrests of a month before noted that "Although our

---

9   "Sin is essentially selfishness. ...The sinful mind is the unsocial and anti-social mind." Walter Rauschenbusch, "A Theology for the Social Gospel," 57. Denouncing corporate authoritarianism, the Social Gospelers also insisted on "the fatherhood of God [i.e., only of God] and the brotherhood of man."

issue has been free speech, our theme has been solidarity. When individual members of our community have acted, we joined together as a community to jointly bear responsibility for their actions." Waxing more philosophic than most leaflets of the time, the statement went on to make a point with which later commune members would agree: "The concept of living cannot be separated from the concept of other people. In our practical, fragmented society, too many of us have been alone. By being willing to stand up for others...we have gained more than political power, we have gained personal strength."[10]

3. *The political context.* These beatnik and civil rights influences came together in a special terrain, on both sides of the Bay. Those active in the later counterculture, attending "happenings" at the Fillmore, hanging out in the Haight or attending meetings at Longshoreman's Hall might not have been aware of the earlier struggles and political activists to whom they were indebted. But the land, the streets and parks they crossed every day were a terrain that had been contoured and shaped by others— people like those who built Golden Gate park atop the original sand dunes and those who had engaged in a long series of local, particularly union, struggles. The latter were epitomized for many by the famous Longshoremen's Strike of 1934, which sparked one of the few general strikes ever launched in the nation. "Beat poets, flower power and Castro Street are...more the lucky heirs, than the ancestors of what is uniquely San Franciscan," noted historian Fred Glass. "[T]he great San Francisco General Strike...laid down the economic and political foundation on which the city's countercultures could flourish."[11]

The International Longshoremen's and Warehousemen's Union (ILWU) was much more than a union as current Americans understand that term. A community institution, its used members' worksite relations as the basis for an organization that created its own housing project, medical plan, credit union and library, and activities for its members like a Writers and Poets Workshop. Local 10 had strong ties with Bay Area ethnic communities because it was racially integrated in the 1930s, long before most other unions. Even after other labor organizations

---

10 "We Want a University," Berkeley, January 4, 1965. Seymour M. Lipset and Sheldon S. Wolin, *The Berkeley Student Revolt* (Garden City: Anchor Books, 1965), 209-210.

11 Fred Glass, "'34 General Strike Laid Base for Counterculture," *San Francisco Chronicle*, April 29, 2009.

succumbed to business unionism during the McCarthy era, the ILWU, drawing among other things on syndicalist roots that went back to the IWW (Industrial Workers of the World), refused to expel its radical and communist members or to sacrifice its social vision.[12]

The value of infrastructure provided by previous struggles proved itself on occasions like the City Hall demonstrations of May 1960, when students from local colleges demonstrated against HUAC (the House Un-American Activities Committee), and those who were subpoenaed by it scorned its attacks on free speech. The pictures of police fire-hosing demonstrators down the steps of City Hall drew thousands more rebellious youth to the Bay Area.

Complementing this San Francisco history was an equally fertile tradition in the East Bay, the cooperative movement brought to the area by its Finnish immigrants. In a state whose cities were once rich with nationality halls, Berkeley by the 1960s was distinguished by having only two—and both were Finnish. Both, intriguingly, were also socialist. (The Communist or Red Finns, joined by IWW activists, took over Finn Hall on Tenth St. after 1917. The anti-Bolshevik socialists met on University Avenue.)

The Finns took the lead in building the Berkeley cooperatives— grocery and hardware stores, a credit union and auto repair shop, a daycare center, and a travel and insurance agency. These ventures showed there were alternatives to the market system for meeting people's needs and taught their members the methods of cooperation. They gave support to the student co-ops which began to be organized at UC Berkeley during the Depression: Barrington Hall, Stebbins Hall, the first women's co-op, Euclid Hall, later Cloyne Court and more. These halls enabled thousands of students arriving in Berkeley (itself a land-grant university) to step easily into something rare in midcentury America: a cooperative milieu in which people handled their common affairs together. Training in cooperative activities became an unexpected part of their college curriculum.

The effect of these backgrounds on both sides of the Bay was to provide the emergent counterculture with a political scaffolding built by earlier activists and complete with inspiring examples, broadminded supporters and not incidentally, friendly lawyers. For rebellious youth

---

12 Bruce Nelson, *Workers on the Waterfront: Seamen, Longshoremen, and Unionism in the 1930s* (University of Illinois Press, 1990), 6, 189, 203.

there were paths through the wilderness that skirted local bureaucracies and compromised political organizations.

4. *Ethnic and racial communities.* The fourth influence on the young in the Bay Area of the '60s were the ethnic communities of San Francisco and Oakland. Those who were active in political organizations or the multiethnic jazz scene noticed many community customs and ceremonies of interdependence in the ghettos and barrios of East Oakland, Hunter's Point, the Mission District—extended families, designated aunts and *primos,* complex rituals of support for illness, incarceration and death, that offered sharp contrasts to life in the lonely crowd.

The African-American churches were the only places outside the unions where people regularly addressed each other as "brother" and "sister." The people around Glide Memorial Church in San Francisco, or the Los Siete defense in the Mission District in 1969, or who had worked in the United Farm Workers demonstrated a degree of concern for each other that most white kids envied. The Black Panther's news was relayed via the InterCommunal News Service; and ghetto kids found food and recreation at their InterCommunal Youth Institute. The crippling myth of the self-made man who admits few debts to others had not made much of an inroad into these communities. The interdependence at the base of everyone's life and growth was freely and openly acknowledged.

A few white radical groups saw these minority communities as the vanguard of revolution because their members were the superexploited in American society. One suspects, however, that those ethnic communities were also given that leadership role because they already presented alternatives to dominant American culture. The desire to change cultural values has always been a key source of the revolutionary impulse. Socialists sought to transform the ownership of the means of production, for example, in order to fulfill the human instincts for solidarity and equality. Many early commune settlers also saw their job as that of developing the cultural path others could follow once the political system collapsed.[13]

---

13 Explaining the founding motive for Black Bear Ranch, Peter Coyote said, that, "We thought that the government was going to be overthrown in two years…And we wanted to have an alternative, a non-mercantile alternative that offered citizens the options of being something other than a consumer or an employee." Elsa and Richard Marley, the couple who bought the ranch's land added: "Our idea was we were going to go and change the world. Our slogan was, 'Free land for free people.'" In Jonathan Berman, *Commune,* (a documentary film), Five Points Media, 2005.

A lot of Bay Area activists felt that the ethnic and racial communities had gone a good deal of the way toward accomplishing this cultural objective.

5. *The Range of Light.* A final, geographically based influence descended from the Sierra to affect the Bay Area outlook of the 1960s, conveyed by the backpackers and early environmentalists. Its influence was immediately evident in some precincts of the region in the appearance of flannel shirts, jeans, and hiking boots, and by many people's regular treks to what John Muir called the Range of Light, or Mount Tamalpais, Mount Shasta, and the Trinity Alps.

Climbers and mountaineers are in many ways individualists. But in the Bay Area, their individual exploits and achievements were also steeped for over a century in collective efforts and organizations. Joseph LeConte, who took generations of geology students to Yosemite in the nineteenth century, taught at UC Berkeley. David Brower, long-term leader of the Sierra Club and founder of Friends of the Earth, grew up in Berkeley and later lived there. The Sierra Club fought to preserve wilderness and introduced thousands of people to the region on its regular camping and hiking trips. The trail to the Sierra for many of those initiates ran through the club's Claire Tappan Lodge in Norden, built in the 1930s by collective effort and maintained by volunteer work parties ever since. A stay at the lodge imparted to campers and hikers the knowledge that the mountain experience was a cooperative experience, just as the Berkeley co-ops taught students that higher education was a collaborative achievement.

The point here is complex given that many Americans imagine a trip to the mountains as a return to unspoiled nature and a rejection of society. But the relationship between mountain and city is tricky, as the writings Thoreau, Muir, and Gary Snyder all attest. California's Sierra are a borderlands, a liminal space from which city people can gain a perspective on their lives but which have also been altered and affected by the city. The founders of the Kaweah Colony in the Sequoia forest emigrated from San Francisco in the 1890s and held their meetings under the canopy of the giant Karl Marx tree, which their countrymen later knew under the disguise of the General Sherman tree. The mountains mean different things to different peoples. But whatever they mean they are not the outcroppings of raw nature. Already in 1844, Fremont descending from the Sierra into Sacramento found red-stemmed filaree, a European plant, growing along the trail.

Kerouac made the narrative pivot of his 1958 novel, *Dharma Bums*, the ascent of the forbidding Matterhorn in the Eastern Sierra, a spiritual test imposed on the book's narrator by Japhy Ryder, a figure modeled after the real Gary Snyder. And during the '60s, backpacking and mountaineering would prove to be the spiritual practice adopted by many as a way to free themselves from "a system of work, produce, consume; work, produce, consume," as Ryder put it, to rediscover the more natural rhythms of life and wilderness. In 1958, Kerouac has Ryder foreseeing "a great rucksack revolution, thousands or even millions of young Americans wandering around with rucksacks, going up to mountains to pray."[14]

California's state parks and forests are not raw nature, then, but a commons too, a combined gift of both nature and earlier people with vision. The forests have been preserved and tended over the years not just to supply water and timber for the cities, but to provide people with access to wilderness and the knowledge that comes with it. "Our relation to the natural world takes place in a *place*," writes Snyder, "and it must be grounded in information and experience."[15] The state's wild areas have been preserved by people who had a sense of place and a respect for place, and wanted to help others acquire them too. Part of the idea of freedom sought by the Bay Area's counterculture assumed a willingness to understand the limits the natural world and accept obligations to it, and a commitment to acquiring a competence in it. That freedom and competence were seen as being gained in the company of others.

III. Conclusion

These were the major geosocial influences acting on those trying to overcome the alienation of American cities and politics in the Bay Area in the '60s and persuading them not to spend their years chasing after a higher standard of living but to try to create a different way of life. Reacting against the deadening weight of mass culture they looked within themselves and found the impulse to reach out and forge genuine social bonds with others. The move was exactly the one traced by Albert Camus in *The Rebel* when he declared: "I rebel, therefore we exist."[16]

---

14   Jack Kerouac, *Dharma Bums* (New York: New American Library, 1958), 78.
15   Snyder, *Practice of the Wild* (San Francisco: North Point Press, 1990), 39.
16   Albert Camus, *The Rebel* (New York: Vintage Books, 1956), 22.

Some have proposed that there were major differences between different parts of the region, those in the City more inspired by the counterculture and Fillmore Auditorium, while those in the East Bay were more political and drawn to Sproul Plaza. But the hippies moving North joined East Bay politicos in denouncing capitalist Amerika. They also sought a political alternative. And Berkeley's New Left helped build People's Park and ran yippie Jerry Rubin for mayor. The traffic on the Bay Bridge moved both ways. Both areas expanded people's sense of possibility and emboldened them to act. And when they acted, both groups of people moved in communal directions.

I have talked about influences and settings. Others in this volume report on how the communes fared, how life was lived, and how these experiments compared to the others of a covenanting people between the seventeenth and nineteenth centuries. At the end of the Oneida Community's thirty-five-year-long experiment in New York, John Humphrey Noyes, its founder, wrote proudly, "We made a raid into an unknown country, charted it, and returned without the loss of a single man, woman or child."[17] The same could not unfortunately be said about the experiments of the '60s.

The Bay Area influences did not inspire the communards and cooperators of the 1960s and 1970s to spell out their founding goals with the same specificity as the state's earlier utopian colonists, nor to give an account of their successes and failures as completely as, their predecessors at the Oneida, Amana, or Icara Speranza. They left few records about their plans to support themselves economically, how they inducted new members or how they organized their internal self-governance.

But the rural communes and urban collectives were a critical part of the 1960s. They gave physical expression to the spirit that informed the period's projects and activities, a grassroots and collectively oriented spirit that found it more rewarding to enrich a common world than to strive for merely private success. The communes and collectives established the space in which their members lived their ideals and newcomers found their footing. They presented inspiring models of how Americans could recast the democratic aspirations that were being betrayed at the time and have grown more furtive and marginal in the years since. Cramped today in large anomic organizations Americans are still looking for forms

---

17 The Oneida community lasted from 1847–1881; the Amana Society from 1859–1932.

of real cooperation. Residents of blighted cities still seek to belong to something more meaningful. That's why the communes of the '60s and '70s still deserve our attention. Life in our debilitated social organizations should no more be permitted to blot out a knowledge of the alternative, Robert Hine rightly noted, than years of air pollution can make us forget the blue sky and clouds.[18]

---

18 Hine, *Community on the American Frontier* (Norman: University of Oklahoma Press, 1980), 256.

The Commune as Badlands as Utopia as Autonomous Zone

Jesse Drew

In March of 1971, I boarded a Greyhound bus headed for a city in Northern New England with three other boys and one girl. All five of us were fifteen years old, and all of us had just run away from home. We held a pocketful of change between us and a phone number to call when we arrived at our destination. The phone number was given to us by one of our entourage's siblings, who had connections to an underground political organization that was then on the FBI's top-ten most wanted list.

The bus pulled into town just after midnight, and we were dropped off into a howling blizzard. Stamping off the snow from our shoes and blinking in the flickering fluorescent lights of a dingy bus station, we nervously made our phone call. Miraculously someone answered the phone, and within minutes we were greeted by a bearded young man, who whisked us off to our first commune, and into a communal network that would be my home, school, and refuge for many years to come.

A popular perception of a "commune" is that of the habitat of the rural "hippie," a peaceful, longhaired vegetarian who longed to go back to the land and be removed from the conflicts of modern social ills. According to this popular myth, in the 1960s and 1970s, thousands of such hippie communes dotted the land, eking out an existence of subsistence agriculture, with no television, little outside contact and infrequent bathing. While such stereotypes are humorous to consider, they ultimately serve to obscure important lasting contributions communes of the 1960s and 1970s have made to North American life. The legacy of these communal and collective projects is too important to surrender to such ignorance. I hope to dispel the urban legend of the "hippie" homestead and revivify the variety, nuance, vitality, and diversity of communal life. I will do so by examining my own personal experience moving through communal and collective life as a teenage runaway in the first half of the 1970s. By providing experience, history, and context, I hope to illustrate that communes differed greatly from the passive hippie stereotype, and stimulated and developed many refreshing and new ideas that still have great relevance to how we live our lives today. By bringing these experiences and analyses to light, I hope to be able to identify more clearly what still remains of the communal project.

Commune + ism = Communism

—Graffito written on commune wall

On that first night in our communal hideout, our group excitedly awaited daybreak and a ride to a more secure rural commune. While snooping around in our hideaway attic space, I came across two books by Abbie Hoffman, *Revolution for the Hell of It* and *Woodstock Nation*. I had never read Abbie Hoffman before, but in the middle of one of the books, I had the revelation that I had spent an afternoon with Mr. Hoffman the year before, while hanging out behind a candy store. He presented himself to my friend and I with the name George Metesky, and said he was interested in teenagers' views of revolutionary politics. After we talked and smoked cigarettes for hours, he bought us a copy of a magazine called *Ramparts*, bought us some French fries and bid us adieu. I had the strong feeling that Mr. Hoffman would approve of us being in our communal way station that night.

The next day all five of us were moved to a commune in the countryside inhabited primarily by the children of numerous communes, with adult collective members as teachers and guardians. As we were teenagers, the thought was that such accommodations were the appropriate choice for our age group. It was all very confusing, because while our energy level was closer to the children and we enjoyed roughhousing and playing games like kids, we were also interested in smoking pot, drinking wine, and having sex like adults. Thus, we called ourselves the "Middle Earth" people in recognition of our intermediate status. We were integrated into the "kid's collective" for about one month before it became obvious that the police and FBI were edging closer to us. We became aware of strange clicking on the telephone, neighbors being questioned by strangers, the feeling of being observed—the usual warning signs that would eventually become routine for us. Thus, we were all packed up in a vehicle one morning and moved to a remote communal farm in the mountains. Here, in the snow-covered hills, our principle activity was digging out firewood from snowdrifts, milking goats, and trying to find dried herbs that would take the place of our cigarettes, which we had run out of. The long dark nights led me to their communal library of Beat and American bohemian literature and poetry that I read ravenously, starting with *Trout Fishing in America*.

From then on, we could not stay too long in any one place and for the greater part of the year, we were moved from commune to commune, one step ahead of law enforcement, which persisted in taking a great interest in our whereabouts. The collective wisdom was that a blundering group of teenage runaways would surely lead the law to the wanted band of political outlaws that had been able to avoid entrapment thus far. We remained always packed and ready to go at a moment's notice, sometimes getting a phone call from a neighboring commune who had just been visited by police, or spotting an unmarked car come up the driveway. Our underground railroad of communes enabled us to experience firsthand many of the communes and collectives throughout Northern New England. To avoid being too much of a liability and a burden to the communes, we happily milked cows on dairy farms, built shelves for new food coops, made candles, tapped sugar bush trees for maple syrup production, plowed the fields with horses, worked on construction projects, rolled logs in saw mills, raised bees, planted crops, cooked, cleaned, took care of babies and children, and helped out in any way we could make ourselves useful. We also discussed racism, imperialism, and guerilla warfare with revolutionaries, sexism and lesbianism with radical feminists, working-class organizing with inner-city activists, prison conditions with radical lawyers, essential medical practice with "barefoot doctors," existentialism and Marxism with avant-garde filmmakers, and bluegrass and folk music with cultural activists. It was a passionate and exhilarating experience for a fifteen-year-old runaway with a ninth-grade education.

In all these travels through the communal network, I couldn't say that I actually came across a "hippie" commune. My communal world was primarily composed of social change activists, who were not escaping as much as seeking to build an alternative vision of the world. Far from cutting ourselves off from society, these communes were attempting to build a positive, working model of a better life in order to influence radical change in mainstream culture. Many communards were active in organized resistance to the social order by fighting logging companies, defending family farms, building food co-ops, organizing demonstrations, assisting military resisters or simply offering refuge or R&R to other activists. Our communes at various times gave respite to Black Panthers, Young Lords, the radical theatre group the Living Theatre, and Lincoln Detox Center medical personnel from the Bronx. We were an integral part of the movement toward a new America, not a hermetically sealed meditation retreat.

As to what exactly constitutes a commune is a somewhat subjective assessment. I differentiate between four types of group living. A commune is how I refer to a group of people who live with shared property, goals, and lives in common. It is a conscious, goal-oriented intentional community with some amount of collectivized property whose daily lives are coordinated in a general consensus. A collective is a group of people who are working on a singular project together, who may or not be living together. I consider communes and collectives differently from what others may confuse as communes or collectives, namely coops and group households. Co-op living is really just based on shared costs and household chores with no other goal than saving some money and adding convenience. A group of friends may live together, but that does not make a commune.

A significant aspect of the alternative offered by communes was the benefits of communal life itself. Many rural communards can attest to the inspiring example communal living offered to rural communities, as when small farmers left to the ravages of bad weather or other misfortune could appeal to the commune for help, picking up hay before a rainstorm perhaps or pulling a tractor out of a ditch. Far from promoting an alien idea, we saw ourselves as reviving a most American tradition of collective work, the barnraising. Bringing our communards together to help a local farmer pull the new roof joists up for a new barn renewed a tradition that had been dying, as family farm culture has been slowly strangled by corporate agriculture, or by suburban encroachment.

Eventually life in New England became too intense, with frequent visitation by snooping police and undercover spies. It was decided that our group of runaways should be split up and moved beyond the area. I would be sent to California, to a remote Northern California commune called Black Bear Ranch. I was moved to a small cabin on a dirt road by myself and told to wait for a car to pick me up. Two days later, a car arrived and we drove nonstop to San Francisco, where I was greeted at the door by two members of The Cockettes, an infamous female-impersonator theatre group. I had clearly arrived in the San Francisco of legend.

Well, I'm going up to California, way up north it's freezing cold,
And that's where we live, off the road

—The Band

Black Bear Ranch

San Francisco was only my stop for an evening however, and the next day I was brought to a house on Stanyan Street in San Francisco, where I was introduced to the comrades who had volunteered to drive me all the way up into the wilderness of Black Bear Ranch—a local household of Hell's Angels.

About seven of us went along for the ride, in an old Ford Econoline van with no passenger seats. We were hunkered down into the empty van back end, drinking Red Mountain wine, stopping along the way to take fruit out of orchards—grapes, peaches, apricots, plums. Up in the mountains, we came across a crew of orange jump-suited fellows clearing the desolate highway. Our driver, a barrel-chested bearded and ponytailed guy, took out a few joints from the glove compartment, and as he passed the prison work gang who were waving red caution flags to slow traffic, he surreptitiously handed a joint to each, with a warm, brotherly glance. The hand-rolled gifts elicited restrained glee and a secret nod of thanks from each prisoner, and were graciously accepted. As we sped beyond the roadwork, I reflected on the scene earlier that morning when our group left the house late because the bikers were glued to the TV set, watching the funeral of George Jackson. I was honored by being accepted into such an intimate moment with strangers, in a roomful of tearful Hell's Angels who watched as prison activist revolutionary George Jackson was eulogized and sent to his grave.

Don't let the past remind us of what we are not now.

—CSN lyrics spray-painted on commune barn

Utopia Now!

The freedom of movement and the brotherly and sisterly solidarity I experienced in my communal travels contributed to the revelation that utopia was not solely the interior, internal dimension of domestic communal living, but the global, universal networked connection of human communion and the shared passion for changing the world. The communal movement enabled my runaway collaborators and me to move from coast to coast as part of an underground railway, offering a truly utopian and alternative existence to the usual fate of teenage runaways that normally revolves around drugs, theft, and exploitation. It is stunning that, in all those years, no one ever turned us away or denied us food and shelter, despite the very serious potential danger from law enforcement as well as the burden we placed on food-strapped communes. What could be more utopian than that?

After traversing the Northern coast of California all day, sloshing around in the Ford Econoline van, we stopped at a commune of fisherpeople on the Northern California coast. The next morning, our van began climbing the long, winding, dusty route up treacherously steep, single-lane dirt roads that lead into the remote virgin timberlands of Black Bear Ranch. After many hours of hard driving, we finally edged past the cabins, teepees, goats, gardens, and domes of Black Bear and stopped in front of the main house, a ramshackle bleached white structure with porches. Several people were milling about and came up to welcome us. The drivers exchanged bear hugs and backslaps with the greeters as I somewhat shyly stepped aside to look around a little at my new refuge. I was immediately invited down to the creek by a young woman, so that we could cool off in the freezing cold mountain water and she could show me the new tattoo on her upper thigh.

Black Bear Ranch in many ways incorporated many of the facets and layers as well as the potential of the communal movement. For that reason, I would like to focus on the Ranch. Unfortunately, during my communal times, I traveled extremely light, living out of a backpack, my primary possession being a packet of phony IDs, a knife, and my toothbrush. I had no camera, no journal, no pens; just my eyes, ears, and memory to capture my surroundings. Fortunately, there are some very good notes and photos on Black Bear Ranch, taken over a period of years, by outside observers, paid for by U.S. taxpayers. Thanks to the Freedom of Information Act, I can rely upon the observations recorded by the Federal Bureau of Investigation, collected by external spies, by infiltrators, and by aerial photography. I will rely on these FBI observations to supply some of the hard facts about Black Bear, though my own analyses may diverge from that of the FBI.

One of the striking things about the Ranch was the sheer remoteness of it, located in an old mining town deep in the Trinity Alps, surrounded by forest. This observation is noted many times by the FBI report:

> Captioned commune is located in an extremely mountainous area in southwestern Siskiyou County, California, which is immediately adjacent to the State of Oregon... The property is surrounded on all sides by U.S. Forest Service land in the Klamath National Forest. Commune located approximately 50 miles from Oregon border and is accessible only after considerable travel on a logging road.

This remoteness made it an ideal hideaway, a Badlands for dissidents and political activists on the run. It had no electricity, no telephone, no running water. In the winter, once the snows came, the land was locked in until spring. There was a telephone booth in the closest town that was used by the commune in emergencies that would take an hour to get to. This public telephone booth was bugged by the FBI, and the list of numbers called out and incoming were meticulously logged. The primary frustration as evidenced by the FBI file is the agency's inability to discern who is actually living and coming and going at the commune. Their traditional spy techniques, telescopes and nightvision from neighboring buildings, wiretapping telephone lines, and tampering with the mail were worthless in the wilderness. Unfortunately for the FBI, to get to know the residents and the visitors, one had to be physically present, a daunting task for outsiders to communal life. To its consternation, the FBI notes that Black Bear was a very hospitable place: "(DELETE) indicated that the individuals located at the Black Bear Ranch were not particularly New Left oriented, but had never been known to refuse food and shelter to individuals in a fugitive status."

This generosity evidently did not extend to government agents, however. It was apparently not wise to get a Black Bear resident suspicious about one's ties to the FBI, as this report attests: "NOTE: ALL OFFICES SHOULD BE AWARE NO INTERVIEWS CAN BE CONDUCTED INSIDE BLACK BEAR DUE TO HOSTILITY OF RESIDENTS."

Of course, the FBI considered all communes to be a menace to society. In this bit of advice, an anonymous FBI supervisor asserts the following: "Experience has shown communes are a haven for revolutionary violence-prone individuals. Any indication that individuals are living in a communal existence should be given immediate investigative attention to establish their identities and determine their propensity to violence."

To live outside the law you must be honest

—Bob Dylan

The remoteness of the commune, far from evoking a feeling of isolation and desolation, encouraged a great feeling of liberation and self-reliance for many of us. It was the clearest example that the new vision many of us had for a new way of living actually worked. The remoteness of our existence created the perfect laboratory environment to explore and develop alternatives to an oppressive and shallow status quo, from social governance to technology to food production. In the main house, there was an excellent research lab and library for exploring homeopathic remedies derived from herbs, roots, and plants, as medical care was entirely up to the communal practitioners. Many babies were born on the commune, creating a training ground for midwives, doulas, and Women's Health practitioners and advocates. I set up a wild mushroom lab to investigate the edible fungi of the forest. Food was gathered, fished, hunted, and cultivated. Despite harboring over a hundred people, the group worked together without coercion and outside of a capitalist economy, from each according to their ability, to each according to their need. Foods that were scarce, such as goats' milk and eggs, were rationed for use by children and pregnant women. We made wine; corned, jerked, and smoked venison and salmon; grew crops; gathered rose hips, herbs and roots for medicines; milked goats; played music; smoked marijuana; ingested hallucinogens; engaged in multiple-partner sex; and did anything else we thought celebratory and liberatory, without regards to the traditions and mandates of any State apparatus.

Even the FBI was impressed with our productive capacity. These were some handwritten notes written to accompany aerial photographs of the land:

Cultivation in fields growing well (more cult. under trees)

25 people in fields (count aprx)

*Note: Considering the number of tents and the extent of cultivation, the total population is estimated at approximately 125. More could possibly be supported by present facilities.

Notes from FBI aerial investigation also point out the extent of dwellings, including two teepees, six "circular tents" (otherwise known as domes), a main building, a barn, and several shacks, checkpoints, and observation posts.

Despite the remoteness of the commune, the outside world was very much in view. The readings, discussions, and debates that ensued into the evenings often revolved around how the communal movement fit within a larger movement for social change. Outside guests, from brother and sister communes to neighboring Indian tribal members to political fugitives, would infuse the conversations with outside reports and new perspectives. Though survival in the wilderness was a high priority in our daily life, there was always something much bigger at stake in our activities.

The questioning, the harnessing and the practicalities of technology were also very much a part of communal existence. Innovation ranged from the modern gas-powered generator used to wash diapers to the *Gilligan's Island*-style construction of dwellings, bridges, and structures. Engineering feats were always being discussed, from improving the smoke flaps on the teepees to constructing a village of domes to developing new ways of drying fruits and grinding grains. The FBI was also interested in the technological accoutrements of the commune, as evidenced from the aerial Cuban Missile Crisis–style photos it took of the land from low-flying planes. An earlier report convinced the FBI that a radio transmitter and a transmitting antenna had been installed at the perimeter of the main house. It later turned out to be the washing machine and a clothesline: "The writer, with the assistance of (DELETE) flew over the captioned commune at an air speed of approximately 85 miles per hour and approximately 50 feet off the ground on two occasions. Particular attention was given to the area in question, no such towers were observed, and the area in question was identified as a laundry area."

East Meets West

Despite being part of one "Movement," there were differences between the East Coast communes and the Western ones, primarily cultural and sexual differences. Sex was a serious issue in the East coast communes, under a scrutiny driven primarily by an insurgent women's liberation movement. The place of sexual pleasure in the revolution was unsure and could be perceived with suspicion and caution. On the West coast, sex was something more celebratory and liberatory, with sexual pleasures taken for granted as healthy and positive. In general, the conversations and discussions around the East coast communal dinner table were more "heavy," and perhaps a bit pessimistic and cerebral, while conversations in the West tended more toward the cultural, spiritual, and literary. The West still seemed somewhat more seeped in a Beat attitude, while the NY intellectual attitude was more dominant in the East.

Communes were based around many different philosophies, structures, and sizes. Though my personal experience consisted primarily of communes geared toward political activism, I also encountered others that were more spiritual in nature, progenitors of what would eventually become considered "New Age." These communities tended to revolve more around "leaders" than our more consensual process. Spiritual existence was an important part of most communal life, whether it was through meditation, or group study or all holding hands around a circle every night. Zen Buddhism, Hinduism, the *I Ching*, Native American ritual, Celtic symbolism, African American spiritual traditions, and good old-fashioned Christian radicalism could all be found in active circulation. Along with spirituality, artistic endeavor and creativity were part of daily life as well, whether it was through crafts, through music, writing, poetry, or drawing. Existence was a question of balance, and life was holy in a Beat kind of way.

Though communes may or may not have had close relationships, communards from all communes took a great interest in how things worked in other communes, and there was a great deal of visiting, exchanging notes and resources. Questions such as how chores were divided up, how much or how little privacy could be expected and whether monogamous relationships were encouraged or discouraged were common discussions. It was some of these questions that led to some particularly infamous and humorous experiments, such as collectivizing all the clothes, or having a roulette wheel that determined who slept with who that night. Everything was up for grabs. With so much at stake, there were many heated disagreements and arguments on the right way to live. But, despite these differences, I witnessed an enormous amount of respect for differing views in the assumption that everyone is looking for wisdom and enlightenment and that everyone had something to say, ranging from widely differing approaches to spirituality, to vegetarianism versus hunting, or the question of violence versus nonviolence, in achieving justice and social change in the United States.

The Communal Legacy

The physical structures of the communes may now be abandoned and dilapidated but the ideas, the vision, the way of working and the ideological conviction still remain. The communes played an important and catalytic role developing an alternative to corporate capitalism and human exploitation. The commune coalesced the critical mass necessary for implementing and realizing an abundance of ideas that are now seen as givens: holistic health practices, alternative fuels and energy, sustainable agricultural processes, challenges to repressive sexual mores, and new forms of participatory culture and grassroots democracy. Whether it's the rise of organic farming, the spread of the so-called slow food movement, co-op food buying, or just a renewed reverence for traditional rural ways, one can often find a communal influence in the background. There are presently many institutions built by communes that still remain vital: food co-ops, free health clinics, alternative schools, healing centers and political organizations spawned by such projects dot the land.

Communes were a proving ground for new forms of appropriate technology, distributed through means such as the *Whole Earth Catalog* or *Mother Earth News*. The hybrid fusion of new technology and the rediscovery of older, traditional ways have made an important, yet perhaps unrecognized impression upon many areas of rural America. Rural farmers deeply enriched the skills and knowledge of communards, as communes relied heavily upon elder knowledge of animal husbandry, blacksmithing, manure composting, wood milling, maple sugar boiling, and other traditional rural craft. Our communes worked with Native American tribes in jerking deer and smoking salmon, gathering and sharing fruits, nuts, rosehips, grains, and other staples. Communal interest in keeping these traditional practices alive are a continuing contribution to maintaining an important knowledge base in a culture that reveres the "new."

Communes and working collectives provided the critical mass, the people power, and the collective wisdom to test out ideas in practice, not just in theory. Many ideas that are reaching mass acceptance now come from such experience, such as organic gardening, home-schooling, home-birthing, and alternative and holistic health. The communal movement instigated many social movements and inspired collective responses to the ills of corporate-dominated agriculture. The communal experience proved to many that an alternative life could be built and maintained without coercion or the threat of starvation and deprivation. It also showed that one's family does not stop at the blood relative's door but extends to the "family of mankind."

But it wasn't just the local impact of the communes that merits reflection. For myself, perhaps the most magical aspect of entering into the communal existence was the networked community of utopian projects I was plugged into by extension. One could travel coast-to-coast within this network and expect a hearty greeting at almost every communal door. In the urban communes of San Francisco, where there were hundreds of such communities, there was a newsletter that enabled and encouraged such door-to-door contact. *Kaliflower*, otherwise known tongue-in-cheek as "the intercommunal handjob," hand delivered by communards in order to increase friendly connections and interchange.

Considering this past is not to suggest that communes and collectives are ancient history. There are still thousands of collectives and communes functioning today and more being organized daily, but perhaps as important are the thousands of people who have been schooled in such collectivity. I see many communards today in leading roles as trade unionists, environmentalists, political activists, media producers, and musicians. Such background experience lives on in the hearts, souls and minds of many, and I know the commune is alive and well.

I left Black Bear Ranch that winter and headed to an urban collective in San Francisco for six months, where I sold underground newspapers on the street, developed a radical film screening series, became involved in the Food Conspiracy, and got to know other urban communes. I then returned to a New England collective farm for several more years. In the mid-1970s, I left the communal living situation in which I was living, as interest waned and people drifted away. I relocated to a small city where I earned the first paycheck that was mine and mine alone. I worked as a palletizer in a syrup factory, stacking boxes for forklifts to take away. I must confess to feeling guilty pleasure at having my first wad of bills in my pocket that I could spend any way I wanted to, not depending on the needs of the collective. Of course, the first thing I bought was a six-pack of beer. I drank that beer on my friend's front stoop, hardhat in my lap thinking about the way ahead on my own. I felt no remorse about the commune's dissolution, no sense of loss, no feeling that a vision had died. I knew that my comrades were all around me and that we had learned and carried forward some valuable skills and knowledge from our experiences.

The communes were a Badlands, a refuge, and a shelter, that brought the euphoria of utopia and the freedom of autonomy, a tonic that showed that a new world is possible. That vision has lasted me a lifetime.

Part II. The City

"*The focus is on the urban pole of the counter-culture and its communal practices. The tone, the styles, and the sheer weirdness of the Bay Area scene are distilled in the fading, embrittled pages of newspapers such as the* Express Times *and the* Berkeley Barb, *which were countercultural organs in the struggle to create communal spaces in which to live, work, and perform. The dimensions of race and class, perhaps more than gender—for example, the issue of Native America and its vexed relation to the counter-culture—are typically occluded in discussions of communalism, partly because communes, especially the rural communes, were overwhelmingly white and so-called middle class.*"

Bulldozers in Utopia: Open Land, Outlaw Territory, and the Code Wars

Felicity D. Scott

Recounting her impressions of Wheeler's Ranch in Sonoma County, Sara Davidson recalled that there was a sign near the community garden reading, "Permit not required to settle here."[1] Wheeler's had been launched as an Open Land commune in late 1967 and by 1970, when Davidson's article "Open Land: Getting Back to the Communal Garden" appeared in *Harper's Magazine*, many had taken up the call to occupy land free of charge, building makeshift structures or setting up temporary dwellings from tents and teepees to customized school buses and vans within this ambiguous territorial zone. The dwellings, Davidson wrote of the scene she encountered, "are straight out of Dogpatch—old boards nailed unevenly together, odd pieces of plastic strung across poles to make wobbly igloos, with round stovepipes poking out the side. Most have dirt floors, though the better ones have wood." The occupants themselves had a similarly poverty-ridden, even preindustrial if slightly theatrical (or fictional) appearance, wearing, as she put, "hillbilly clothes, with funny hats and sashes," outfits also described as "pioneer clothes."[2] The scene in the patchwork-like garden, she went on to suggest, "presents the image of a nineteenth century tableau: women in long skirts and shawls, men in lace-up boots, coveralls, and patched jeans tied with pieces of rope, sitting on the grass playing banjos, guitars, lyres, wood flutes, dulcimers, and an

---

1 Sara Davidson, "Open Land: Getting Back to the Communal Garden," *Harper's Magazine* (June 1970): 92.
2 Ibid., 92 and 96, respectively.

accordion. In a field to the right are the community animals—chickens, cows, goats, donkeys, and horses."[3]

Wheeler's was not, of course, alone in adopting such anachronistic and seemingly vernacular customs and aesthetic trappings or in adopting an ethos of communal stewardship of land and minimal exploitation of resources. Indeed, these practices were characteristic of many back-to-the-land "pioneers" and they have often been regarded to be manifestations of an escapist desire to return to simpler modes of existence in response to increasingly complex, competitive, and even hostile urban environments, socioeconomic, and political forces, or as simply romantic searches for a life more meaningful than the spiritual void characteristic of their parents' generation. If these widespread and genuine sentiments were certainly important motivating factors in returning to the land, I want to suggest that much more was at stake in the Open Land component of this movement, as evidenced in the rapid and often violent, even crushing responses such attempts to "open" or "free" the land elicited from the state. We might, I think, read the movement instead as a symptomatic and tactical response to specific historical pressures, as a form of counterconduct which (wittingly or unwittingly) articulated with some precision a type of knowledge about and engagement with contemporaneous techniques of power and control.

Exodus from official systems of managing land and the built environment—from property rights and trespass laws to building codes as well as health and safety regulations—was not, as soon demonstrated at Wheeler's, as easy as declaring, "Permit not required to settle here." Indeed, the sign served less as a performative or speech act in the sense theorized by J.L. Austin (actually declaring the land to be free of the need for permits) than it did as a polemical and political gesture.[4] It was at once a manifesto for freeing the land or ceding it (back) to the commons and an invitation to participate in testing the limits of the police and legal system's (let alone the neighbors') tolerance for the commune's battle against private ownership of land and their unconventional behavior. And the local authorities (like the neighbors) did, of course, fight back, giving rise to what came to be known as "code

---

3   Ibid., 93.
4   For an important reading of Austin see Thomas Keenan, "Drift: Politics and the Simulation of Real Life," *Grey Room* 21 (Fall 2005): 94–111.

wars" and with them an escalating set of tactical and countertactical maneuvers between the commune, on the one hand, and local and state governing institutions, on the other. It was during this battle that the ad hoc shelters and other nonnormative structures (we cannot quite call this architecture) that served not only as an expression of identity but also as a mechanism of "settling" Open Land emerged as key sites and key components both of this countercultural refusal of normative modes of life and of the local government's mode of defense against it. If these low-tech shelters proved to be powerful material on the part of the communards—easy to produce, affordable, and garnering both anxiety and publicity—they proved ultimately insufficient against the laws regulating human habitation, codes which quickly came to replace the charge of harboring dangerous persons as the police and legal system's most effective ammunition. Davidson ended her account of Wheeler's Ranch by recounting that she had accompanied members of the commune to a court-appearance for "charges of assaulting a policeman when a squad came to the ranch looking for juvenile runaways and Army deserters." Although the judge had declared a mistrial in this instance, she went on to note, "The county fathers are not finished though. They are still attempting to close the access road to Wheeler's and to get an injunction to raze all buildings on the ranch as health hazards."[5] County officials would eventually triumph on both fronts; with the exception of Wheeler's studio (protected as the owner's private residence) all buildings were later demolished and the access road closed to all but Wheeler and a few select guests. Normalcy of occupation was enforced.

Happiness People

Wheeler's Ranch was not of course the first property in Sonoma County to have "opened" its land to those wishing to depart from urban life and join an alternative rural community. Nor was it the first to have elicited a crushing response from law enforcement and the judiciary system. When Bill Wheeler opened his 320-acre property in the winter of 1967 to whoever wished to settle there, he did so partially in response to the rapid foreclosure of Morning Star Ranch, an earlier attempt to

---

5   Davidson, "Open Land," 95 and 96, respectively.

forge such a "liberated" territory within the United States. In spring of 1966, Lou Gottlieb and Ramón Sender had declared Gottlieb's ranch to be Open Land, a place without rules, regulations, or organization. In a sympathetic article on Morning Star and its "happiness people" published by the local *Press Democrat*, Gottlieb was described as "a patriarch who doesn't govern, a landlord who doesn't charge."[6] Morning Star was to be a utopia of the nongoverned, a nonhierarchical community, a place that sought to exist far beyond the domain of patriarchs and landlords as well as of extant social and material norms. Gottlieb, a former singer with The Limelighters, and Sender, an important protagonist within the early development of electronic music and synthesizers at the San Francisco Tape Music Center, met at the legendary "Trips Festival" at San Francisco's Longshoremen's Hall in late January of 1966. This connection to electronics (and to LSD) does not in retrospect seem incidental. Morning Star was very much haunted by the sense that electronic technologies and computerization heralded a future of pure automation, a future in which human labor would be replaced by information machines. "The people here," Gottlieb remarked to a journalist while touring the commune's "primitive houses," "are the first wave of an ocean of technologically unemployables. The cybernation is in its early snowball stages."[7] That human labor would become outmoded on account of "cybernation" harbored, on the one hand, a utopian promise: freedom from work and from scarcity. And the embrace of manual labor—building houses, farming the land, doing-it-yourself—also reads in retrospect as a compensatory shift away from that very "cybernation," a largely unselfconscious if for many therapeutic attempt to deal with the prospect of a withdrawal of material activities by the first generation for whom this shift toward the vicissitudes of immaterial labor was not only imminent but palpable.

On the other hand, we also find the recognition of a dystopian underside heralded by advanced technologies—the eradication of opportunities for work and loss of the dignity of labor, and beyond this the specter of atomic and nuclear warfare. This sense of a looming

---

6   Dick Torkelson, "Happiness People II: Gratan Ranch Hippie Retreat," *Press Democrat* (1967), included in *The Morning Star Scrapbook: In the Pursuit of Happiness,* eds. Unohoo, Coyote, Rick and the Mighty Avengers (Occidental, CA: Friends of Morning Star, n.d. [circa 1973]), 26.

7   Torkelson, "The Happiness People II," 26.

threat of being forced into a condition of basic survival gives a very different valence to the embrace of archaisms and the identification with less privileged persons characteristic of the "voluntary primitivism" practiced on Open Land communes. The two sides of this equation were not necessarily dialectically opposed. Sender himself noted that such "voluntary primitivism" "could only evolve within an economy of abundance, such as the United States today. It proposes a synthesis of the technologically sophisticated life style with a voluntary return to the ancient, tested ways—living close to God's nature and in harmony with the elements."[8] Here, in a microcosm, me might say, was a strange, distorted reiteration of the radical ruptures within, and unjust adjacencies emerging in, global access to technology, a reiteration marked by the shifting topology of relations between industrial and postindustrial modes of production. If "voluntary" for those living within an economy of abundance, for many others—whether the poorer sector of the American populace or those rapidly industrializing areas of the so-called Third World, including countries recently gaining independence from colonial rule (increasingly becoming industrial labor pools)—such "primitivism" born of limited access to advanced technology was of course hardly voluntary. It raises the question of the historical limitations of the communards' identification with social injustice, or the identification "down," whether to poor farmers, to itinerant populations, to Native Americans, to the nineteenth century, or to survivors of a nuclear apocalypse.[9]

The history of Morning Star and Wheeler's Ranch has been recounted in detail elsewhere.[10] Here, I want to offer a brief account of what might have been at stake in the particular conjunction of an attempted opening or freeing of the land, an underdeveloped form of shelter, rejection of many aspects of modernity, and the ethics of "care"—at once of the

---

8   See Ramón Sender "Morning Star Faith," *The Modern Utopian* 4, nos. 3 and 4 (Summer–Fall 1970): 22.

9   This text forms part of a much larger study in which these questions are addressed in detail.

10   See, for instance, Hugh Gardner, "The War of Sonoma County: Wheeler Ranch," in *The Children of Prosperity: Thirteen Modern American Communes* (New York: St. Martins Press, 1978), 134–49; and Ramón Sender Barayon, Gwen Leeds, Near Morning Star, Bill Wheeler, et al., "Home Free Home: A History of Two Open-Door California Communes: Morning Star Ranch and Wheeler's (Ahimsa) Ranch," http://www.diggers.org/home_free.htm.

land, of the planet, of other persons, and of the self. Following a mention of the "Morning Star Colonists" in "The Hippies: The Philosophy of a Subculture," *Time*'s famous cover story of July 7, 1967, the 31.7-acre property quickly attracted large numbers of residents and visitors and with them the attention (and wrath) of Sonoma Country officials. As documented in the *Morning Star Scrapbook*, an anthology of news-clippings, writings, drawings, and photographs, breaking up the commune became a concerted project among county law enforcement, building inspectors, public health officers, and sanitation officials. In late June 1967, Gottlieb was charged with operating an organized camp in violation of State public health regulations. The *San Francisco Chronicle* recounted that, upon being arrested, he had wryly announced, "If they find any evidence of organization here, I wish they would show it to me."[11] Having constructed a bathroom and fixed up the kitchen facilities in an attempt to be in accordance with the law, Gottlieb pleaded no contest to the initial charges on September 12. But within hours of the plea, the "hippie colony" was raided by what one paper called "a small army of county officials," including Sheriff John Ellis, sheriff's deputies, probation officers, FBI officers, the director of environmental health, building inspectors, a Sonoma County supervisor, Municipal County Judge James E. Jones, and others. Signs were posted condemning the structures and residents were given twenty-four hours to evacuate.[12] Following this raid, many early settlers moved to Wheeler's Ranch and others relocated to New Mexico to found Morning Star East amid a growing field of Southwestern communes. (An important part of the story of rural communes during this period was the search for cheap land that remained less regulated by local and state authorities, somehow below the radar whether on account of remoteness or lack of economic profitability for commercial land use.)[13] Those remaining or subsequently arriving at Morning Star were repeatedly raided, rounded up, the property repeatedly condemned. The organized camp charge was eventually dropped, but further charges followed from contempt of court and trespass to fire and safety code violations; anything to discourage this nuisance.

---

11 Lou Gottlieb, cited in Ralph J. Gleason, "A Limelighter's New Thing," clipping reproduced in *Morning Star Scrapbook*, 19.
12 See *Morning Star Scrapbook*, 42–47.
13 See Gardiner, "Love and Hate on Duncan's Mesa: Morning Star East and the Reality Construction Company," in *Children of Prosperity*, 102–19.

In January of 1969, with Gottlieb still refusing to forcibly remove people from the land on the grounds that it went against his religious belief, twenty-one people were arrested on charges of violating the Superior Court order to vacate. Faced with ever-mounting violations and fines, Gottlieb went to the county courthouse in May of 1969 and deeded the land to God in a notorious attempt to render the property in public domain, to return it to the commons. This savvy legal maneuver served to stay the injunctions for a period, with judges unwilling to declare that God didn't exist. But in July of 1970, Sonoma County Superior Court Judge Kenneth Eymann ruled that "Whatever be the nature of the Deity, God is neither a natural nor an artificial person capable of taking title (of Morning Star Ranch) under existing California law"[14] and instructed local authorities to carry out the writ against the property and demolish all inhabited structures with the exception (as in turn with Wheeler's) of Gottlieb's studio, understood as his private residence. Gottlieb denounced the ruling as "idolatry," "blasphemous," "sacrilegious," but the appeals to freedom of religion also proved useless.[15] Sonoma County had, as the communards observed, "started a broad-based policy of repression, including a punitive and discriminatory enforcement of the health and building codes... It became a political issue for Sonoma County's officials to rid themselves of their *undesirable* neighbors."[16]

Bulldozing the unskilled, ad hoc settlements at Morning Star and later at Wheeler's can be read, on a first-order level, as simply a way to remove structures considered to be threats to human health and safety, as unfit for human habitation, as an instance of the state acting on behalf of the welfare of its citizens, as a simple act of enforcing the law when faced with buildings not up to code. (Such regulatory codes do, of course, play an important role in keeping people safe and slumlords in check). Yet, if we are to judge by the vehemence of the county's response, the political stakes appear to have been much higher than the health and safety of those who had chosen to live in such conditions. (That the structures at Morning Star enjoyed a two-year stay of destruc-

---

14   Judge Kenneth Eymann, ruling cited in "Judge's Ruling: God Can't Own Morning Star," clipping reproduced in *Morning Star Scrapbook*, 151.

15   See Bony Saludes, "Gottlieb Thunders Against the Judge," clipping reproduced in *Morning Star Scrapbook*, 149.

16   *Open Land: A Manifesto*.

tion is testament to the fact that they were not posing an imminent danger.) For the communards, these structures were a principle means for articulating and disseminating prospects for and images of alternative modes of life; they were strategic vehicles in their attempts to withdraw from the state's regulation of environment controls, and hence weapons in the battle over opening land. Mirroring these tactics, building codes and bulldozers had thus become ammunition in the state's defense against these "attacks" on the norms of mainstream America. The state's response might raise in turn the question of whether what we find here is something like the intentional destruction of a particular built environment as a means of destroying a corresponding culture, something like an act of war that, were it a war between states, would be prohibited by the Geneva Convention. Before deeding the land to God, Gottlieb had in fact proposed deeding Morning Star to the county as a museum of folk architecture, a proposal indicating that the eccentric dwellings exemplified for him the emergence of way of life proper to Open Land, and in which preservation of the structures would serve both as a form of testimony and to protect this "cultural heritage" from the code wars.

By the late 1960s, bulldozers had of course become a key technology for the destruction of ways of life deemed crucibles of insecurity. Whether we recall the destruction of low-income inner-city neighborhoods as crime-filled "ghettoes" under the rubric of urban renewal or (in a distinct register) the destruction of villages and forests in Vietnam as part of the ecocidal war machine in Indochina, and later of Palestinian refugee camps on the basis of their harboring terrorists, the bulldozer increasingly served as one component of a political and technological apparatus mobilized for what came to be called urbicide and/or ecocide.[17] To try to unpack some of the issues raised here, I want to return and take a closer look at what informed these highly idiosyncratic built assemblies and how they might possibly have posed a challenge to security—of land prices, of the health of the population, of

---

17   Steven Graham, "Lessons in Urbicide," *New Left Review* 19 (January–February 2003): 63–78. See also its updated version "Constructing Urbicide by Bulldozer in the Occupied Territories," in *Cities, War, and Terrorism: Towards an Urban Geopolitics*, ed. Stephen Graham (Malden, MA: Blackwell Publishing, 2004), 192–213. Eyal Weizman, *Hollow Land: Israel's Architecture of Occupation* (London: Verso, 2007). Andrew Herscher and András Riedlmayer, "The Destruction of Historic Architecture in Kosovo," *Grey Room* 1 (Fall 2000): 108–22.

moral and social values, of the productivity and hence profitability of the workforce.

Shelter

A section of *Open Land: A Manifesto* entitled "Our Beleaguered Homes," outlined the ethos of self-build, no-code homes. "How about building yourself a house? No, no, you don't need money, architect, plans, permits. Why not use what's there." Suggesting that in the mild climate of Northern California one could simply join the bluejays and squirrels in the branches of trees, or dig a hole hidden from the cops, the text asserted that "Man has a nest-building instinct just like the other animals, and it is totally frustrated by our lock-step society whose restrictive codes on home-building make it just about impossible to build a *code* home that doesn't sterilize, insulate, and rigidify the inhabitants... So it falls down in the first wind storm. The second one won't. Dirt floors are easy to keep clean. Domes are full of light and air."[18] If the cost of materials and do-it-yourself ethos certainly informed the nonnormative character of the ad hoc constructions springing up at Morning Star, Wheeler's, and beyond, as suggested in this manifesto, their forms cannot be explained simply as the product of a lack of building expertise (although this did of course often factor in) or, in the case of the automobiles, lack of skill in customization. The teepees, lean-tos, tents, open-sided A-frames, simple tarpaulins, tree-houses, geodesic structures, vans, school buses, brushwood hogans, and "other miscellaneous shelters, including a Cadillac hearse, being used as homes"[19] were, to reiterate, not simply expediencies but in many regards a form of protest, one that took the form of demonstrating (and disseminating) an alternative mode of life.

Many believed, moreover, that in working against the grain of the normative logics inscribed within conventional architectural and urban forms and instituted through planning and building codes, that these alternative structures in themselves facilitated a mode of liberation from those forces which "sterilize, insulate, and rigidify the inhabitants." There are many reasons to be suspicious of such functionalist

---

18 See "Judge's Ruling: God Can't Own Morning Star," 157.

19 See "Gottlieb and County At it Again at Morning Star," April 25, 1971, clipping reproduced in *The Morning Star Scrapbook*, 161.

claims (claims that the forms themselves were liberatory). We need think only of the degree to which many of these forms, such as geodesic domes and the wood-butcher aesthetic, became rather mainstream by the 1970s, assimilated without significantly altering forms of life. Yet it does seem that at the moment of their emergence these structures had identified points within the architectural process in which contemporary forms of governmentality impinged most directly upon the subject, where techniques of power were most evident within the organization and regulation of the built environment. And it is perhaps at this register (rather than, say, their aesthetic value or simplistic ideas of their liberatory function) that such alternative built environments might offer lessons for thinking about architecture and the built environment: lessons regarding how buildings might serve not simply to give a spatial form to dominant institutions and techniques of power, to materialize the very *dispositif* or apparatus of power, but how they might also operate as tactical maneuvers, even as a counter-*dispositif* or site of refusal of official forms of social and ideological regulation.

War

Open Land was initially conceived as a utopian experiment. Yet, it quickly came to operate as a battlefield, the site of a mêlée with county authorities, the place from which, as Gottlieb suggested to Davidson, was launched a confrontation against the nationalist logic of the "territorial imperative." "What kind of country is this," the communards asked, "that can allow mobs of armed men to vent their savagery upon villages of unarmed brothers and sisters? Is this America?"[20] The often ad hoc dwelling structures and settlements, as noted above, proved to be important components of this violent encounter, tactical if low-tech materiel that prompted a cycle of raids by building inspectors and subsequent demolition. "When he opened the land," Fairfield recalled of Wheeler's, "the county authorities were quick to move in and condemn his home as not up to code standards. They wanted to discourage another Morning Star." He went on to argue in a long parenthesis, "(Punitive measures are always the first to be used by government and those in power. The effects of such measures have always been to increase resistance rather than

---

20 *Open Land: A Manifesto.*

suppress it. I would theorize that authority wishes to encourage opposition rather than extinguish it as this gives them the opportunity to show power, boost ego, vent hostility. Without opposition, what use is authority? Military men need wars to make their existence meaningful; so too with those who wage other battles.)"[21]

This passage speaks to a certain knowingness regarding dynamics of power and the ways in which these battles served not only to identify points of insecurity but also to aid the state in closing them down. It also suggests the way in which the state served to prompt, even promote, a turn to violence. *Open Land: A Manifesto* noted that response to constant harassment by county authorities had led in two opposite directions: "many of the older established residents with children made ready to escape further North. Other folk are returning to the city ghetto life or going on the road. Some will end up in jails or hospitals. Some, discouraged and disillusioned, may join the violent revolution in the city streets." When the county razed structures at Morning Star again in May 1971 (enlisting a company that had been contracted to demolish unsafe structures after a natural disaster, the 1969 Santa Rosa earthquake), Gottlieb, as one journalist noted, "struck an ominous chord. 'This was peaceful. But think how easy [*sic*] it could have changed. One insane act—and...' he swept an outstretched arm toward the cluster of officials standing some 50 yards away. 'Sooner or later, it will no longer be a peaceful confrontation. Someday...it will be bestial, worse than the Civil War.'"[22]

That opening the land was already conceived as a form of militancy (if not yet a violent form with respect to persons) was noted by Gottlieb: "Morning Star is a training replacement center, or rest and recuperation area, for the army of occupation in the war against the exclusive ownership of land."[23] Wheeler reiterated and extended this theme, suggesting that the struggle with Sonoma County over the communal use of land was in fact already akin to a state of civil warfare, the clash of two ideologies with radically unequal military strength. Likening the commune to the Viet Cong, he declared, "We're an underground movement. We're going to take some

---

21 Richard Fairfield, "Sheep Ridge Ranch," in "Communes, U.S.A." special issue of *The Modern Utopian* 5, nos. 1–3 (1971): 121. Sheep Ridge Ranch was another name for Wheeler's Ranch.

22 Lou Gottlieb cited in James E. Reid, "Lou Gottlieb Thunders as County Again Plows Over 'God's Land,'" clipping reproduced in *The Morning Star Scrapbook*, 165.

23 Gottlieb, cited by Richard Fairfield, "Morning Star," in "Communes, U.S.A," special issue of *The Modern Utopian* 5, nos. 1–3 (1971): 113.

very hard blows for sure. It's not inconceivable that the County will succeed in tearing down all the buildings on the Ranch... But we are a form of guerilla warfare and we're going to take our losses."[24] In this context he also recalled a meeting with a Sonoma County supervisor at the tax window, and associated their actions with revolutionary battles: "You know, we've *got* to fight against you," the supervisor had said. "Every revolution that's ever happened has had resistance against it and if you think this one's going to be any different you're crazy." "I thought about it," Wheeler added, "And he's right—we need it. It's gotta happen that way. For us to come together we've got to fight for what we believe in, in the same way the Israeli's fought for what they believed in."[25] If the comparison with Israel spoke largely to a widespread fascination with kibbutzim as a paradigm of new communalism, and if they identified with the founding of a new country, it nevertheless reminds us of the important and complicated set of issues regarding the relation of the utopian imaginaries of these "pioneers" and settlers to the native population.

Morning Star and Wheeler's had become "Outlaw Territory."[26] Indeed, Open Land was widely assumed to provide shelter to those avoiding the law. In October 1968 Wheeler's was raided: "twenty-five police officers, FBI, juvenile, narcotics, military police, without benefit of a search warrant, converged from two directions on Wheeler's," a transgression that prompted Wheeler to accuse the county of civil rights abuses.[27] Open Land was, however, quite literally conceived as an "outlaw area;" it was an attempt to open territory beyond the sanction (and protection) of legal codes, an attempt to demarcate and declare an extraterritorial enclave in which the usual rule of law and functioning of state legislature could somehow be suspended. As Gottlieb proposed during an interview with Fairfield, "What we need in this country are statute free sanctuaries, because many people who fall ill in this country fall ill from an allergy to statutes; there has never been a society that has been as burdened by statutes."[28] While they sought escape from the impact of regulatory codes,

24 Wheeler in "Interview with Bill Wheeler," 127.
25 Wheeler in "Interview with Bill Wheeler," 129.
26 "A Fast Run-Through, Part Two," typescript page in *The Morning Star Scrapbook*, 40.
27 *Open Land: A Manifesto.*
28 Lou Gottlieb cited in "Interview with Lou Gottlieb, Founder of Morning Star Ranch (February, 1971)," in "Communes, U.S.A.," 115. This would take on a semireligious dimension under the pressures impacting their beliefs. "Statutory law defines the life style that the Morning Star Faith renounces." "Morning Star Faith."

refusing to abide by legal statutes deemed oppressive if not harmful to one's person, these formulations raise the question of what sort of legal protection and citizenship rights were assumed to remain. Are we faced here with something like a perverse mirror image of declaring martial law, or of the state's ability to suspend the usual functioning of the law through declaring a "state of emergency"? Can we read these hippie colonies, that is, to have formulated a camp in the expanded sense theorized by Giorgio Agamben, wherein "the functional nexus" between territory, the state, and citizenship (nation) become unsecured? Certainly the communards hoped to complicate a simple topology of citizen and foreigner, or inside versus outside America, to produce a new spatial arrangement that "remains constantly outside the normal state of law?²⁹

The members of Morning Star and Wheeler's were treading a fine line between civil disobedience and a total disregard for the institutions of the law and its enforcement, the institutions through which civility is maintained and citizens are protected and represented, but also, as they acknowledged, through which dominant techniques of power and the normalizing function of the State operated to particular (and, to the communards minds, oppressive) ends. Motivating these actions was the belief that a property-less relation to land would lead to a distinct form of social organization (tribalism) and new geopolitical relations (Open Earth). But in retrospect we need to ask, of course, how such a self-organizing system could ensure that what would come to replace that governmental rationality and its attendant institutions would be equitable, non-hierarchical or even non-violent relations and systems of organization. What sort of political space were Open Land communes actually imagining?

Conclusion

I want to come back in concluding to underscore what might be at stake in these struggles over Open Land for the discipline of architecture. The rural commune movement spoke most overtly to the desire for a simpler or more meaningful existence, a desire often coupled with apocalyptic beliefs that following an imminent ecological catastrophe one's very survival might depend on having learnt basic techniques for living, tech-

---

29 Giorgio Agamben, "What Is a Camp?" in *Means Without End: Notes on Politics* (Minneapolis: University of Minnesota Press, 2000), 37–45; Giorgio Agamben, *State of Exception*, trans. Kevin Attell (Chicago: University of Chicago Press, 2005).

niques not dependent upon the technical infrastructure and political governance of the state—such as control and distribution of resources and services (water, power, food, land, shelter, education, health care, etc.). Their forms of counter-conduct, including their modes of habitation, appear in retrospect as historically symptomatic attempts to loosen the grip of, or even to sponsor a mass exit from the regulatory and administrative functioning of the contemporary state and its dispersed apparatus of control. Rejecting normative and scientifically justified approaches to health, hygiene, education, sanitation, birthrates, labor, housing, and the organization of the environment, Open Land communards were *not*, to stress, fighting for access to or equitable inclusion within the system. Rather, they were actively withdrawing from the institutions, practices and sites through which micropolitical techniques of power had developed under a modern form of governmental rationality, they were withdrawing from the points at which the logic of governmentality systematically met the body and psyche of the contemporary subject in their everyday lives.[30] Open Land thus also implicitly questioned the relation between the state's more benevolent role in ensuring the health and welfare of its citizens and the forms of control it exerted over them in the name of maintaining productivity, or more precisely, maintaining profitability for the capitalist machinery under the impact of a transforming modernity.

Despite the successful crushing of Morning Star and Wheeler's, we might ask whether the "code wars" were in fact won by the state. Certainly the widespread fascination with communes and returning to the land would soon subside. Yet, as Steve Durkee once characterized the aims of the Lama commune, these experimental communities "[left] behind accurate maps of the territory."[31] Some of these maps are being recovered by a new generation seeking, for instance, to leave the city and found ecovillages, to fight the closing of the commons, to renew the Open Land movement, or to extend its ambitions to questions of intellectual property in the information age.[32] These maps have many flaws and points of

---

30 On Foucault's notion of governmentality, see, for instance, Michel Foucault, *Security, Territory, Population: Lectures at the Collège de France, 1977–1978*, trans. Graham Burchell (New York: Palgrave, 2007).

31 Steve Durkee cited in Hedgepeth, *The Alternative*, 164.

32 See, for instance, *This Is the Public Domain*, an art project by San Francisco–based artist Amy Balkin [http://www.thisisthepublicdomain.org]; LAND [http://www.n55.dk/land.html]; the project to renew People's Park [http://www.peoplespark.org]; or organizations such as First Monday [http://www.firstmonday.org].

blindness and certainly they need to be redrawn, even to have updated user's guides. And the State is of course familiar with them too. But they harbor important lessons regarding the need to critically, and with great specificity, interrogate the complex matrix of forces at work in a particular historical and geopolitical condition.

The Dome and the Shack: The Dialectics of Hippie Enlightenment

Simon Sadler

" "Just what *was* the fascination with the geodesic dome?" If I could answer this question, one organizer of the University of California, Berkeley's 2006 "West of Eden" symposium told me, I would have made my preliminary contribution to a discussion of Bay Area communalism and utopianism.

This came initially as a relief, as the answer seems fairly obvious—the geodesic dome was so extraordinarily different from standard shelter. Living in a geodesic dome was an act of such obvious dissent from existence in the "Little Boxes" of Cold War era "ticky-tacky" suburban sprawl that swept the Bay Area.[1] The domes' small footprint allowed them to be dotted among California's Arcadian orchards and groves, which would be spared the indignity of being torn up to lend their names to new blacktop ribbons. Square thinking came from square buildings; the expanded mind would bloom in a space without corners.[2] The geodesic dome's beguiling geometry gave alternative society a visible image, and its relative lightness and portability promised stealth and autonomy. More than this, an authorless mathematical certainty connected the geodesic dome's builder-occupant to patterns underlying nothing less than cosmological order.

---

1   I refer here to Malvina Reynolds's song "Little Boxes," made famous by performer Pete Seeger in 1962.

2   "To live in a dome is—psychologically—to be in closer harmony with natural structure. Macrocosm and microcosm are recreated, both the celestial sphere and molecular and crystalline forms. ...Corners constrict the mind. Domes break into new dimensions." Bill Voyd, "Funk Architecture," in *Shelter and Society,* ed. Paul Oliver (New York: Praeger, 1969), 158.

On closer consideration, needless to say, the question about the counterculture's fascination with the dome is not so simple. The myriad worries about Richard Buckminster Fuller's disputed claim to have invented the geodesic dome, about Fuller's attraction to technocracy and the military-industrial complex, about the unsuitability of his designs for self-builders without access to machine shops, are well known now and were becoming well known to the counterculture four decades ago. In fact the geodesic dome, and to some extent the charismatic leadership of its supposed inventor, Fuller, functioned more discursively and iconically than practically, and the counterculture largely abandoned both Fuller and his dome in the early 1970s. If anything, this loss of faith made the geodesic dome even more valuable as a material-object focus for Bay Area design theorists concerned with the telos, the ends, of counterculture. Counterculture, I think it is fair to say, approached design as a means by which to make the world intelligible—design was not simply the means to a style, or a protest, or a necessity, but an ontology and epistemology, a means of knowledge about the world and being in the world. Within that equation the geodesic dome promised a certain ideal of shelter—with the dome, Fuller had honed his *pragmatism* to an *ideal*. Now his hippie students would deconstruct that ideal back to something more pragmatic, sidelining the dome with shelters "imperfected" like shacks, cabins, and assemblies of tools, all as works-in-progress. Within the tension between the ideal and the pragmatic was a dialectic of hippie enlightenment.

Remembered for its civilian adaptation of the geodesic dome, countercultural design was nonetheless multifarious. Initial fascination with Fuller's dome and with his model of design and ecology at large ignited interest in the potential of design generally. For example the *Whole Earth Catalog*, the fantastically popular merchandise catalog founded in the Bay Area in 1968, putatively to furnish provisions to the rising commune movement, openly declaimed itself to be an homage to Fuller and his vision of the world as a whole system, and it was surely the key agent in the dissemination of Fuller's ideas through the counterculture. But Fuller's epistemology was to some considerable extent pushed aside, notably by the *Catalog*'s increasing interest in another Bay Area thinker, UC Santa Cruz anthropologist Gregory Bateson, whose theories of "ecology of mind" were based on the premise that there is no outside from which to observe ecology's inside, meaning that we are all bound to all the things in the world as coevolutionists.

Was it possible to coevolve with a dome? The removal of a single bolt would ensure structural catastrophe. In 1962, the British architect-critic Alan Colquhoun criticized Richard Buckminster Fuller for presenting "a final form—the image of a technique which has reached an optimum of undifferentiation," and something of the same suspicion seems to have motivated the changed opinions of the geodesic system first by Lloyd Kahn, a design editor with the *Whole Earth Catalog*, then by the *Catalog*'s founder Stewart Brand.[3] Kahn actually ordered that copies of his celebrated *Domebooks*, which recorded the dome-building exercises (as inspected by Fuller) at the experimental Pacific High School in Santa Cruz, be withdrawn from bookstores. Kahn dismantled the exemplary dome which he had built for himself at Bolinas, California, and renouncing his interest in Fuller's worldview, in geometry, and in high-tech materials like acrylic, Kahn returned in 1973 to his love of carpentry and timber, publishing his still more popular books about vernacular and handmade architecture.

Brand too denounced architecture that utilizes advanced materials and technologies in his detailed treatise of 1994, *How Buildings Learn: What Happens After They're Built*, even though he heretically (or pragmatically) advocated for advanced technological solutions such as space colonies in the 1970s and nuclear energy in the 1990s. (Urbanization itself—once considered an evil that the communal movement hoped to redress—has been forgiven in Brand's most recent work.) Brand came to delight in reused industrial buildings and traditional building typologies; Kahn became passionate about the slow and local craft of building. So permissive does the countercultural aesthetic become, indeed, that it apparently goes in any number of directions—from the misshapen domes of the pioneering Drop City settlement in Trinidad, Colorado (where Brand first envisaged the *Whole Earth Catalog*), to the shacks of the Morning Star commune in Sonoma County, California; from rudely shaped sheet scrap metal to shingles and logs, then to the gaudily painted inner-city Victorians reclaimed in the late 1960s and 1970s by the hippies and other subcultures, notably the Gay community of the Castro.

---

3   Alan Colquhoun, "The Modern Movement in Architecture," *British Journal of Aesthetics* (January 1962): 59–65, reprinted in *Architecture Culture 1943–1968: A Documentary Anthology*, eds. Joan Ockman and Edward Eigen (New York: Rizzoli, 1993), 342–46.

Literature on countercultural design has had a tendency to fall into two camps. The counterculture proved adept at managing its own literature since the initial self-published tomes of the 1960s, whereas a secondary critical literature has vigorously fulfilled its duty to be critical. The irritation with countercultural design which critical observers feel is prompted in part by the counterculture's tendency to be enamored by "fixes"—crazes, we might say, not inappropriately about a social movement centered on a generation that grew up in the decade of the Davy Crockett cult. Cynically, we might see the geodesic dome as the counterculture's Davy Crockett hat, part of a drop-out package completed by other fixes like LSD and communalism. And as this craze wanes it is replaced by another (the bricolage of wildly erratic handmade shelter), then another (online communities, starting with the *Whole Earth Catalog*'s WELL), then another (New Age). Yet the critiques brought externally to the movement, however legitimately, appear to be disregarded by those within it, as though participants regard external criticism as redundant: the movement operated its own internal "peer review" (notably through its publications such as those of *Whole Earth*), its own lampooning (for instance through the Bay Area's Ant Farm collective) and by dint of the counterculture's tendency toward self-criticism and enquiry—toward a relentless pragmatism, in fact.

The theme of pragmatism guides this chapter hereon, because it is so prevalent in countercultural design. Placing at its center the relationship between idealism and pragmatism dialectically oversimplifies the dynamics of countercultural design, and it is cruelly reductive for a movement that wanted to transcend any trace of dialecticism and linearity—that espoused, instead, an ecological view of the world, with its culture and nature and things interconnected. As part of this effort the *Catalog* urged its readers to read around evolutionary science, cybernetics, mysticism. But a dialectical analysis provisionally opens countercultural design to political scrutiny, something resisted by counterculture's preferred evolutionary and cybernetic analogies, in which "self-organization" becomes a ghost in the machine that mitigates human agency.

The geodesic dome itself looked like a freeze-framed dialectic between the ideal and pragmatic. Though the rigid struts and links and circular plan of the geodesic dome could not coevolve, rigidified as they were into a technoscientific ideal, it was nonetheless possible to take a pragmatist's delight in the form of the geodesic dome, so visibly different as it was from western architecture's traditional preference for orthogonal structure, classicism, Cartesian rationality and serial production. Fuller seemed less to have designed the geodesic dome than intuited it, to have discovered it, plucked it from nature, where it stood comparison alongside things like crystals which seemed like ideal designs but were also shaped by accident. Since Darwin, Nature was understood as the great pragmatist, the great self-organizer, ever rearranging matter and pattern into best fits. Darwin's great insight was itself a spur to the American tradition of political philosophy known as Pragmatism. Indeed the counterculture is so reminiscent of nineteenth century American bootstrapping traditions: for instance Transcendentalism, with its spiritual emphases upon the alliance of intuition, individualism, and nature, was another nineteenth-century influence upon the counterculture that relates to Pragmatism via such figures as Ralph Waldo Emerson and Henry David Thoreau, themselves searching restlessly for that spark connecting the ideal and the pragmatic.

In Pragmatism, abstract propositions hold true when they are shown to *work*. Lloyd Kahn, concomitantly we might say, pulled copies of his *Domebooks* from the bookshelves in scorn at their impracticality, while his colleague Jay Baldwin insisted, on no less pragmatic grounds, that "Bucky Works."[4] Stewart Brand, in a manner worthy of Pragmatist John Dewey, wanted to know "how buildings learn." Baer's Zomes, meantime, were a clear command to the geodesic system to learn—to learn, for example, how to enclose a space that is not round, and thus how to accommodate human behaviors and functions that fall outside of a circle. The *Catalog*'s famous strapline—"Access to Tools"—announced a veritable portal to the pragmatic. The *Catalog* drew from and gave back to a certain Bay Area design ethos, one traceable to the "Bay Region Style" of architectural modernism that was distinguished from the Eurocentric "International Style" (which elsewhere stood as the quintessence of twentieth century architecture) by being much more pragmatic in its acceptance of local building manners, topography, and climate. "Bay Region Style" was inaugurated by architects like William Wurster and Bernard Maybeck, and was so-named by Lewis Mumford, a liberal critic well regarded by the counterculture both for his architectural criticism and his distinctive reading of history as an emergent, systematic, and organic

---

4   Jay Baldwin, *Bucky Works: Buckminster Fuller's Ideas for Today* (New York: Wiley, 1997).

biotechnical complex synchronizing people, thought, and culture. (Design Thinking, with its Dewey-esque bid to transcend the opposition of theory and practice via an "intelligent" practice of lateral analysis and rapid prototyping, is the best example today of the survival of a pragmatist design culture with strong Bay Area links.)

The danger of pragmatism, with its Pollyanna belief in the next fix, is known to all critics of the liberalism within which pragmatism finds lodging. Pragmatism and liberalism alike posit ingenuity—instrumental logic—ahead of any more profound truth. Bay Area counterculture sequestered the god-like powers over destiny, over the whole earth, that the Frankfurt School philosophers had already argued were the path to global ruination. "We are as gods," the *Catalog* reminded its readers, "and may as well get good at it"; "the distinction between God and man," Max Horkheimer and Theodor Adorno warned about instrumental rationality, "is reduced to an irrelevance... In their mastery of nature, the creative God and the ordering mind are alike."[5] If the *Catalog* set out (as Brand has claimed) in the tradition of that incorrigibly inquiring eighteenth century volume of the Enlightenment, the *Encyclopédie*, then the epistemological revolution of the counterculture followed something of the same tragic trajectory that Horkheimer and Adorno claimed in 1944 had beset the Enlightenment. The Enlightenment transitioned, they claimed, from critique to affirmation, that is, from the skepticism of the *Encyclopédistes* to the positivism of Auguste Comte or, to transfer the thesis to counterculture, from a distrust of modern America to an embrace of technoculture and, by the 1990s, even of economic libertarianism. Pragmatism indeed; as Adorno and Horkheimer said of Enlightenment, much the same could be said too of what critics have usefully termed the Californian Ideology of euphoric innovation: "By leaving consideration of the destructive side of progress to its enemies, thought in its headlong rush into pragmatism is forfeiting its sublating character, and therefore its relation to truth."[6] In other words, thought becomes diverted from a critical enquiry *outward* into the truth of the whole—which was surely one promise of the title "Whole Earth"—into a search for *local* fixes. Counterculture's distrust of "the system" (the American system of industrial production, the system of

---

5   Max Horkheimer and Theodor Adorno, *Dialectic of Enlightenment: Philosophical Fragments* (Stanford: Stanford University Press, 2002), 5–6.

6   Ibid., xv.

education, and so on) ironically depended on a blind trust of another "system"—the system of Nature, and analogously of ecologies thriving on "bottom-up" pragmatism. Rejecting a system of speculatively built suburban shacks, counterculture had accepted a system of self-built ex-urban shacks (or, to borrow Emerson's famous quip, it rejected brand-name mousetraps in favor of better mousetraps).

But we should supplement this political-philosophical criticism of counterculture with an acknowledgment of its peculiar historical context, wherein pragmatism countered the unproductive ideological polarization of Cold War and the delirium of postwar plenty.[7] To some extent, the counterculture addressed the conundrums of late-capitalist societies identified by Frankfurt School philosophers. In *One-Dimensional Man* (1964) Herbert Marcuse suggested that Karl Marx's theory of the estrangement of people and objects we call alienation requires revision when producers and consumers come to identify with commodities as *extensions* of themselves. Counterculture's DIY culture, one might suggest, correspondingly sought an ethical cleansing of its adherents' relationship to consumption, in a way reminiscent of the way that the Arts and Crafts movement of the late nineteenth century hoped that commodity production and exchange could be reformed into a social bond. True, the *Catalog* encouraged a degree of commodity fetishism and prototyped the "communal consumption" model now familiar through user-review sales systems like Amazon.com. But few of the objects featured in the *Catalog* promised instant consumer gratification, suggesting instead actions upon the world, the reformation of subjectivity, the betterment of social relations. One might then object that the *Catalog* was marketing experience and self-invention, but the same could be said of many aesthetics. The counterculture's aesthetic bears a better resemblance to Dewey's contention in *Art as Experience* (1934) that creators, audiences and objects are not autonomous and based on disinterested relations (as in the Kantian tradition), but are brought together when creativity serves as an integrator for a constructive everyday life.

To its credit, counterculture's linkage of theory and practice aimed to ground politics in real matter, real places, in temporality and in praxis, in the rethinking of myth, technology, self, and nature. The

---

7   Ibid., xvi.

Pragmatist merging of theory and practice invites comparison too with anarchist political philosophies promoting the diminution of central- ized authority in the conduct of human relations. One point of cross- over is the high esteem in which the counterculture held the book *Communitas* (1947) by Paul and Percival Goodman, which imagined a society founded upon a commonwealth that maximized liberty and creativity. Less to its credit, Bay Area counterculture was seduced by a libertarian anarchism (an ultrapragmatism, indeed), eventually made notorious in *Out of Control* (1995), a book in which former *Catalog* editor Kevin Kelly's greeted the techno-economic market complex as a ground-up, self-organized, hybridized, neonature writ large—that is, as a pure positivism.

My discussion seems to have strayed from an initial inquiry into the design ethos of Bay Area counterculture. But I would argue that the counterculture's design ethos, pragmatically weighing-up the strengths and weakness of Fuller, of self-taught architecture, of tool distribution mechanisms and information exchanges, provides a case study of the telos of Bay Area communalism and utopianism. As just another design, community was an ideal made without end—*this* was the ideal. The movement's general rejection of Fuller spurned patentable images of the whole in favor of an older understanding of modernity as a thing in becoming, its components forming a whole through ceaseless dif- ferential and synchromesh. In his meditation on the geodesic dome, Alan Colquhoun cautioned that its ultrafunctionalism implied "a rejec- tion of mediate steps between man and the absolute."[8] By contrast, Bay Area shacks, building manuals, and tool culture attempted to restore, whether successfully or not, a respect for nature, for spirit, for matter, for contingency, for a distinct "objecthood" beyond mere conceptual- ization. It wanted "to grasp," as Horkheimer and Adorno put it, "exist- ing things as such, not merely to note their abstract spatial-temporal relationships, by which they can be seized, but, on the contrary, to think of them as surface, as mediated conceptual moments which are only fulfilled by revealing their social, historical, and human meaning."[9] "What the primitive experiences as supernatural," we might recall of Horkheimer and Adorno's argument when pondering hippie "neoprim-

---

8   On the role of Pragmatism in American life, see Louis Menand, *The Metaphysical Club: A Story of Ideas in America* (New York: Farrar, Straus and Giroux, 2002).

9   Colquhoun, "The Modern Movement in Architecture," 243.

itivism," "is not a spiritual substance in contradistinction to the material world but the complex concatenation of nature in contrast to its individual link."[10] Bay Area counterculture made peculiarly explicit a dialectic between idealism and pragmatism that is probably secreted in designs of many types and scales.

---

10 Horkheimer and Adorno, *Dialectic of Enlightenment*, 20.

Occupied Alcatraz: Native American Community and Activism

Janferie Stone

One late November day in 1969, a car drew up to Pier 39 in San Francisco. Four women, two young, two middle-aged, emerged. They were Mono, native Californians from a small rancheria near Dunlap, where the Central Valley rises into the Sierra Foothills. They had driven over five hours and began to search the line of seacraft waiting to take Indians out to Alcatraz to join the Occupation. The news had spread as if on the wind; natives of all tribes had set foot on the Rock to reclaim it for the dispossessed peoples of America. The Rock was in the center of the whole San Francisco Bay Area scene. Antiwar protests rocked the campuses at Berkeley and San Francisco State, the Black Power movement surged in the East Bay, the Summer of Love and the music scene reverberated in the Haight-Ashbury, and Gay power found its niche between The Castro and Polk Street. As back-to-the-landers trekked out across the bridges, looking for communal land where they could test newfound values, they might glimpse Alcatraz, where young Indian activists were staking their claim, continuing their road of contention, activism, and cultural revival. They would hold the Rock in an Indian way.

As Shirley Guevera tells it, she was a nineteen-year-old student at Fresno State; her EOPS grant had come in and classes had started. She was one of four girls and four boys in a rancheria family. Her roots were in the soil of California, her routine the many chores done before going to school each morning. She wanted to be off the rez; she wanted adventure. She had never been to a large city, had never participated in the Disneylands of American culture. When she heard about Alcatraz, the call was clear, irresistible. Pride and longing rose up in her. On those docks the smells, the sounds, the sway of the ocean caused immediate seasickness. But she knew she wanted to go to the Rock. The four women engaged "a guy with a two-man speedboat" and climbed aboard. Shirley cowered in the prow of the boat as it slammed wave after wave, the water spraying over the bow, the salt against her tongue, crusting her hair. She thought, "Oh my...now we are going to die!" The boat did not split apart, but sped through the Coast Guard cordon and sidled up to the dock where banners fluttered: THIS IS INDIAN LAND and RED POWER. Gratefully, the four women tumbled ashore. Up the long steps, through the short cut. They were part of the occupation of Alcatraz. Her sister stayed only a few days, heeding the voice her mother had instilled in all her children about education and opportunity; her aunts stayed about a month; Shirley stayed until the last day of the Occupation. On June 11, 1971, she had gone to San Francisco to do chores when the U.S. Marshals rounded up the last fifteen occupiers physically present on Alcatraz. The pain of separation from the Rock lodges to this day. "I would still be there."

Shirley casts the Occupation as a moment that became momentum. With the taste of salt she first learned to ask, "How do we all connect, the you and the I, none beneath and none above, all breathing the same air? How do we care for the generations? How do we take care of the earth, acknowledging that everything we do affects everyone else?" She and many of the others who were on the Rock over the eighteen months of the Occupation have had forty years to move beyond acrid disappointment, beyond the body and soul trauma, to contemplate ongoing movement and activism.

The Federal Bureau of Prisons had vacated Alcatraz Island in 1963. Sioux Indians first occupied the island in 1964, signing a formal claim statement "under an 1868 Sioux treaty that entitled them to take possession of surplus land."[1] Young Indians from tribes that had lost federal trusteeship status during the Indian Termination of the 1950s–60s had relocated to the Bay Area. Or, if their tribes still had a reservation, the agents of relocation had played on the theme of opportunity in the wide world in contrast to the destitution of their

---

1   Troy R. Johnson, *We Hold the Rock: The Indian Occupation of Alcatraz, 1969 to 1971* (San Francisco: Golden Gate National Parks Foundation, 1997), 10.

rez lives. The young were a generation or two distant from knowledge of the land and seasons. In the Bay Area, their anger rose, faced with (more) broken promises of jobs and assistance. The hidden price tag of a college education was to sever from being Indian, sell one's share in the reservation, to become an exile in one's own country. Energy coalesced around centers such as the Intertribal Friendship House in Oakland and the American Indian Center in San Francisco.[2] Coupled with the energy of radicalized students from San Francisco State and UC Berkeley, the activists set the (re)occupation of Alcatraz into motion, establishing hold by November 20, 1969. They claimed the island as Indian Land, for "Alcatraz shared qualities common to most Indian reservations, including isolation and the lack of resources necessary for human life."[3] They put out the call to universities and reservations for Indians to come and stand with them. The eighteen-month course of the occupation, and its portrayal in the media, moving from press accounts of student idealism and initial popular support to headlines about infighting, factionalism, and power struggles has been documented elsewhere.[4] But the long-range depth of the Indian power movement seems to be rooted in the sociability of the experience, of how the group managed the ever-changing faces of the communal body at the core of the Occupation.

Alcatraz was where tribes could cross-pollinate their historic common grounds and reconnect across the generations. Each occupier brought a body of traditions and history, surfacing to create a tribal commons on the Rock. What they did not know could be learned. On the first sailing to the island, the number gathered on the docks had to be trimmed to induce the skipper of the Monte Cristo, to take them aboard. Adam Fortunate Eagle writes, "Children and Elders had to stay behind. This old Lakota Couple...felt such an overwhelming grief— their grandparents had been at Wounded Knee in 1890. They'd been

---

2   See Susan Lobo, *Urban Voices: The Bay Area American Indian Community* (Tucson: University of Arizona Press, 2002).

3   Johnson, *We Hold the Rock*, 12–13.

4   See Edward D. Castillo, "Native American Activism" in *The Whole World's Watching Berkeley* (Berkeley Art Center Association), 94–97; Jack Forbes, "The Native Struggle for Liberation: Alcatraz," *American Indian Culture and Research Journal* 18, no. 4 (1994): 93–102; Adam Fortunate Eagle and Tim Findley, *Heart of the Rock: the Indian Invasion of Alcatraz* (Norman: University of Oklahoma Press, 2002); Johnson, *We Hold the Rock*.

in a teepee when the bullets of the 7th, 11th, and 14th Cavalry came slamming through the buffalo hide."[5] Coming to Alcatraz was a political decision that restructured families who had forgotten Indian Ways. Millie Ketcheshawno, Muskoke, stated that her desire to come with her children met objections from their non-Indian father. "So that was the end of him." Edward Willie remembers the hardships experienced by families in Relocation: "Indians lost in the urban tundra that was the East Oakland ghetto... My poor mother was singlehandedly trying to raise five children." The Occupation opened up new vistas and understandings for all, from his eleven-year-old self to the Elders. "It was not until years later that I was able to pinpoint the cause of the good feeling in my heart. I realized this was the important ingredient that had been missing in our lives. These were our people: Indians, Indians, and more Indians."[6] In succeeding waves, the elders came, the families came, and if at first they did not know anyone, it felt like coming home. The home was not the Rock in its chilled stone, but the spiral of kin and Indian ways of organization. If the loops of the barbed wire of imprisonment lay in loose hanks, whistling and singing in the wind, the voices of playing children piped all over the island, from the folds of the tepee in the gardens to the depths of the old citadel dungeons, where Hopi elders had once been manacled for not sending their children to the white man's schools.

The first Occupiers held daily morning meetings to come up with governing principles and a structure. The injunction was always to think and act Indian. The principle of egalitarianism led to the consensus governing style, with each and every resident of the Rock able to give voice. The non-Indian Press, for lack of understanding, and the federal government, for political purposes, confused consensus with factionalism. "When one person does not agree with the decision of the majority, this should be construed as the exercise of consensus government, not factionalism."[7] From the beginning, disinformation obscured the idealism and indeed the successes of the residents of the Rock.

---

5   Johnson, *We Hold the Rock*, 15.
6   Edward Willie, "Rock Memories" in *News From Native California*, 23, no. 4, Summer 2010.
7   Troy R. Johnson, *The American Indian Occupation of Alcatraz Island: Red Power and Self-Determination* (Urbana: University of Illinois Press, 1996).

Elections for the Council of Seven (brothers and sisters) were every ninety days. The council set up committees for publicity, security, housing, clothing, education, with work assigned to each woman, man and child. The weekly Friday meetings were forums for decisions and for keeping all residents informed of political strategies and current events. The entire population of the island voted on any major decisions. "Alcatraz was always a community. Whoever was living on the island always had a say in what was going on through our weekly council meeting. Our general meetings. The direction did not come from the leadership. It always came from the community," said John Trudell, a Santee-Sioux.[8]

Certain young men had already stepped into the glare of the needed publicity. While there were many women active in the years of organization, they followed a familiar understanding of the complementary nature of male and female power that had served their peoples for millennia. In these political organizations, the unseen hand is as powerful as the face that speaks. As Shirley said, "If it was a man in front of the camera there was always a woman right behind," her hand steering his back. For many tribes and polities such as the Iroquois League of Six Nations, matrilineality had been the kinship principle that guided stewardship of the land until the Europeans came. Senior women appointed chiefs. And for Alcatraz, "the women pretty well selected the leaders and we went ahead and selected Richard Oakes to represent us," according to LaNada Boyer, a Shoshone-Bannock.[9] Boyer emphasizes how young and in the moment those first student occupiers were, but they quickly had to make important organizational decisions, done in an Indian way. Boyer herself stayed on the mainland as the public face and "handled public relations and dealt with government officials."[10]

There were those who were the face of the Occupation. And there were those whom Shirley dubbed "the worker bees," feeding, housing, and caring for bodies. Her voice conveyed the pride of being a worker, of coping with the real issues of looking after others and a place. In the early days, before the federal government made it obvious that they would take a "hands-off-for-now stance," the siege mentality meant

---

8   Ibid., 28.
9   Ibid., 27.
10 Johnson, *The American Indian Occupation*.

sleeping in the cellblocks or arranging the hospital in areas that could be secured if they came under attack. Shirley conveys the sense of play that wove through the serious matters of governance. "The children would do things, because they could." Kids quickly figured out the cell lockdown mechanism and "they would lock us in there." Discipline was within the family, but such escapades lead to the opening of a schooling center and nursery on the third floor of the apartment buildings, formerly residences for the prison guards. The rooms were beautiful spaces, windows all around, with the light playing between sun and fog; the views changed from mere glimmers to a panoramic dome holding the city, the bay, and the buzz of boats around the Rock. In this space the elders came to teach their remembered arts, stories, and songs.

While their teachings were for the children, Shirley commented that even the young men might sometimes be seen here, learning the heart words of their people and the hand skills of beading, working leather, and weaving, arts that allowed the mind to roam and to plan. These skills had almost disappeared in the decades of boarding schools and Relocation. As Boyer emphasized, the boarding school experience (from the 1870s to the 1960s) had wrenched youngsters from their families to ship them hundreds, thousands of miles, to institutions where they were forbidden to speak their languages or practice rituals. Federal Indian policy explicitly sought to break the bonds of Indian communities, to create compliant individuals and isolate tribes on reservations with few resources for communal and individual viability. The boarding school experience was instrumental in severing ties between the generations and stopping the passage of knowledge linked to land, society, and ecology. While (ironically) pan-Indian consciousness found roots in these cells of institutional isolation, the angry youthful generation that returned to the rez could barely speak with their elders. The languages had been stripped from them. Individuals were particularly prey to the diseases of dislocation, such as alcoholism. At Alcatraz the torn edges between the generations began to knit as they worked over the hand arts, songs, and words.

When elders arrived on the dock, they were met and honored, carried by the "Take a Chance" pickup truck into the hive of activity, up the steep lanes of the prison complex. Creedence Clearwater had donated a boat to transport goods and people from Pier 40, the first boundary between the United States and Indian land, where food, clothing, and supplies amassed. If Indians were living on handouts, these were not from the government but from people sympathetic to the justice of their cause, a gifting ring that opened up possibility rather than narrowing down acceptable reciprocity. This circle of giving and learning, while fragile, is still open forty years later.

The kitchen, when the occupiers first arrived, was fully operational, from refrigerators to ovens to running hot water. Men who had been chefs in the army such as Peter Blue Cloud, Mohawk, coordinated the constant demand for meals, inspired by whatever was at hand. Edward Willie recounts how he and his brother were put on KP duty to sweep out the accumulated dust and shortly thereafter spent a wild night stuffing turkeys for Thanksgiving. The former exercise yard of the prison was the site for this feast, with long tables laid out with huge bins of turkey, mashed potatoes, and green beans. But the early bounty turned to hardship as the federal government cut off access to the essentials for life, including water, over the course of the Occupation. Whatever came out by boat, the food and drink were shared in the dining hall, as people sat at the long tables and benches and the energy eddied around family groupings. Manners were taught, and organization pulsed at the corners of the hall. These were the moments of the occupation whose force was felt in the lives of the occupiers long after the glaring, wrenching end of the Occupation.

The lives and sometimes tragedies of a few of the Occupiers have been part of the stories of succeeding decades, leaving many residents of the Island disinclined to dredge up memories. But the experience of the Rock has suffused into many small activisms. An instance of such a legacy is found in Shirley's story. In the mid-'70s, she and her husband returned to the Bay Area from Northern California to care for his grandmother. Shirley volunteered at the Hintul Kuu Ca (the Indian children's place) founded within the Oakland School district by a group of Indian mothers. After a year or so, the director suggested she take a job there and, gradually, over the years she earned the academic degrees to back up her experience. At the Hintul Ku Caa, young children learn what is expected of them as young ladies and gentlemen, in an Indian way of being. In its current location on Campus Drive in the hills of Oakland, the community nurtures its children from preschool through college. Alumni of the school, such as Shirley's daughter, wish to arrange their working lives so that their own children can experience the support that allowed them to grow into responsibility, community, and activism. The seeds for these values were nurtured on the Rock.

The story of the Occupation is evoked each year with the Thanksgiving Dawn Ceremonies, attended by thousands, Indian and other. As Shirley said, in a teaching for teachers, "After thirty-eight years the words come. Grandfather finds a way." While she was directly referring to the establishment of the Indian Occupation as a major focus of the current tourist experience of Alcatraz, she was also evoking the narratives that have nurtured the Indian community itself, even as these stories found their way into the wider community. The first transmissions were from "Radio Free Alcatraz." Words are powerful, medicine that can injure or heal. The story of the Occupation is not a story that belongs to one person, family, clan, or even one people. In this understanding, I suggest that there is a finding ground between the back-to-the-land communal movement and the Occupation of the Rock.

The Indian occupation of Alcatraz was a key moment in an imaginary of California. The Rock was a place where land was held, group living was practiced, and consciousness evolved within social and political bodies. Many young Native students have told mentors such as Edward Castillo that the Alcatraz Occupation was of deep importance to their sense of self; they recognize the action as the crucible of the American Indian political movement. Forty years later, patterns emerge. The harsh course of being Indian on Alcatraz takes its place in the history of tribal generations within federal government policies; those policies were in turn affected by the Occupation. The significance of the Occupation to the new wave of communalism that was sweeping California in the '60s and '70s has not been considered in analyses of the outcomes of the occupation of the Island, simply because it is not central to Indian issues. But the Occupation was one prominent happening that marked the San Francisco Bay Area as a vortex of change and had both direct and indirect influences on California communalism.

Native actors turned a moment of opportunity into momentum. At the same time, the visibility and symbolic power of Alcatraz coalesced in the imaginary of California that led young back-to-the-landers to settle in the northern state and to support the Alcatraz action. Non-Indian supporters aided in any capacity they could, especially as contributors of aid (food, clothing, and money), for the actions at Alcatraz, Washington, and Wounded Knee. Many communes followed rituals learned in contact with Native sources, participating in ceremonies of solidarity and exchange. But there are significant contrasts in the outcomes and social impact of the Red Power and the back-to-the-land movements.

The occupiers of Alcatraz were at first a youthful generation, very much aware of being in contention with the dominant culture of America at the time. When they sought modes of organization within the group, the ways of ancient cultures rose in them, their memories quickly reinforced by elders who saw the action as significant to all their people. Prayers, circles, and complementary gender roles were all part of recent memory and habit. Connection with the elders stabilized the surge of energy even after the bitter disappointment of not being able to hold onto the Rock. In contrast, the youth of the back-to-the-land movement were in rebellion against the values of their elders and thus largely unsupported by older generations. In their efforts to come up with new ways of interacting and making decisions, they turned to other philosophies: Buddhist, anarchist, tribal, and often Native American, with the tinges of appropriation. Nuclear family upbringing had instilled habits that could be intractable in communal settings. When personal issues disrupted the group ethos, there were no elders to advise patience and counseling. Long hours spent in acrimonious meetings left groups in political and emotional shards. Just as elders gave depth and a sense of obligation to the generations beyond the group formation found on Alcatraz, the Indian understanding of complementary gender roles obviated many of the strident issues of feminism that put communalists through emotional maelstroms. A number of women's communes spun off the back-to-the-land movement, to give women the support to develop skills, enterprises, and arts, without the inhibiting judgment of men. Native women largely rejected Feminism, preferring their ways of growing stronger in alliance with their men, working on Indian issues first and foremost.

Both groups saw land/space as essential to their endeavors. The Rock was a symbol of the reservation system, of the loss and endurance of all native peoples. Influenced by the moment of Alcatraz and subsequent widespread occupations and activism, tribes that had been terminated continued to organize, to get federal re-recognition, and moved toward enterprises (including casinos) that could support their peoples and cultures on their lands. The land that was the magnet for communalists was logged over forest, amenable to slow regeneration as back-to-the-landers established their homesteads, singularly or in experimental groups. Communes had to deal with the politics of working on the commune, for no obvious monetary gain, versus working off the land in professions or trades with salaries and status. But the economics of backcountry living meant that many individuals turned to marijuana cultivation, an enterprise linked with a secrecy that challenged the group ethos. Land itself, acquired at low prices in the early days, gained in value in the market economy, as the small communities came to be seen as attractive for projects such as food co-ops, health foods, medical clinics, and alternative schools that were outgrowths of communal groups within the general aura of humanistic values.

While back-to-the-landers may originally have thought they could isolate themselves from the dominant society and drop from sight, the Occupiers of Alcatraz knew that they had to grab the attention of that society in order to effect changes to the treatment of Native Americans. They could count President Nixon's repudiation of the policy of termination for Indian tribes as one major outcome that was positive.[11] While the immediate goals of an Indian Spiritual Center and University on Alcatraz were not achieved, the momentum continued, working through uneasy accommodations with capitalism and its social orders. Looking back forty years later, the Occupation of Alcatraz was a crucial moment for organizing an Indian activism based in an Indian way of being, found within the body of the occupiers. In the back-to-the-land movement there were also myriad moments of opening up land to new ways of owning, of organizing labor, and of making group decisions. Despite the backlash against the Indians that came later with AIM and Pine Ridge, and despite the media's implicit denigration of the back-to-the-land impulse as "hippies dropping out," a comparison of the two movements continues to inform and inspire.

Alcatraz was the site where Native peoples began to recover culture that had been disappearing for several generations. The communes were

---

11   Ibid.

an exploration of common land, unmapped in social dimensions for the participants. The occupiers of Alcatraz rediscovered the strength of old Indian ways of doing and being together. The communards searched for new ways outside of their natal cultures. But the attempts changed the lives of the participants permanently. Both these actions opened social networks and generated broad community activism. Contemplation of the histories has much to offer to people in a corporate society, divorced from the land and each other.

This writing has relied on testimony from participants of the Occupation (Shirley Guevera, Edward Castillo, Jack Forbes), the writings of participants, and conversations with activists and teachers in the Native American Program at UC Davis. I thank all for their time and insights.

Communalism and the Black Panther Party in Oakland, California

Robyn C. Spencer

The Black Panther Party (BPP), founded in 1966 by Huey Newton and Bobby Seale in Oakland, California, grew to become one of the leading organizations of the Black Power movement. The BPP believed that revolution was both internal and external and strove to create an organization that would be a microcosm of the world they were trying to create. Party members grappled with sexism, classism, individualism, and materialism and attempted to create alternative structures, institutions, and lifestyles. Their goal was not only to challenge and change the social and political conditions in the United States, but to politicize their membership and their mass following to challenge American cultural norms and values. Due to the Panthers' belief in communalism, politics infused all areas of Party members' lives and the borders between workplace and home space, public and private were blurred. The Party promoted a collective structure to facilitate the total commitment of its membership. They attempted to meet the needs of its cadre for food, clothing, and shelter. In short, Black Panther Party members not only tried to transform the world, they tried to transform themselves. They were not alone. Many social movements of this period grappled with the politics of personal transformation. However, these movements' histories are rarely brought together and systematically examined.

There has been little scholarly investigation into African Americans' engagement with the theory and practice of communalism in the 1960s and 1970s. Communalist ideas, often associated with the counterculture, have been assumed to have limited relevance to the history of the black

freedom movement. Situating communal practices with the counterculture has taken it out of the purview of black liberation according to the
dominant stratified view of the 1960s and 1970s. Many scholars have
drawn clear lines of distinction between the black freedom movement and
the other movements of the 1960s: feminism and women's rights; anti-
Vietnam; the counter culture; the Native American movement; Gay and
Lesbian liberation, etc. Some scholars such as Premilla Nadasen whose
work connects welfare rights to feminism and Black Power, have challenged how the movements of this period are categorized. However, most
scholars have remained within a framework that focuses on differences
between movements rather than similarities. When movement intersec-
tions are highlighted, they appear as fleeting and symbolic—usually represented as border crossing by highly visible individuals (Martin Luther
King's speech connecting civil rights to Vietnam; Mario Savio connecting Free Speech to civil rights; Jimi Hendrix as a link between the hippie
movement and Black Power) or prophetic moments (Waveland connecting women's rights to civil rights) rather than sustained engagement,
common origins and related trajectories.[1] Cross-pollination between and
among social movements has been a tangential concern for scholars of
the black freedom movement.

The Long Movement thesis and Black Power studies, two provoc-
ative interpretational frameworks being used to interpret the black
freedom movement, have raised other questions about the boundaries
of the black freedom movement. While the Long Movement thesis has
concerned itself with redefining the movement's chronology and antecedents, Black Power studies has tried to provide a full accounting of the
Black Power phase of the black freedom movement's trajectory nationwide; while Black Power studies are rooted in sharp distinctions between
civil rights and Black Power, the long movement thesis is rooted in blur-
ring boundaries. However, both frameworks have left the question of
how Black Power has overlapped with other social protest movements
and broader trends in American culture unanswered. The assumption
that the politics of personal transformation that was so central to the
other movements of the time was tangential to Black Power has obscured

---

1   However, Lauren Onkey has written provocatively work about Jimi Hendrix as
     a "black hippie" who was a central part of the counterculture and interacted with
     key elements of the Black Power movement but was not part and parcel of the
     movement.

some of the nuances of the movement. Yet there is much to be gained when considering Black Power as a mass movement, akin not only to civil rights but conceived in a larger context and subject to the same trends in American cultural history. The Black Power movement included politics that were personal, experimental, transformative, and rooted in the bold redefinition of self and community.

The Panthers' embrace of communalism has remained invisible in the scholarly literature not only because of assumptions about the nature of Black Power, but because of assumptions about the nature of the counterculture. The first assumption is that communards equates to hippies. In actuality, although hippie communes have come to define the popular and scholarly understanding of the communal phenomena, they were the minority of intentional communities. Miller has called the tens of thousands of communes of the '60s "enormously, endlessly diverse" in terms of activities, goals, origins, and trajectories. They included "Asian religious ashrams, group marriage experiments, communal rock bands, 'Jesus freak' houses, centers of radical politics, and back-to-the-land experiments in agricultural self sufficiency."[2] They were "a social phenomenon of remarkable proportions" and an important, if overlooked, part of American cultural history.[3] The second assumption is that the counterculture was completely apolitical in nature. Newer scholarship has begun to challenge this assumption by linking cultural revolution with political change. Jeff Hale has traced roots of the White Panther Party in Detroit to beatnik culture's engagement with radical politics. Doug Russinow has looked at how the New Left engaged in social radicalism under the banner of the slogan "the revolution is about our lives." He considers the New Left as "the Left wing of the larger white youth counterculture" that pursued activities with a "sharper political edge" such as building counter institutions, cooperatives and grappling with issues around sexual freedom and empowerment.[4] These scholars have begun the process of expanding the definition of the counterculture to a broader sense of cultural radicalism and challenging analyses of counterculture that simply focus on bohemian notions of escapism and tuning out poli-

2   Timothy Miller, "The Sixties-Era Communes," in *Imagine Nation: The American Counterculture of the 1960s and 1970s*, eds. Peter Braunstein and Michael William Doyle (New York: Routledge, 2002), 328–29.
3   Ibid.
4   Ibid., 100.

tics. The third assumption is about race. Although there has been some attention to the role of gender and class in collectivist ideology, race has not been a well-mined area in studies of communal living. The rejection of materialism and voluntary poverty that were hallmarks of communes were luxuries of the haves rather than the have-nots.[5] Timothy Miller points out that "communes were almost as thoroughly middle–class (or higher) as they were white; their residents were better educated than the average American peers, and they typically came from intact nuclear families." One study noted that communes were less than 1 percent nonwhite in the 1970s.[6] Scholars have assumed that because African Americans have been largely absent from the ranks of the counterculture means that the exploration of their engagement with these ideas is of limited utility.

However, a revaluation of the counterculture that moves hippies to the margins and radical politics to center stage would reveal the filiations between the counterculture, feminist arguments about the personal being political and Black Power's redefinition of self. African Americans in general and the Black Panther Party in particular cannot be separated from these larger historical forces. The BPP was part of that less than 1 percent of nonwhites living in communes. Miller notes that "Probably the largest African American participation in communal living" in the 1960s "came with the occasional organization of an all-black or nearly all-black commune—as in the cases of the Black Panthers, who operated communes in several cities for a time."[7] In the 1960s and 1970s, the Panthers grappled with the theory and practice of communalism in the attempt to craft an expansive vision of liberation and adapted collective ideology to suit their needs—this translated into communal living, collective parenting and the creation of alternative institutions. Although this led them to confront the tension between individualism and collectivism, leadership and accountability, internal democracy and hierarchy, sexism and egalitarianism, expressions of communalism in the Panthers' history were not always self-actualizing or progressive in practice. Ironically, the Marxist Leninist ideology that undergirded the Panthers' openness to communal ideas at the rank and file level also provided a parallel impetus toward centralization and hierarchy at the top under the banner of democratic centralism. The Panthers' engagement with communalism was fraught

---

5   Ibid., 343.
6   Ibid.
7   Timothy Miller, *The 60s Communes: Hippies and Beyond* (Syracuse Univ. Press, 1999), 171.

with tension and contestation from its very inception in the late 1960s and by the late 1970s, rank-and-file members were articulating feelings of exploitation and dissatisfaction. Yet, the Panthers' attempts to pose concrete alternatives to mainstream culture can provide a widow into alternative definitions and trajectories of Black Power. It also reveals another aspect of the social history of the BPP: for many members, the attempts to shed individualism, confront ingrained ideas about gender and sexuality, build genuine bonds of mutual trust and respect with comrades, and provide social services to both comrades and communities in need were some of the most politicizing experiences of their time in the BPP. An examination of these lived experiences that helped members maintain their commitment to the organization, even as it eroded in viability by the late 1970s, holds the potential of giving scholars a more nuanced understanding of the successes and failures of personal political transformation in the 1960s and 1970s. For too long, sexism and nihilism have defined the scholarly inquiry into the internal life of the BPP. Analyzing how the Panthers engaged with collectivism opens the door to different analytical questions and answers.

The Panthers' embrace of Marxist Leninism in the late 1960s was an important impetus to their adoption of collective strategies. Miller has pointed out that there were many points in American history when "socialists have concluded that the best way to have some sort of real socialism is to pursue it in voluntary groups; such groups, they argue, can provide some of the benefits of socialism within a larger capitalistic society, and they can serve as examples which demonstrate the merits of socialism."[8] According to Kathleen Cleaver, Marxist theory both "clarified the role of the Black Panther Party as a vanguard party in the revolutionary struggle for black liberation," and "helped combat the debilitating collapse of intra-party discipline left in the wake of the death, imprisonment, or exile of key leaders."[9]

In the late 1960s financial pressures, the devastating impact of political repression due to COINTELPRO coupled with the Panthers' embrace of socialist principles and their deep sense of comradeship, led some members to live collectively. These initial collectives were born out of

---

8   Timothy Miller, *American Communes, 1860–1960: a Bibliography* (New York: Garland, 1990), xxiii–xxiv.

9   Kathleen Cleaver, "Back to Africa: The Evolution of the International Section of the Black Panther Party (1969–1972)," 28. Unpublished paper in author's possession.

expediency and consisted of rank and file members who lived together in Panther dwellings. These spaces became mixed living quarters, work-spaces, and guest accommodations for visiting comrades. Although some Panther leaders lived modestly, none of them lived collectively. As such, the first Panther collectives coexisted with deep inequalities, hierarchies and a lack of organizational democracy. As rank-and-file Panthers began to engage in this collective experience, which included financial auster-ity and collective spending, the financial hierarchies within the organiza-tion became clearer. According to Panther Janice Garrett-Forte, full-time rank-and-file Panthers often had no jobs and few financial resources: "The only income we got was what we got from the Party. And so that income meant money for you to buy food, if you needed some shoes or whatever you got it any way you could. Plus people were donating things. ...Nobody was going without." However, the standard of living of rank and file members contrasted sharply with that of some leaders. Garrett-Forte observed, "Central committee members were living pretty good. A lot of money was going for their defense funds and that kind of thing. The foot soldiers, who were dedicating their lives, had to get things the best way they could. There wasn't money filtered down to the ones who were doing the righteous legwork."[10] This inequity weakened rank-and-file members' commitment to the collective idea. Bobby Bowen recalled that "some of the leadership had leather jackets, fancy 'gater shoes and access to cars" while rank and file were "sleeping on top of each other in Panther houses." He admitted being influenced by this dynamic and striving to emulate the debonair fashion sense of some leaders.[11]

Collective living, which involved shared responsibilities for cooking and housecleaning, also highlighted tensions around gender issues within the organization that were becoming more prominent in this period.[12] Although Panther rhetoric promoted egalitarian gender roles, Roberta Alexander noted that there were many debates around issues such as: "women leadership; women being able to be armed, to defend themselves as well as the brothers; on whether or not the women do all the typing or whether or not they also take part in the running of the offices, not just behind the typewriters; and it even goes down to the sexual levels, whether or not the women are supposed to do so and so for

---

10   Janice Garrett-Forte, interview with author, October 9, 1997.
11   Bobby Bowen, interview with author, October 22, 1997.
12   Ibid.

the cause of the revolution."[13] Domestic labor became a source of contestation and debate as the Panthers moved to designate household task and chores collectively. The ideal situation heralded by Bobby Seale: "When there's cooking to be done, both brothers and sisters cook. Both wash the dishes. The sisters don't just serve and wait on the brothers" in reality rarely prevailed.[14]

The fact that women comprised two-thirds of the organization's membership by 1969 suggested that gender was but one of many factors that governed women's political choices or shaped their experiences.[15] The Party's official support for gender equality and stated commitment to ridding its membership of the male chauvinism that pervaded the larger society provided space for women to maneuver and challenge gender discrimination.[16] Emory Douglas noted that despite the "mechanism[s] in place," sometimes even Party leaders, just like rank-and-file members, resisted taking orders from women, "or didn't want to because of their ego." The politicization process central to Party membership was designed to undermine this attitude: "It's just that the cleansing process was an ongoing thing. We tried to maintain it and not let it get out of control by having rules and regulations and PE classes and sisters in leadership that brothers had to work under. There was adjustment."[17] The potential of this "cleansing process" probably strengthened the resolve of some Panther women, who argued that the Panthers were moving toward the realization that "male chauvinism and all its manifestations are bourgeois and...the success of the revolution depends upon the women."[18] In 1969, the struggles between men and women had become so central that Roberta Alexander could declare, "we think more...about the contradictions...between the sisters and the brothers than we do about the pigs."[19] The day-to-day life in the Panthers nascent collectives became a place where these tensions were most deeply expressed.

13 "Roberta Alexander at Conference," *The Black Panther*, August 2, 1969, 7.
14 Bobby Seale, *Seize the Time: The Story of the Black Panther Party & Huey P. Newton* (New York: Random, 1970), 403. According to Kathleen Cleaver, Seale surveyed the Party in 1969 to make this assessment.
15 Kathleen Cleaver, "Women, Power, and Revolution," in *Liberation, Imagination, and the Black Panther Party: A New Look at the Panthers and Their Legacy*, eds. Kathleen Cleaver and George Katsiaficas (New York: Routledge, 2001), 125.
16 Seale, *Seize the Time*, 403.
17 Emory Douglas, interview with author, October 9, 1997.
18 "Black Panther Sisters Talk about Women's Liberation." *The Movement* (September 1969).
19 "Roberta Alexander at Conference," *The Black Panther*, August 2, 1969, 7.

The Collective Comes of Age

The institutionalization of the Panther collective was also done to accommodate an influx of members. The Panthers had responded to dwindling membership with the impetus to centralize their membership base, skills, and resources in Oakland.[20] Chapters in Vallejo, California; Chattanooga, Tennessee; Houston; Sacramento; Detroit; Washington, DC; Winston Salem, NC; Philadelphia; Seattle; and Boston were relocated to Oakland after they closed down.[21] These relocated members transformed the Panthers' collective structure. The Panthers who came to Oakland had remained in the organization through the chaos of COINTELPRO and internal disputes. Some were leaving behind chapters and branches decimated by COINTELPRO and internal squabbles, but others were dismantling the foundations they had struggled to build in local communities. They left behind family members, friends, and the familiarity of "home." McCall, who relocated to Oakland from Philadelphia, exemplified this mindset. He stated, "I had totally dedicated myself to this organization. Regardless of what happened internally, I knew this was what I wanted to do, this was who I wanted to be, this was what I wanted my life to be about: uplifting the black community by any means necessary no matter what it took and I was determined to do that by any means necessary through this organization, the Black Panther Party. So, no matter what contradictions occurred, I just said well, that's a part of life and moved on. Just keep progressing forward. You have the whole community depending on you to show you some hope."[22]

The BPP justified the expansion and institutionalization of its collective as a means to facilitate the total commitment of its rank and file membership. They attempted to meet members' needs for food, clothing, shelter, and even health care. They created a Health Cadre whose job included keeping track of ill comrades and children, and tracking epidemics of the flu and other contagious illnesses that could spread quickly in a collective living situation. Routine paperwork, such as typed memos from meetings, directives, and work reports from rank and file

---

20 Memo to Central Headquarters, Black Panther Party from Massachusetts State Chapter, Black Panther Party, folder: "General Reports from Chapter & Branches," box 14, HPN Papers; "Notes from Central Body Meeting, October 2, 1972," folder: "Central Committee Info," box 10, HPN Papers.

21 Panther answers to interrogatories, 19–24, box 80, HPN Papers.

22 Bobby McCall, interview with author, October 14, 1997.

cadre provide a vantage point into the BPP's operations. Agenda items for central committee meetings included comrades' appearance and clothing needs, interpersonal conflicts, and the maintenance of cleanliness in work areas.[23] An agenda item for the July 21, 1972, meeting was "Discuss the way *some* party leadership talk to the comrades (rank & file) and the way in which *some* party leadership give instructions to rank & file comrades."[24] The collective distribution of Panther funds to buy shoes and clothing for comrades was discussed at the October 2, 1972, meeting.[25] A memo to central body members dated August 16, 1972, brought up the need for a dialogue on Planned Parenthood within the Party, policies for expectant mothers, creation of an infirmary, and teaching remedial reading and math skills.[26] The Panthers adopted "collective parenting." They founded the Child Development Center, a boarding school for Panther children staffed by Panther members who took on the role of parents. This collective parenting provided a space for parents to have free childcare and continue their full participation in the organization. A November 1973 memo reminded members about the centrality of the Center and the importance of shared responsibility: "No comrades should mistreat our children. They should be well-fed, kept clean and treated like growing, developing young people with their own specific needs and desires that must be, until they are capable, met by us. We are all their parents."

According to James Abron, "The Party basically took care of you from dusk to dawn if you had kids. The people who worked at the school, those were the ones who were basically in charge of your kids. You were basically given your kids on the weekends, but Monday through Friday, we would teach 'em, feed 'em, take 'em to our dormitories and wash 'em, help them with their homework, put 'em to bed, clean their clothes, wipe their butts and then [laughter] the process would start over again. And we had three or four dorms plus the Child Development Center."[27]

---

23 "Memo re: Agenda Items to be discussed," May 22, 1973, folder: "Central Committee Info," box 10, HPN Papers; "Notes from Central Body Meeting October 2, 1972," folder "Central Committee Info," box 10, HPN Papers.
24 "Agenda for Meeting with Responsible Comrades," folder: "Central Committee Info" July 21, 1972, box 10, HPN Papers.
25 "Notes from Central Body Meeting October 2, 1972," folder: "Central Committee Info," box 10, HPN Papers.
26 Folder: "Central Committee Info," box 10, HPN Papers.
27 James Abron, interview with author, October 6, 1997.

The organization also attempted to provide for the political education (PE) of membership. In October 1972, the Panthers held an internal dialogue about the creation of study groups within the organization. Panther members expressed interest in studying subjects ranging from Fanon's *The Wretched of the Earth* to Oakland urban politics.[28] PE classes were used as a forum for discussion of issues. The Central body considered a proposal to renew PE efforts which suggested dividing the collective, approximately one hundred people, into two groups based on skill to study a curriculum that would include "remedial math and English, Party History, Party Ideology and lectures in Sociology (progressive), Psychology (study of the self and others), Biology (the human body, other living things) and advanced math (mathematics in relationship to dialectical materialism." Instructors would be central body members as well as guest speakers and lecturers. The Panthers laid out a schedule with a plan for a yearlong program of PE along these lines.[29] These classes were not optional. A memo dated August 29, 1973 stated, "It is mandatory that comrades go to P.E. class."[30]

PE classes attempted to make the link between personal shortcomings and politics. One memo from the Editing Cadre noted, "Following completion of the newspaper, we had a cadre P.E. class on Discipline (from the *Red Book*) and Party Structure. The class was a good one; informative, necessary and well-timed. Certain contradictions arose on the last night's work on this newspaper; tendencies toward laxity, individualism, and a disregard of organizational structure. Criticism, self-criticism and a re-education were appropriate methods of correction. It was a class the entire cadre needed."[31]

The Panthers created an internal review quiz to test Party members' knowledge of current events, Party history, and ideology. The first quiz centered on the relationship between Party policies and the ten-point platform and program. Panthers had a fixed time period in which to complete the quiz and were encouraged to utilize reference materials. Questions ranged from short answer questions such as "list three major

28 Memo from Joan Kelley October 31, 1972, to Comrade Servant, box 14, HPN Papers. General Reports from Chapters and Branches.
29 "Memo to all members of the Central Body, August 28, 1973," folder: "Central Committee Info," box 10, HPN Papers.
30 "Innerparty Memorandum," August 29, 1973, box 14, HPN Papers.
31 "Memo to the Servant from the Editing Cadre," January 3, 1973, folder: "Information Regarding our Newspaper," Box 11, HPN Papers.

institutions which must be controlled by the people" to analytical and interpretive questions such as "What is an education relevant to Black people? What does the Public School System have to offer children in the inner-city?"[32] It also tested knowledge of current affairs with questions such as: "Where are three major wars of aggression being waged by the United States?" "What is happening in Rhodesia, Mozambique and Angola?"[33] The second review quiz centered on the history of the black church, the development of black businesses and the history of the Black Panther Party. Questions on Party history asked: "Name 20 fallen comrades (and dates slain);"[34] "When was the first Black Panther newspaper issued and tell something about the front page story;"[35] "Name at least two laws that have been created, changed or eliminated because of the activities of the Black Panther Party."[36]

Weekly reports from the different ministries of operation within the BPP chronicled everything from meetings attended to political work accomplished to financial reports and interpersonal conflicts.[37] The Panthers created a daily work report form with spaces to fill in hours of fieldwork, number of paper sold, and hours and subjects of study.[38] To help keep Party members abreast of current events, the Panthers created memos called "news of the day" which gave brief summaries of the local, national, and international news.[39] Inner-party memoranda were created to facilitate communication within the Party. The first memorandum dated July 29, 1972, stated, "The issuance of this memorandum comes as a result of the July 27, 1972, Political Education Class. There, comrades voiced criticisms/self-criticisms regarding the interrelationships of comrades, while suggesting methods of how to best bring about more warmth and love among all comrades." The memos included a list of items to be discussed during PE class such as Mao's "On Contradiction" and "Criticism and Selfcriticism" as well as Newton's Boston College speech on intercommunalism, and books such as *To Die for the People* by Newton, *Seize the Time* by Seale and *Blood in My Eye* by Jackson. Inner-party memoran-

---

32   "1973 Review Quiz No. 1," 4, folder: "Central Committee Info," box 10, HPN Papers.
33   Ibid., 8.
34   "1973 Review Quiz No. 2," 5, folder: "Central Committee Info," box 10, HPN Papers.
35   Ibid., 9.
36   Ibid.
37   Folder: "General Reports form Chapters and Branches," box 13, HPN Papers.
38   Folder: "General Info We Have Printed," box 14, HPN Papers.
39   See folder "News of the Day," August 1972–February 1973, box 14, HPN Papers.

dum began to appear regularly in 1972. They served as an internal news-letter and provided a place for chronicling arrests, advising about legal defense issues, disseminating mobilization updates, announcing recreational activities and deaths in the family, and reminding Panther parents to pick up their children from the school and comrades to write letters to political prisoners.[40] Memos were also used to reinforce discipline and rules. A memo dated September 27, 1973, directed all comrades to go the field every day: "Comrades who go to school or work should go into the field for a couple of hours each day also. The coordinators are to decide how long each person will stay in the field."[41]

For many rank and file Panthers, membership in the collective required strict discipline and free time was a function of the needs of the organization as determined by leadership. The dependency of rank and file members on the BPP to meet their material needs, and in effect, provide a family structure, had a dampening impact on dissent. However, it is clear that the allocation of work time on Sundays became a contested issue. A memo dated October 18, 1972, commented that members had been taking advantage of the recreation time on Sunday to disappear without notice. The memo warned that those people who were not going to the park should inform the office coordinator of their whereabouts.[42] A memo dated November 14, 1973, directed all comrades to attend PE class on Sunday morning at 8:30 a.m.[43] After the Panthers founded the Son of Man Temple in October 1973, Sundays became even more circumscribed for rank-and-file members. Panther literature described the Son of Man Temple as an "Interdenominational Community Church dedicated to Community Survival"[44] and proclaimed:

"Our belief is that every human being has the right to be free. We can all agree that we are not. Therefore, we come together to express our agreement on that belief every Sunday at the Son of Man Temple. It is a place where we can come to discover and learn. If we begin the week with this kind of unity and understanding we can carry through each day, our concern, an enthusiastic feeling, about our survival and freedom."[45]

---

40 See box 14, HPN Papers.
41 "Innerparty Memorandum," September 27, 1973, box 14, HPN Papers.
42 "Innerparty Memorandum," October 18, 1972, box 14, HPN Papers.
43 "Innerparty Memorandum," November 14, 1973, box 14, HPN Papers.
44 "Son of Man Temple," box 14, HPN Papers.
45 *CoEvolution Quarterly* 3 (Fall 1974): 17.

The temple held a community forum every Sunday with guest speakers as well as entertainment. Although the temple was aimed at the Oakland community, Panthers were expected to support it as well. Attendance was not optional. A memo dated August 8, 1973, noted "All Party members are to attend church every Sunday. There are no exceptions."[46] A directive on January 31, 1974, warned that comrades who were late to Son of Man temple service would have to pay a $5 fine. If they did not attend and had no prior permission, they would be fined $10. There would be a sign-in book to monitor attendance.[47] The prevalence of punitive measures in the memos is striking and a reflection of dissent. Decision-making was far from collective. Central committee members met on a regular basis, usually bimonthly.[48] At these meetings, usually held at Newton's apartment, Panther leaders discussed political strategies and organizational procedures and priorities. It is clear that there was some resistance to some of the strictures of collective life. However, there were many Panthers who saw the tight schedule of activities as part and parcel of their commitment to the organization, to the community and to each other.

Ericka Huggins wrote a poem called "In Oakland" describing the mixture of hard work and comradeship that framed reality for many Panthers:

east 14th street—
cement,
tar,
blinking traffic lights;
    the yellow of yesterday,
the red of today
the green of tomorrow..
our lives have never been 'normal'...
we are part of tomorrow,
our todays and yesterdays
quickly become a vague memory
(so quickly do we move).
Sometimes we can stop to look at ourselves, in motion

---

46 "Innerparty Memorandum," August 8, 1973, box 14, HPN Papers.
47 "Innerparty Memorandum," January 31, 1974, box 14, HPN Papers.
48 Folder: "Central Committee Info," box 10, HPN Papers.

and love ourselves and each other.
These are the good times,
the comradely times,
when we can celebrate life.[49]

McCall remembered, "We ate together. We slept together. We lived together. We did everything together like a family, like an organization should... We were a bunch of disciplined, organized young brothers and sisters who were determined to uplift the black community. It wasn't no joke being in the Party. It might have been called a party, but it was no party. We had a lot of fun with each other because we loved each other. We had a lot of family affairs. We always celebrated each other's birthdays...in a big way. We didn't celebrate holidays but we did celebrate life with each other."[50]

Creating Counterinstitutions

Panther leaders envisioned making the BPP into a lasting institution to prepare for the long haul. Newton defined a revolutionary vehicle as a "revolutionary concept set into motion by a dedicated cadre through a particular organized structure."[51] Collective living was entrenched as the Panthers moved from being an organization that applauded "revolutionary" action against the police to an organization that emphasized day-to-day work. Much of that day-to-day work was done by committed rank and file members who could be mobilized to meet organizational goals. Panther Amar Casey, who had come to Oakland in 1973, recalled how impressed he was by the Party's infrastructure: "When I arrived in Oakland, there were Panthers coming from all over the country. There must have been 350–400 Panthers in Oakland at that time. What they were doing was busy trying to build this big institutional infrastructure. I was amazed at what they owned, it blew me away, they had the school, they had the dormitory for the children, they had a newspaper, they had a restaurant, a medical clinic. They had an amazing infrastructure."[52]

The community programs were the lynchpin of the Panthers' new vision. The Panthers expanded the range and scope of these programs

---

49 Ericka Huggins, "Servant: Insights and Poems," March 1972, box 14, HPN Papers.
50 Bobby McCall, interview with author, October 14, 1997.
51 Huey P. Newton, *To Die for the People* (New York: Random House, 1972), 56.
52 Amar Casey, interview with author, October 28, 1997.

and renamed them "community survival programs." According to Newton these programs were called "survival programs pending revolution," since we needed long-term programs and a disciplined organization to carry them out. They were designed to help the people survive until their consciousness is raised, which is only the first step in the revolution to produce a new America."[53] In the Panthers' analysis, survival programs were temporary models aimed at alleviating economic distress and teaching self-help and community control. They were supposed to meet the concrete needs of the masses of people as well as highlight the inability of the state to resolve these problems, thus providing mass political education. According to Newton, "Our programs are not a revolutionary program or a reformist program, it is a strategy through which we are organizing people for revolution. [It is] impossible to wage an armed struggle if you don't have the masses organized."[54] The Panthers touted their survival programs as a strategic measure; however, they failed to actively engage in community based political education to teach Oakland residents about the politics behind these programs. As a result, these programs achieved many successes but were rarely a catalyst for community political action.

Graphic artist Emory Douglas visually represented the Panthers' new focus in the image of the "Survival Nurse," a black female nurse standing near a bus from the People's Free Busing Program holding clothing from the People's Free Clothing Program, shoes from the People's Free Shoes Program, a book from the People's Liberation Schools, and a bag of groceries from the People's Free Food Program in her arms. The cap on her head indicated that she was a worker for the People's Free Health Clinic. A gun was holstered to her side, and she wore a button that proclaimed: "I am a Revolutionary."[55]

Within this panoply of programs, the Panthers' main focus became health and education. In 1971, the BPP opened a health clinic in Berkeley to provide free medical attention, medication, referrals, sickle cell testing, immunization, prenatal instruction, first aid kits, and community health surveys. Doctors and other health care professionals volunteered their

---

53 Huey P. Newton, *Revolutionary Suicide* (New York: Harcourt, Brace & Jovanovich, 1973), 297.
54 "Huey Newton talks to French reporters/HPN on party ideology," September 20, 1974, tape recording, HPN Papers.
55 *The Black Panther*, March 20, 1970.

services.[56] The Panthers also created a free ambulance service.[57] They believed that by showing the community that "it is possible to receive professional, competent and, above all, preventative, medical help without paying any money for it," they were teaching "the people...to understand that as taxpayers they do not have to stand for the lackadaisical treatment given to them by county hospitals and other public health facilities."[58] Party supporters Tolbert Small, Reverend Neil and Herman Blake were the Clinic's first Directors.[59] One of their major community health initiatives was raising awareness about sickle cell anemia. They established a Sickle Cell Anemia Foundation chaired by Small in 1971 to test people, focus publicity on the disease, and work toward a cure.[60] In an open letter dated July 8, 1971, Small announced, "The Sickle Cell Anemia Foundation of the Black Panther Party will be performing genetic counseling nationally both to redefine the accurate incidence of sickle cell anemia and to decrease the incidence of sickle cell disease in this country by making sickle cell tests available free for every black person. The foundation hopes to raise the consciousness of black people towards this disease and to stiiulate [sic] an environment of research into this long neglected disease."[61]

A January 1973, memo noted that doctors were available at the clinic four days a week for approximately sixteen hours total. In one week, sixty-five patients, many of who were white, received medical attention. Although the memo pointed out that more doctors and more supplies were needed, it was clear that the clinic was serving community needs.[62]

However, in order for the clinic to be successful according to the Panthers' conceptualization of the survival programs community members had to "begin to ask questions and to organize themselves to change existing health services so that they truly serve the people."[63] The clinic had little success meshing an overt political agenda with the

---

56 "Budget, 1971," Folder: "Black Panther Party No-Profit Corporations Including Black United Front," box 34, HPN Papers.
57 *CoEvolution Quarterly* 3 (Fall 1974): 1.
58 Ibid., 22.
59 "Articles of Incorporation of People's Free Health Clinic, Inc," folder: "Black Panther Party No-Profit Corporations Including Black United Front," box 34, HPN Papers.
60 *CoEvolution Quarterly* 3 (Fall 1974).
61 Folder: "Black Panther Party No-Profit Corporations Including Black United Front," box 34, HPN Papers.
62 Health Cadre Reports, HPN Papers, box 36.
63 *CoEvolution Quarterly* 3 (Fall 1974), 22.

provision of social service, especially when the diversion of organizational resources to the Panthers' election campaigns in 1972–73 further reduced staff. A January 1973 memo noted that "outside of the Saturday paper sales, still no work is being done outside of the infirmary and the clinic."[64] A few weeks later another memo complained, "Again this week, no community work was done because of the great amount of work required to maintain the infirmary and the clinic with such a minimal staff."[65] The Health cadre implemented plans for forming community outreach teams to bridge this gap.[66] However, by April, the Health cadre reported that outreach efforts were at a low, and the clinic was attracting fewer patients: "During the period between March 27 and April 5, fifty-six people were seen at the clinic. The patient load has dropped considerably over the last six months. This is due to the shortage of doctors available at the clinic. ...The clinic's participation in community affairs and functions (such as the outreach program) is non-existent, because of the staff's inability to get out due to the school, and things to be done in order to catch up. (Situation will worsen as a result of going into the field on Friday and Saturday.)"[67] Health Cadre reports warned that low staff, inadequate funding, and inability to do community work would eventually lead to the clinic's decline.

The Oakland Community School (OCS), which provided a model for community-based education, was one of the Panthers' strongest community survival programs. The Learning Center began as the Intercommunal Youth Institute in 1971, a school program catering to Party members' children. Huggins, the Director of the School, discussed its evolution: "We started in 1971, in an apartment. Then we moved to a house, then to a number of other apartments and houses. As we moved along and as we developed, people came to our support and our aid and great numbers of students, student teachers, parents, all kinds of people wanted to know why we didn't get a school building and open up our school to more children. Because at first, we were just a supplement to public school education, and not quite an alternative because we only gave supplementary language and math instruction after school to children whose parents

---

64 Health Cadre Reports, HPN Papers, box 36.
65 Ibid.
66 Ibid.
67 Memo dated March 27–April 5, 1974. Folder: Health Cadre Reports, box 36, HPN Papers.

were then members of the BPP....We started doing all these things because we knew that the children of the BPP had no hope unless we did something for them. They were being thrown out of school just for being sons and daughters of members of the Party. They were being chastised for wearing Free Huey buttons. They never said a word, but were bearing the brunt of all of this, because of the views of their parents."[68]

The Institute taught a variety of subjects such as math, language arts, science, people's art, environmental studies, and political education. Field experience and critical thinking were central to the Panthers' approach. Oakland parents appreciated the academic rigor and progressive educational philosophy that the Institute provided and soon the student base of the school expanded.

The OCS was housed in the Panthers' Oakland Community Learning Center (OCLC), the central terminus for many Panther activities and community events. The OCLC was the site of the Panthers Legal and Educational Program which offered legal counseling, free busing to prisons, free commissary for prisoners, food stamps, and welfare counseling. Drama workshops, Party fundraisers, lectures on African politics, debates on police brutality, forums on the rights of the handicapped and disabled, sports programs, GED classes, consumer education classes, plays, and films were offered at the OCLC.[69] It also provided teen and youth service programs such as Teen Counseling, Junior High and High School Tutorial Program, Martial Arts Program and Youth Training and Development. The OCS held events at the OCLC that brought together the Panthers community service mission with their goal of community education. In November 1976, the OCS sponsored an event that included African speakers lecturing about politics and liberation, coupled with a performance by OCS students and a give-away of five hundred bags of groceries. Through the OCLC, the Panthers were able to create a core group of community supporters, anchored by the parents of the children who attended the OCS.

The Panthers created a collective environment where students and teachers lived and learned together. Students stayed in dorms and were grouped according to ability rather than age. Panther literature stated: "Our students participate in determining the policies that govern them.

---

68 Michele Russell, "Conversation with Ericka Huggins. Oakland, California, 4/20/77," 17, 20, box 1, HPN Papers.

69 Folder: "Misc. Articles," HPN Papers.

They criticize each other (and their instructors) in order to correct mistakes and mistaken ideas. If they violate the rules that they themselves helped to make, then they are criticized before the collective. All of this is done with the understanding that we criticize with love, never with hatred. Never are children called stupid, dull, or dumb. No one child is forced to make a better grade than another. There are no grades. There is no negative competition. There is only the competition that will produce enthusiasm and prove, through action, that our capabilities are endless."[70]

The initial goal for the OCS was to provide a social service in a way that would politicize those who received it. Over time, however, these programs became more institutionalized and entrenched. For example, funding for the Oakland Community School was sought from corporate and private contributions.[71] In 1973, the Panthers created the Educational Opportunities Corporation (EOC), a nonprofit corporation to oversee the Oakland Community School. Its initial trustees were Party supporters Berton Schneider, David Horowitz, and Richard Kaldenbach. The EOC's articles of incorporation described its purpose as "to provide general and vocational educational opportunities to individuals, both adults and minors, at the primary, secondary, and high school grade levels, and to offer adult educational extension services, all of which educational activities shall meet the requirements of Section 214 of the Revenue and Taxation Code."[72] The EOC began to apply for and receive government grants. In March 1974, it received its first grant from the city of Oakland. By 1974, the Oakland Community School had a staff of nineteen. An EOC annual report dated February 1975 stated that enrollment in the school doubled in January 1974 as a total of 110 students returned or were accepted at the school.[73]

The OCS had earned a nationwide reputation for excellence in community based education. In February 1976, the OCS was featured on the cover of one of the most popular magazines in black America, *Jet*. OCS students ranged in age from two to eleven years old. They received full tuition, and health care and lived in dorms where they received three nutritious meals a day.[74] They received individualized attention in classes

---

70 "General Articles. Re: Youth Institute," box 48, HPN Papers.
71 Black Panther Party, *CoEvolution Quarterly* 3 (Fall 1974).
72 Folder: "Huey's Personnel File," box 18, HPN Papers.
73 Folder: "Montclair Article," box 5, HPN Papers.
74 February 1976 article. Folder: "OCS Brochure," box 4, HPN Papers.

that rarely exceeded ten students per teacher. The staff of twenty-seven full-time accredited teachers taught students art, music, science, Spanish, environmental studies, and physical education.[75] In the summer, students participated in a structured program of trips, classes, and recreational activities.[76] By May 12, 1976, approximately 125 children attended the OCS.[77] While this was a measure of success on one level, on another it represented a shift in the vision of the school as a counter institution.

The Dialogue about Dating

Collective living and rigorous work routines bred an insularity that left many rank and file Panthers with feelings of isolation. After the topic of loneliness was broached at a political education class, Newton invited comment on the Party's unspoken policy of female Panthers dating solely within the organization.[78] This custom was rooted in the chauvinistic assumption that women were more likely to let personal emotions weaken their political commitment and allow men outside of the Party to influence them to leave the organization. Although this policy was not uniformly applied, some women bought into the notion that BPP members could best understand and support each other's unorthodox lifestyles and strong political commitments. For them, politics had a role in the choice of a partner. In this equation, male Panthers were free to date community women (on the assumption that they could influence the women to join the organization) as well as Panther women.[79] Panther women (who were heterosexual) were limited to Panther men. BPP members responded to Newton's request with an outpouring of emotions, opinions, and grievances that reflected a deep dissatisfaction with the organization's gender dynamics, internal structure, and relationship to the community. One Panther woman wrote:

> I feel that the great sense of loneliness which I feel and know that others feel can be greatly helped with the coming of people in the community being able to spend time with us. ...But, let us consider

---

75 "July 1977 Corporate Overview EOC," folder: EOC, box 4, HPN Papers.

76 Folder: "Montclair Article," Box 5, HPN Papers.

77 Steve McCutchen, interview with author, October 11, 1997.

78 "Memo to: Huey, From: Dale re: Women in the Perty [sic]," October 4, 1977, folder: "Reports on Comrades," box 14, HPN Papers.

79 Ibid.

the amount of people who have left out of reasons of loneliness. No animosity, or breech of party policy just sheer loneliness and the desire to feel needed has chased many a person away. Apart form [sic] the accepted and obvious feelings of alienation of being a party member and all those stigmas attached to that and the very real sense of family separation, we must also undergo a type of alienation from our sex. We Black Panther women who dont [sic] like to go out, who dont like to receive flowerss [sic], who dont want to spend time alone with a person unless we are in bed, or who are suppose to be available for those late night runs, can become lost. Now I really don't think that that any individual in the streets holds the answer to a more enjoyable life and wholesome selfm [sic] yet the attention is needed, and wanted. Also I believe that there would be an eventual end to the feelings of sexual oppression and jealousy. More equal grounds could be gained and this would promote more male appreciation of the female and more female appreciation of herself.[80]

This letter went on to state that women had played a major educative role in many revolutions but due to the lifestyles of some Party workers, "we barely see the masses much less have a chance to educate them." Consequently, she argued, myths of Panther women as "robots or some type of Black humanoid" abounded both inside and outside the BPP. Within the BPP women often faced "abuse and misuse" at the hands of their male comrades.[81] She complained, "Whithin [sic] past months a comrade slopped into bed with me and began to disrobe me and have sex, to which I firmly objected and he did finally give up. But this same comrade barely speaks to me or trys [sic] to take me out or anything like that. Its not as if this happens daily, but it happens too much. Incidents like this that dont [sic] get reported and are just thought of casually perpetuate all of the terrible misconceptions of the Black Panther woman."[82]

Jonina Abron wrote, "Throughout the 29 years of my life, I have experienced the dual pain of being a Black woman in America. When I joined the Party five years ago, I was thrilled about becoming part of an organization that believes in the equality of men and women. However, I have since learned that my comrades and I have yet to overcome many of our backward ideas." Abron argued that all Party members should be free

---

80 Ibid.
81 Ibid.
82 Ibid.

to choose partners outside of the organization if they chose people "who have ideals and goals common to us."

"My concern about male-female relationships extends beyond the sexual aspect. Ultimately it will take a new and humane society to alter the ways in which men and women in America treat each other. Within our Party, it bothers me that there are a couple of comrade brothers who still view women as sexual objects. We should have *no* men in the Black Panther Party who feel this way or women for that matter. It bothers me that there are a few brothers who seem unable to carry on a conversation with me once I explain that I am not interested in going to bed with them. It makes me feel that they feel I have no value beyond my body. ...I would like to see the Party seriously begin to deal with this issue. While we have a number of women in leadership positions in our Party, they are respected by the men *because* they are in the leadership."

Women, she conceded, were sometimes guilty of the same attitude toward men who are not in leadership. "I know we are all products of this society, but we should expect more from each other because we are members of the Black Panther Party. Why can't we love and respect each other as human beings instead of males and female?"[83]

Veronica "Roni" Hagopian argued that external relationships could root the Party more deeply in the community. She wrote, "If the sister has been around for a good while and her practice has proven her to be a responsible person, I think this can be a positive thing for the Party and for the particular man we may see. It may not even be with the intention of bringing him in as a member, but bringing us closer as friends and allies."[84]

Amar Casey and Melvin Dickson argued that men and women should be bound by the same restrictions. They stated that guidelines and principles should govern all external relationships. "We all, we are sure, can personally remember past instances when brothers who left the Party or their work suffered as a result of their relationships with a community sister. With both brothers and sisters adhering to such policies as have been mentioned, perhaps a sense of personal equality would prevail among comrades' internal relationships."[85]

---

83 Ibid.
84 Memo from Roni Hagopian, August 21, 1977, folder: "Reports on Comrades," box 14, HPN Papers.
85 Memo from Amar Casey and Melvin Dickson, August 12, 1977, folder: "Reports on Comrades," box 14, HPN Papers.

Another woman wrote in stating that she agreed with the policy of women not dating outside the Party because she believed that men from the community would have a hard time understanding the rigors of a Panther woman's life and might express jealousy or influence the woman to leave. She protested against the ways in which the collective structure limited individual choice about pregnancy. She poignantly argued, "I think a sister who don'nt [sic] have any children should be able to have one. I hated to write this one down because I know it is selfish feeling this way. If 10 women got pregnant it would really slow down the work, but maybe if two got pregnant at a time?"[86]

The outcome of this dialogue, which largely took the form of memos to Newton, is uncertain. It created a space, however, for rank and file members to collectively discuss organizational policies, customs, and norms around a range of issues, including how courtship and sexuality related to politics.

The Undoing of the Collective Structure

By 1974, the BPP had fewer than a hundred members. The Party's collective structure required total commitment and bred an insularity that was only partially mitigated by the creation of avenues of entry for community volunteers. Although membership in the Party had always been fluid, attrition markedly increased during the 1972–73 election campaigns. Party members had made many personal sacrifices to keep the campaign alive. Hagopian recalled, "For a while during the campaign, we didn't see much of our children. It wasn't until the campaign ended that we started a weekend program where the kids would come home for the weekend."[87] According to Douglas, "The campaign was almost a twenty-four hour thing. We had to close down a lot of the other operations or keep them going on a smaller scale cause we had to focus people to take on leadership in the different levels to make sure voters got out, our literature got out. All those things took a drain on people. [This led to] burnout."[88]

Reduced membership affected the viability of the Panthers' Survival Programs. The Elections committee noted the connection between over-

86 "Memo To: The Servant From: Arlene Clark," August 9, 1977, folder: "Reports on Comrades," box 14, HPN Papers.
87 Veronica "Roni" Hagopian, interview with author, October 23, 1997.
88 Emory Douglas, interview with author, October 9, 1997.

work and diminished focus on community programs: "At times, this [pace of the campaign] puts a tremendous strain on othe [sic] facilities, committees and party survival programs. However, this wa [sic] expected, when the elections committee first expanded."[89]

As financial problems grew and the survival programs faltered, Party members played a larger role in sustaining the organization. Memos directed "Comrades to buy collectively, an item at a time, for the Child Development Center and the Institute,"[90] and "give $10 to the Institute for food and transportation each month. ...The above-mentioned $10 is not to be confused with the $10 due each week from each cadre for field trips."[91] In addition, Panthers were ordered to "bring fifty cents ($.50) with them to Son of Man Temple Services every Sunday to contribute to the fund to buy lunch for the children during services."[92] Some Panthers took jobs and donated all or part of their salary to the organization.

Weak PE structures and social isolation taxed Party members' commitment to the collective structure. In April 1978, the Panthers held a meeting to discuss the children's collective. Some Panther parents viewed the dorms as a temporary measure, rather than a political program, questioned the need for the children's collective, and argued that they could teach their children individually. Huggins argued that the dorms were a socialist program born out of the desire to expose children to a collective experience and the need to distribute parental responsibilities. She suggested that the Central committee create new dorms that would appeal to parents and disseminate a statement of purpose for the children's collective. She also advised that Party leaders should meet with collective parents more often.[93]

Innerparty memoranda chronicled many attempts to reform the Party's political education structure and reach out to the community in 1977–78. One memo called for more meetings and dialogue among the central body to carry out work, and pursue better communications and dialogue. It warned, "we have lost our balance: our cadres function in isolation, our political education has been neither consistent nor strong

---

89 Memo from Melainee King March 10, 1973, folder: "General Reports from Chapters and Branches," box 14, HPN Papers.
90 Agenda Items to be discussed June 13, 1974, folder: "Central Committee Info," box 10, HPN Papers.
91 Innerparty Memorandum, March 21, 1974, box 14, HPN Papers.
92 Ibid.
93 "Memo to Huey from Ericka re: Collective Parents meeting," box 4, HPN Papers.

enough (though recent improvement has been made), our tasks are often carried out in a non-structural manner, *and* our children (who follow our example) suffer in their overall educational development. We cannot and do not deny external pressures, harrassment [sic] and forces which work against us. We are a revolutionary Party! But, because criticism and self-criticism are essential to an organization which functions through democratic centralism, we must place and accept blame."[94]

On March 31, 1978, Jonina Abron wrote a memo to Newton requesting that central body members address PE classes on a regular basis "about the development of Party programs, the trial and other internal matters."[95] A few weeks later, Abron pointed out that PE classes were plagued by lateness and low attendance despite the fact that the Ministry cadre was changing the structure of the classes to include weekly PE quizzes and other interactive mechanisms such as films, guest speakers, and member presentations.[96] She warned that Party members needed to "improve our overall attitude toward PE classes."[97]

Panthers recognized that community political education was central to their survival as an organization. In another memo to Newton, Abron noted that the Panthers had not held regular community political education classes for three years and advised, "we need to be doing more to inform the people who work with us and others who just want general information about the BPP and current events. This is particularly important now because of the upcoming murder trial."[98] The Ministry cadre wrote Newton recommending that community members be allowed to attend Panther PE classes because "there are a few non-Party members who attend regularly now, but there are many others who would like to."[99] Casey wrote Newton in July to ask him to speak at one of the PE sessions for teens working at the OCS over the summer.[100]

---

94 "Central Body Info," box 5, HPN Papers.
95 "Inner Party Memorandum," box 4, HPN Papers.
96 Editing and Distribution Report, August 4, 1978, folder: "The Black Panther Party Newspaper," box 35, HPN Papers.
97 "Memo from Jonina re: PE classes," April 11, 1978, folder: "Innerparty Memorandum," box 4, HPN Papers.
98 Editing and Distribution Report, August 4, 1978, folder: "The Black Panther Party Newspaper," box 35, HPN Papers.
99 Memo dated October 2, 1978, folder: "Innerparty Memorandum," box 4, HPN Papers.
100 Memo to Newton from Amar Casey dated July 31, 1978, folder: "Innerparty Memorandum," box 4, HPN Papers.

Ironically, these reform efforts were centralized. Rank and file members' proclivity to work in partnership with leadership blunted the critical edge of their efforts. Rather than explicitly defining Newton's activities as problematic, BPP members petitioned him to seek solutions or to join them in reform efforts.[101] By March 1979, Newton's legal problems and the continuing harassment from the FBI and IRS had a devastating impact of organizational finances. After trying a variety of fundraising measure, the OCS had to borrow money to meet its payroll.[102] The Black Panther Party could no longer sustain its survival programs or the material needs of full time members. Party members were asked to fill out questionnaires about their income and expenses, and their potential interest in participating in collective buying with Amway, a bulk sales company.[103] Their field operation was discontinued because they didn't have enough personnel to secure permits to collect donations. Instead, members were instructed to get part time jobs on the weekends to supplement the $100 they would now receive monthly from the Party.[104] A memo from the Central Body dated September 15, 1979, announced, "Every comrade, regardless of stature, will be getting money, according to need."[105]

Ideologically weakened and no longer a financially self-sustaining close knit family-like unit, the Panthers could not recover from this downward spiral. Internal contradictions and the fundamental need for individual self-actualization drove the last remaining members from the organization. Casey recalled how the total commitment of the membership made their potential exploitation total as well:

> It was a system based upon sometimes brutal exploitation of the collective. Okay. So you have these people who are committed 100 percent, twenty-four hours a day, seven days a week to the Black Panther Party and...the system basically would exploit that collective until a person would get tired and just leave, that's basically what it was...we're talking about from when you get up at five o'clock in the morning because you're working in the dormitory with the children

---

101 March 1, 1979 OCS meeting, folder: "EOC," box 4, HPN Papers.
102 OCS Weekly reports, March 10, 1979, box 4, HPN Papers.
103 OCS Weekly reports, July 11, 1979, box 4, HPN Papers.
104 Memo from Central Body Meeting, September 15, 1979, folder: "Central Body Meetings," box 5, HPN Papers.
105 Ibid.

and you have to bathe them and get them dressed and ready for school. You ride in the van and come to school, you teach school all day. Either when the kids leave at the end of the day at 5:00 either you ride in the van and go the dormitory and clean up and bathe them and get them ready for bed and go through that whole process again or you stayed in the school and you cleaned the whole school, you see. Which could mean you don't leave that school until twelve midnight and then you go home and you got to be back there by eight the next morning. ...Now when you went through that five days a week and then on Saturday you went into the field [collecting donations], okay, and then Sundays you usually had some sort of meetings to go to. So you end up having half a day on Sunday really to yourself. That was pretty much it. That's what exploitation of the collective means. Now you're doing this week after week, after week after week, after week after year after year, you're doing this. No holidays, ain't none of that, ain't no break. Constant...there was very little balance in terms of the development of the individual, the development of the capacity of the individual to be able to maintain themselves.[106]

Many Panthers wrote to the leadership expressing similar views. Party members found it increasingly difficult to subsume individual needs to the collective, especially when they believed that the collective was flawed. One Party member requested time to go to complete a graduate degree and go to law school.[107] Another pleaded for his own apartment "rather than being a grasshopper and stayiing [sic] any an [sic] every where." He complained, "I can't even keep my own child because of me not having my own place."[108] Another recounted a bitter story about being arrested on traffic ticket violations and bailed out at $65. Upon her release, she was hurt to discover that despite the many financial sacrifices she had borne and her contributions to the Party in the role of legal defense coordinator, some of her comrades had whispered that she should have spent the weekend in jail. She questioned the Party's financial priorities which could allow someone who worked ten hours a day, five days a week to be

---

106 Amar Casey, interview with author, October 28, 1997.
107 Letter to Newton from Beatrice Kelly re: Request to complete Masters Degree, January 18, 1978, box 14, HPN Papers.
108 Letter to Newton from Lonnie Dee, Folder: "Reports on Comrades," box 14, HPN Papers.

denied money and the lack of basic moral support within the Party which allowed comrades to be sometimes treated "unlike anyone campaigning for humanity should treat another human being." The final straw came when her desire to attend law school was greeted with veiled accusations of individualism. Ironically, when she called in to resign from the Party, she discovered that she had been expelled.[109]

Tommye Williams wrote that she had "come to a crossroads in my life—one path is the Party and the other path is my personal happiness." She pointed out that the Party was rife with inequities: "some comrades have to struggle each month to pay rent, bills, food, and to buy necessities for their children, and some comrades don't have a source of income at all. Other comrades do not have to worry about their financial necessities."[110] She critiqued the Party's collective parenting system, arguing that Panther parents needed to spend more individual time with their children. "Our children are growing up—half the children don't know their parents or their parents don't know their children. They need a sense of security, to know who they are. At the present, the children still do not receive enough time with their own parents." This affected her relationship with her son: "As it stand now, I spend Sundays (when there is not a meeting) with him and a couple of hours each evening three nights a week with my son. I would like to spend Saturdays with him also and participate with him in different activities, which interest him. I spoke with Ericka about this particular issue. It was worked out that I go home early a couple of days of the week. This might work temporarily for me but it is still an issue which affects most of the mothers in the Party."[111]

McCutchen wrote that he had faith in the Party's ideology but "the human error...caused me to move away, to withdraw. What was left of the party could not produce, could not encourage those ideas, those dreams, those products. ...What was left was a shell. I did not want to be part of a shell and call myself a revolutionary. I stayed for as long as I thought was feasible."[112] He argued that financial problems were a major factor in the Party's decline:

---

109 Folder: "Reports on Comrades," box 14, HPN Papers.
110 Letter to Newton from Tommye Williams, folder: "Reports on Comrades," box 14, HPN Papers.
111 Ibid.
112 Steve McCutchen, interview with author, October 11, 1997.

We weren't attracting new party members because of economics. We lost members because of economics. Party members had to weigh the advantages and disadvantages of twenty-four-hour commitment and were being forced to find their own places and pool resources. How were they going to pool resources without having access to funds? We were losing members for that reason. Other party members wanted to go to school or return to school. So those who have to have a choice between staying in the Party and going to school, then they were gone. Community workers would come in, primarily a lot of the parents from the school and other members of the youth, the teens... those were primarily the workers who supported the Party during this time period.[113]

Allen offered a bittersweet blend of criticism of the organization and homage to the impact of membership on his life:

I think I've had things I've agreed with and disagreed with over the years like any other comrade, but a lot of it is I guess I've lost the desire to struggle hard to bring up my points of view. I've learned a tremendous amount of things about myself and the world by being in the Party for the past 7 ½ years, and I owe this to my comrades that have been understanding when I needed it. I don't take any of the experiences I've gained while in the Party lightly at all. And I doubt I could have learned as much as I have anywhere else.[114]

Casey's letter of resignation contained a systematic organizational critique:

You [Newton] once said that personal problems can be expressed through politics. This is true. However, it is also true that personal problems can be expressed politically. The line seperating [sic] the two is thin indeed. But many people that are still with us have personal problems which are the result of a political policy or line. They are unable to express their personal problems as they relate to the rules, policys [sic] and guidelines of the Party. Consequently they just leave or "hang in" as many comrades say these days. What they don't realize is that this Party, the peoples and that it is what we

---

113   Ibid.
114   Letter to Central Body from Austin Allen, folder: "Reports on Comrades," box 14, HPN Papers.

make it. That Huey Newton is not a god or prophet, as you constantly remind people all the time.[115]

He pointed out that "so many comrades have left and so many are on the verge of leaving because we suffer from lonliness [sic], the lack of personal lives, extreme poverty and the lack of personal development. These problems are often expressed in contradictions, between the leadership and the lead [sic], parents and their children, men and women and comrades and the community." Internal development of the Party had been "negligible." "[P]arty members don't socialize, don't transfer skills in an organized manner, don't study party ideology or revolutionary theory, [they] lack of physical development, weapons training, medical education." They faced the "personal indignity" of going into the field to solicit donations while their basic needs were not being met. He queried, "How can we as revolutionaries hope to administer thousands perhaps millions one day through the city, state or federal governments when we don't have the financial self-reliance to manage our personal money?" He suggested that the Panthers adopt socialism for their organization: "Free medical care, education, food, etc. A guaranteed income and a revolutionary spirit. Perhaps in this way we could overcome our selfishness and become true Communists."[116]

Conclusions

Only twenty-seven Panthers were left by the Party's fourteenth anniversary in October 1980. One third of Panthers were over thirty-five years old and had taken part-time jobs to sustain themselves.[117] The Party had been reduced to the OCS, where the vast majority of members worked, and a legal defense structure centered on Newton. After Newton was accused of embezzlement of funds from the OCS in 1982, the Oakland Community School was closed and the last remaining members left the organization.

---

115   Letter to Newton from Amar, folder: "Reports on Comrades," box 14, HPN Papers.
116   Ibid.
117   Memo from Jonina to Newton, October 1, 1980, box 69, HPN Papers.

Magus of the Counterculture
Ramón Sender talks with Iain Boal

Ramón Sender is a central figure in the history of the greater Bay Area counterculture: electronic music pioneer, lightshow technician at the first Acid Test in San Francisco, consigliore and chief remembrancer of Morning Star and Wheeler's Ranch communes. Born in Spain in 1934, he is a living link between the radical communal traditions of the Old and the New World—through his father, the Spanish Republican novelist Ramón J. Sender, and his first wife's great grandfather, John Humphrey Noyes, founder of the nineteenth century religious utopian Oneida Community, by way of the authoritarian communism of the Bruderhof. In exile from fascist Spain with his father and sister—as "citizens of the planet, without attachments...radical cosmopolitans"—*Ramón fetched up in New York. Just out of high school in 1954, Ramón fell madly in love with Sybil, Noyes's great-granddaughter.*

" **I** met Sybil's parents and her grandparents when I visited the site of Oneida in Kenwood. Her father had been a planned child, known as a *stirpicult*, during the Oneida heyday.[1] A eugenics committee, including Yale professors, matched people up, but oddly enough John Humphrey was selected more often then anybody to reproduce. The whole idea of intentional community remained in my mind and in hers. The free love aspect remained more in hers than in mine."

Ramón spent a year in Rome at the Conservatory of Music then returned to Brandeis to be near Sybil who was attending Radcliffe.

---

1   Stirpiculture was the experiment in eugenics practiced at Oneida.

"We both dropped out, got married at the Harvard Chapel because it was free, and dissolved into poverty. I'd never had a job in my life. She hadn't either. We were very naïve. In the back of our heads was this dream of intentional community...knowing nothing about working things out. She immediately got pregnant and we moved to New York. We broke up and I came out here in 1955 just to get distance from this insane relationship. I spent the summer in North Beach reading Zen poetry and working at the Bank of America, an interesting combination. I go up to City Lights. Ferlinghetti's talking to Mike McClure and I introduce myself. 'Who are the young composers I should meet?' They tell me. Two years later, I'm starting this taped music center that turned into early avant-garde electronic music. I saved up money and took a two weeks retreat up on Mount Tam. Hiked up there with my Zen books. One evening I had a kind of epiphany as the sun was setting through the fog. I decided to go East, get rid of all my stuff, and move out West, become a hermit living in the redwoods."

While back East, Ramón met a friend who had just returned from a Gandhian community in Georgia, called Macedonia, in the process of merging with the Bruderhof. Ramón decided to explore that community, catching a ride up to the Bruderhof, on the Hudson, near Kingston.

"All I saw were smiling mothers, children playing on the swings, very idyllic, bucolic... Here I was, this father, missing my two-year old daughter, for I had been the house parent in her early months. I thought, if only she was here, this would be so ideal. I went back to the city, grabbed my stuff, and came for a stay, which lasted almost two years. The Bruderhof came from South America through a series of jumps. Hitler kicked them out of Germany. When World War II started, England said, 'We either intern your German members or you leave as a group.' The only country that would accept them was Paraguay. They bought a large ranch in Paraguay and from 1943 to 1953 evolved as three villages in the backwoods, very primitive. They started sending people up here, contacting peace groups. Between the Quakers, some Brethren, some Mennonites and Hutterites, they gathered together a group at the Kingston place. Half of Macedonia joined them, bringing their educational play equipment business. About the time I came, the rest of Macedonia caved in and joined. The play equipment, mostly wooden toys made of maple, was their livelihood. The government put a lot of money into early childhood programs and that was a huge bonus for them. They started making money hand over fist. They didn't have to pay salaries. One, Flori's husband, had had a successful steel business in Philadelphia and was a really astute businessman. He took over the educational play business and rapidly developed it into a multimillion-dollar affair. Flori was willing to help if you had any problems. She became the go-between for me and my wife. I was able to reconnect with my little girl, Xabi [Xabiri]. I convinced Sybil to visit. She spoke to the Elder and was very moved by the whole experience. Within six months she was back because the community challenged her. Not as my wife. First you become a novice, then you go into the preparation group for a 'baptism' into the community. Which was my second epiphany. Up on Mount Tam I had had the big 'yes, yes, yes.' Here I had the big 'no, no, no'—the neti, neti, not this, confess all your sins, grovel, die to your ego. Very painful, but very enlightening. I think the Elder didn't trust my experience, considering it too emotional. I cried for three days straight. As a novitiate in the Bruderhof you commit yourself totally, including all your real property now and all your future assets. The year was adventurous. The Elder decided that one woman was haunted by demons. We had an ongoing exorcism. What a trip. The community was bringing Sybil and myself closer together. I was having breakfasts (taken privately with family) with her and Xabi. It was such a thrill to have my little girl. In a way my scheme had worked."

A year later they were asked to prepare again for baptism. Sybil, working as the office manager, had caught fire while Ramón hung back.

"One day we were driving with the Elder. Sybil, sitting in front with the Elder, turns, challenging me. 'You're not talking up in meetings. What's wrong? I think you love me more than you love Jesus.' That fairly put a spear through me. I suddenly lost trust in the whole situation. I saw it in a dark light; Sybil was attracted to the Elder—oh, here we go again. I thought we'd be where Sybil wouldn't play out her sexual attractions and here she is with the Elder, of all people, the man I'd idolized. I went into a complete state of anxiety. I'd been celibate. My first months there I was masturbating in the shower but realized it was not kosher and purposefully held that urge down. The minute I lost trust, an overwhelming sexual thing took over. I started masturbating, then confessed it to one of the Elder's acolytes. Gradually they pushed me out, saying 'You'd better not come to the worship for a while.' I'd continue doing it. 'Maybe you should move to another Bruderhof.' My mind couldn't say, 'I want out of here.' My body took over and said, 'I'm gonna move you out. This place isn't healthy.' I went to work at a local camp for the summer. Things didn't get better. Questioned by the group, I said, 'The way I feel, I'm in a cage and there's one door you want me to walk through and I'm not going through that door.' They all departed very sorrowfully. I drove out to California in 1959, like the wrath of god was chasing me across country. It took a while to get over all this. I met someone and instigated divorce proceedings. Sybil and the Elder showed up. They didn't believe in divorce and they were going to try and talk me out of it. Really spooky."

Tape Music Pioneer

"I studied at the San Francisco Conservatory and in my last year I started a concert series and met my partner, Mort Subotnick. 1962 was our first year in an old Victorian, slated to be demolished, on Russian Hill. We put an ad in the *Chronicle* saying we were looking for an electronics engineer; this guy showed up and built us a synthesizer, taking about eight months. He beat Moog by a year. We realized that the visual aspect of a concert is important. Of course, it's possible to do it in total darkness—we had a composer friend who started Audium, which has been playing electronic music in total darkness for forty years.[2] But Mort and I wanted light and tried two already known lightshow people, each with their own agendas. I knew Tony Martin and said, 'Please come do our lightshow stuff,' and finally talked him into it. It was never his first love but he did a very, very good job. We collaborated with local artists, poets. We had Ronnie Davis do an experimental show. It cost us a fellowship from Ampex, the Redwood City tape recording company, when an Ampex guy came and the show was so scatological that he walked out. Mort ran out after him crying, 'This is not what we usually do!'

Ron Davis found a place on Divisadero, He said 'How about we share this place?' We liked it and thought about sharing with the Mime Troupe, but knew we'd be swamped. So we rented it without Ron and invited Anna Halprin and her dance workshop to rent space for $75, and

---

2   Audium, Theatre of Sound-Sculptured Space, http://www.audium.org.

invited KPFA to share the concert hall for $100. The monthly $175 paid the rent; all we had to do was pay utilities for our concerts. We had the third-floor studio almost four years, hand to mouthing it. We would get calls from people saying, 'There's a bunch of equipment that just fell off a truck, selling for pennies on the dollar, would you be interested?' The Rockefeller Foundation sent someone out who really liked us. He said, 'Look, I can give you $15,000 just myself, but if you want a bigger grant, you'll have to affiliate with a college.' Mort was teaching at Mills College and I just had gotten my Masters there because Mills had a long tradition of avant-garde music through Darius Milhaud. We made a deal with Mills and the grant went up to $150,000 including a performing group."

Acid Test Impresario

"By the summer of '65, I had taken my first peyote trip. It had totally blown me away. I had never even smoked pot. The energies were a lot more potent than I had thought. I just smoked pot for six months, then LSD came along. I was getting pretty burnt out on the concert format. I really wanted to do Sunday morning church services, running through all the ancient religions, and do things like sacrifice a cow on stage so people would know where their meat came from. It was suggested I talk to Stewart Brand, who had a multimedia show called *America Needs Indians*. I got together with Stewart, told him about my church idea. He said, 'Let's go down to Big Sur and talk to the grand old man of Gestalt psychology, Fritz Perls. Maybe he'll be your first guest sermon giver.' We went down to Big Sur. I invited Fritz. He looked at me and said, 'What? Are you crazy? A sermon? A cow?' So that was that. A month later Stewart called me up: 'Ken Kesey's in town doing Acid Tests with the Grateful Dead and the Trips Festival, which would be a weekend blowout with all the most interesting groups in the city.' Things were beginning to percolate. Kesey was busted for the second time on Stewart's roof. He was up there with Mountain Girl smoking pot and they decided to throw pebbles on the roof of a nearby building where they thought a friend lived, and whoever lived there called the cops. When the cops arrived, Kesey grabbed the bag of pot from the cop and threw it off the roof. He was already awaiting sentencing on another bust down the Peninsula at La Honda.

He was in the papers every day, December '65. We couldn't have asked for better publicity for the Trips Festival. The energy kept building and building. Stewart and I are thinking: we're riding a cyclone here, we need help. I suggested, 'This guy Bill Graham just did a benefit for the Mime Troupe, a great success and maybe he would come on as the manager.' I phoned Bill and asked 'Would you take it on?' He said 'Sure.' I said, 'How much do you want? I'm taking $200 and Stewart is taking $200.' He said, 'Pay me whatever you think I'm worth after it's over.' So he made the tickets, he made the posters, he got word out. We had a massive turnout at Longshoremen's Hall, which could handle five to six hundred people. Packed every night. There were sideshows, some filmmakers. Anna Halprin and her dancers came, climbing up into a cargo net strung over the main area. There's a warrant out for Kesey. He has a twin brother, Bud, looks just like him. The first night Bud showed up in a NASA space suit. Once he established his identity, Ken came in as Bud for the rest of the event, and then afterward disappeared over the Mexican border. We met Monday to count the proceeds. There was $14,000 in little paper bags Bill Graham had thrown into the trunk of his car. That same day he signed a lease for the Fillmore. You could see the writing on the wall. I was so burnt out by the energy. I had stayed very straight, probably the only person not on LSD at the Trips Festival. I didn't like getting high in public, would rather have my setting under control. I decided I needed to go to the desert with fifty caps of acid and think it all over. Oh, one thing—before the Trips Festival, the *Chronicle* sent their temporary journalist, Lou Gottlieb, to interview us. Lou was taking time off from the Limeliters after their near fatal plane crash in Colorado. A friend on the *Chronicle* said, 'Hey, Lou, you're not with the Limeliters, why don't you review concerts for us?' He reviewed a Beethoven piano recital and compared it to the *Tibetan Book of the Dead*. He had already done LSD in Los Angeles. Lou and I got talking about the Bruderhof and intentional communities. He said, 'You know, I have thirty acres up in Sonoma County, an old ranch I invested in. If you ever get the urge to try something communal, there it sits.'"

Communing

"I went off to the Mojave and communed with whatever powers there are. I tripped, living in a cave, South of Needles. I drove to Phoenix. My car broke down. I had my engine rebuilt in Truth or Consequences. I drove North to Colorado to visit Drop City, the only commune I knew of. A group of domes of cut-out car parts and muddy as hell, with planks from dome to dome. I'm writing newsletters back to Stewart on this hectograph with a tray of gel. You draw or type on special paper, with carbon backing. You lay it on the gel, pull it off and the words stay on the gel; you put a piece of blank paper on it, cool it off. An early photocopy. You could get about six copies before it became so faint that nobody could read it. I was using this on my travels to send newsletters out. On my way out of town, I checked in with Steve and Barbara Durkee, living with Ram Dass (Dick Alpert) in Palo Alto. They were on my newsletter list. I wrote them about how beautiful northern New Mexico is and the next thing I know Durkee is out there with his money man buying land for the Lama Foundation, now a Sufi shrine because Sufi Sam is buried there. I returned to San Francisco and realized I couldn't live in the city anymore. I went up Mount Tam with my girlfriend Joan, whom I had met at a John Cage Event. We took our clothes off and started running around, when a ranger appeared. Right then Joan reminded me of Lou's offer. We went to Morning Star with Stewart, his wife, and Lou with his pockets full of hashish cookies, provided by his dear friend Buckwheat from Sausalito, a famous jazz player and provider of goodies. Springtime '66 and the apple blossoms were at their height. I fell madly in love with the place. I said, 'I'm staying or coming back as soon as I can.' Lou, embarrassed, said, 'I've never spent any time here. I read an ad in the KPFA folio about a property. Just as I was reading it, Bud, Malvina Reynolds' husband called me saying, 'There's an interesting investment opportunity here.' I figured, 'The gods have spoken, so I bought the place sight unseen, and went back on the road.' He looked into subdividing and they were going to rename the road through the property Gottleib Lane. Lou thought it was hilarious. When I said, 'I'm moving up.' Lou said, 'That's fine, I will too later this summer. I intend to practice piano and have my Carnegie Hall debut in five years.' He was a really fine pianist.

I moved up. Jacob Pettis, from an open theater group in Berkeley, moved up, as did Walter Bentley and the filmmaker Bruce Bailey. Fall '66 we went to an Intentional Communities conference in Ben Lomond and introduced ourselves as a Sri Aurobindo ashram. I had become a mad aficionado of sun-gazing, doing it in semishaded redwood groves. My thoughts would stop; I could enter a no-mind state very easily. I felt sure that all religions had started with sun worship. I studied until I found Sri Aurobindo, who used sun worship metaphorically. We got into a correspondence with the mother who was running the Sri Aurobindo ashram,

Aurobindo having died. Lou and the mother corresponded about LSD and she sat in on someone's trip just to figure it out. When we ran into trouble as an open gate community, Lou wrote, 'What am I to do? We have these people who just keep showing up.' She said, 'Take their photograph and mail it to me and I will decide who should stay and who should go.' I ran out one evening and bought a camera and took everybody's photo.

The word was out. November '66, we identified ourselves as an ashram, interested in new members. By January '67, people were starting to show up. Lou moved in, renovating the old egg storage shed, just big enough for a Bechstein concert grand, a mattress on the floor beneath. Bach and Mozart tinkled through the premises all day long. As people started showing up, I hurriedly put the rules of the ashram on the wall, which nobody paid any attention to.

Lenny, a fourteen-year-old half-Jewish, half-black girl, from New York was traveling with her teacher from some New Age Summerhill school in Florida. She went into Social Services or the emergency room in Santa Rosa with the kind of infection you only get from intercourse. An underage girl with a yeast infection definitely brought some attention to us. We had our first visit from a social worker and the chief narc. I decided my little sessions in the redwood grove were not going to be too groovy. In March, Joan and I rented a cabin in Bodega Bay. We came over frequently. One time Lou said, 'Oh, the Diggers came up from the city and asked if they could plant the garden, take care of the orchards and could they have the fruits and vegetables to feed the thousands of hippies that are coming for the Summer of Love?' Next time I visited, there were ten more people, including Peter Coyote. In six months, we had gone from ten to fifty people; the energies were very good, everyone working in the garden and building little huts. They had their first bust—an April Fools' bust. The cops sent someone out from jail and he said, 'I'm here to set you up.' The place was clean as a whistle by the time they came.

Shortly after, the back-corner neighbor complained about nudity and love making, visible to his daughters over the back fence. He was a retired businessman. Lou was his nightmare. His nubile daughters wanted nothing more than to jump the fence. He started a petition around Occidental for people to sign a complaint against Morning Star that went to Santa Rosa. The authorities got even more interested.

By July, we were feeding three hundred people every night. The pots in the kitchen were getting larger and larger. We were making food runs to the city. I put an ad in the local paper: 'We'll trade work for food.' One lady, who ran a dairy, signed up a bunch of Diggers to fix her fence; later we figured they were making fifteen cents an hour, but getting eggs and milk. Then the winos moved in and set up camp outside Lou's studio. They had a fire circle in the driveway and would sit up all night drinking, shouting, screaming, occasionally stabbing or punching each other out. We already had families with kids so we had our first and only meeting, where it was decided that Lou, as the owner of the property, had to ask these people to leave. He went to the most outrageous of the group and said, 'We really have to ask you to leave.' He said 'Well, you know, Lou, it's gonna take me a couple of months to get my stuff together.' That's the night Lou had his migraine and decided it was God telling him he should never ever ask anyone to leave.

Cars started streaming through, with these faces at the window, looking out, with eyes: OO. Occasionally somebody would roll their window down, asking, 'Where is the free love?' I'd always point to the back exit 'Just go out that road.' We blocked the driveway so people couldn't drive through. The winos moved down to the front, clearing a flat space for a parking lot. They became the parking attendants. You'd arrive and half-toothless, weird looking characters would come up and go, 'Can I watch your car for you? It's only five bucks.' You got the impression that if you didn't hand over the five bucks you'd come back to a car without any tires.

July was crisis month. The septic tank overflowed and the Health Department insisted on leach fields. We didn't want to take trees out so we were digging the trenches by hand. The perfect set up for hepatitis. Everybody came down with it. I got it. Went down to the city. Got better. Joan showed up and said, 'Let's drive up to Tolstoy Farm; you'll love it!' We spent two months at Tolstoy. It was not seriously hippified then, although it became so later, and maybe somebody burnt down their main house on purpose to get rid of the crashers. We came back to Morning Star in September for the arrest of the Morning Star 12. The County said, 'Lou you have to arrest these people as trespassers.' So Lou said, 'OK, who wants to get arrested?' We came on the day that he was going down the road saying, 'I arrest thee. I arrest thee.' People tried to not live on the land but nearby in a neighbor's summer housing for apple pickers. Still, folks drifted back to Morning Star putting up tents and teepees. The cops would come in the morning, warning then busting people who didn't leave. Eventually they bulldozed everything three times. Lou had to pay for the bulldozing and they left Lou's cabin the first time. He donated it to Ed Walkingstick, who rebuilt it on the back of a two-ton truck and drove off into the sunset with the equivalent of Lou's cabin on the back of Lou's truck. So that was '68—sleeping in the bushes, avoiding the cops. In early summer, Lou deeded the land to God and left for India. He had gotten a little sidetracked from Carnegie Hall.

That year, I went to a party in Olompali, a Marin County weekend hippy resort. The Grateful Dead had leased the place before Don McCoy, the founding father. We looked down our noses at them because it wasn't "open" land. One problem with Olompali was that they had a 10 mile-per-hour dirt road leading right to Highway 101 without any entry lane. Stoned hippies going 10 mph had to enter 60 mph traffic, which was not good. Then the horses escaped and got out on the freeway and somebody hit one. Then two children drowned in the pool. It was looking like the adults were not exactly there. Shortly after, the main house caught fire and the Novato fire chief died of a heart attack on the way to the fire. I was there that night. Nobody set the fire; it was one of those stupid electrical ones. Nobody died except the fire chief and the Chihuahua that lived on the land.

At Olompali I met a psychiatrist from Philadelphia, Ira Einhorn [subsequently the notorious "Unicorn Killer"]. He said, "I run a half-way house along the lines of that English psychiatrist, that blowout center guy, Ronnie Laing." I said, "That's funny, we run a sort of blowout center at Morning Star. Would you like to see it?" We hopped in his VW van. Lou wasn't there, but I decided to give the tour. There was a crew in the apple orchard, two or three black guys, one named Tarzan, and a black woman, Mama. They saw us coming and started screaming. The closer we got, the louder they screamed. One guy pulled a revolver; another guy a linoleum knife. I backed up, slowly. I had gotten along with these people. They didn't like us that day. Mama jumped in between, tearing off her shirt and baring her breast. One of the guys had his arms in plaster casts from knife wounds and he hit Mama, knocked her down. Later we heard he'd broken her jaw. The screams were heard all over the land. By the time we'd retreated, John Butler, one of the dearest men in the world, a black guy, is standing there with an African spear in his hand. He was really worried. Terrified, Ira jumps in his VW and takes off. I spent the night in the bushes listening to Tarzan shooting off his goddamn revolver in the air and decided the land was telling me it was time to leave.

I'd parked my van, with flattened tires, to keep people from driving into the meadow. I pumped them up with a bicycle pump and headed down the front drive. A girl I'd met at Olompali was writing for the *Modern Utopian* magazine. She said 'Hey, let's tour the New Mexico communes and I'll write 'em up.' We left for New Mexico, went down to the Domes, visited New Buffalo, and Morning Star, New Mexico. We went up to Lama. We did write something, published in one of Richard Fairfield's magazines. I came back. I didn't reject the idea of communal living; it had run off.

I planned to join Lou in India and made it as far as Hawaii. A note came from Lou, saying, 'I found him, my hash-smoking hippy guru and he's coming to Morning Star to chant the Bhagavad Gita and raise the vibes.' I returned to San Francisco. My ex-girlfriend Joanie was working as a topless dancer to support her scene, running a crash pad at the corner of Haight and Ashbury, with a bouncer to keep speed freaks out. I convinced her it was time to drop all and return to the country.

At a party out at Bill Wheeler's ranch, someone said, 'Why don't you open your land? You've got 360 acres and nothing happening. People have been kicked off Morning Star.' Bill said, 'I've never closed it.' Silence. You could feel the silence. Within a week, the Reeds had moved there. In May '69 Joan and I came. An empty cabin. We stayed. A wonderful experience from May '68 till December '70. I always felt Morning Star would never become a viable community. It was too close to straight neighbors and too accessible for the winos. Whatever problems the main society had would show up. Wheeler's was more remote with a very long, bad dirt road. The winos did not like it.

Given time Wheeler's would have become a viable community. Bill had to learn to let go, although he was willing to play cop (while Lou wasn't). If somebody was really impossible, Bill would punch them out, tell them to leave, or take them to the nearest mental health facility. That kept the place relatively peaceful. Bill tended to be very sarcastic. At first he would wander into the hippy sites on horseback and play the lord of the manor. He got over that. 'I never declared it closed or never said it wasn't open.' He had, in some sense, a critique of private property. Lou's theory was that you should let the land select who lives there. However, you may get too many people to make it a viable place for children and families to live. The cops and the county made Morning Star unsafe for families because if parents were arrested the children would get taken to Social Services. Morning Star families moved off. The yogis moved off. The rear guard action was pretty tough, AWOLs and Vietnam vets.

Wheeler's, on the other hand, was more remote. Access to Wheeler's was over the land of a very uptight neighbor who got increasingly angry as more and more hippies went across his land, not knowing which was Wheeler's and which was his. They'd camp on his land or make love in the bushes. He hired a front guard to check people's IDs and take photographs as they came in. When the guard quit his job, he gave us all his stuff. We got portrait photographs of people with their name and license plate numbers on the back.

After the bulldozing that closed Wheeler's, Bill moved to Bolinas for two years. He met Peter, who was willing to sell a million-dollar home in Tiburon and buy out the bad neighbor. This 1,200 acres front ranch was a gorgeous piece of property, renamed Ocean Song. For a while, the Ananda community from the Sierras ran a school there but that didn't work out. I think Peter donated a big chunk of it to a nonprofit group.

Bill was finally forced to build a code house and put in a flush toilet that he never uses. With one 'code house' on the property then other people could build their shacks and not be bothered, since the neighbors are cool.

I go every May Day and play accordion for the May Pole dance, occasionally other times. When Bill was in danger of losing his access, he bought the ranch to the West, Star Mountain, in his wife's name, and then sold it to a mutual friend of ours, Alan Wood. Then Delia Moon came by and bought 1,200 acres in Bodega at the height of the hassle at Wheeler's. We thought, 'Now we've really got it made.' But she never opened it up. She invited people to settle it and formed a viable community, but very different. People have their individual little landscapes.

I left Wheeler's when our son was born, in December of '70. Winter was coming on. I'd extended our little hut and it wasn't gonna be warm enough. A lot of the couples were breaking up through the Stephen Gaskin influence: experimenting with double couples, foursomes, different types of relationships. One Wheeler couple joined that Gaskin trek East. Bill and his wife broke up. An unsettled relationships scene. I felt very old-fashioned there. Our baby came down with pneumonia. When he was out of the hospital, I decided we'd go to the desert to dry out. I started writing my history of Morning Star and Wheeler's. I was feeling really "communed out." The end of an epoch. I got a good advance from the book and bought a place on the edge of all the communities. I boasted I could walk nude out the back of my land and travel through four different pieces of communally owned property for miles from mine to Delia's Sheep Ridge, to Ryan's, to Wheeler's, to Star Mountain, to Ocean Song. Basically a square mile, all friendly. I lived there for five years and did a lot of writing. I wrote two or three novels, a couple of nonfiction books. When my first novel was coming out in '79, I decided I had to make the scene down here in San Francisco if I was going to become a writer that anybody ever heard of."

The Diggers delivering free food in Golden Gate Park.

1966 or 1967 ©William Gedney Collection, Duke University, David M. Rubenstein Rare Book & Manuscript Library.

"Hippies in Golden Gate Park," 1969.

Photographs from the Jefferson F. Poland papers.
Photographer unknown. BANC PIC 1971.130—PIC. Courtesy
of The Bancroft Library, University of California, Berkeley.

"People's Park," 1969.

Harold Adler. Berkeley
Scenes from the 1960s
[graphic], BANC PIC
1992.063—PIC. Courtesy
of the Bancroft Library,
University of California,
Berkeley.

People's Park Free
Church posters.

The Berkeley Free
Church Collection,
1967–72, Graduate
Theological Union
Special Collections
and Archives, Berkeley,
California.

Noon: We will gather at the People's Park Annex (Grove and　st Streets in the
Bart land) for a rally at 12:00

1:00: We will march in several groups to the People's Park .　There we will
surround the Park and demand the fence be taken down.

6:30: We will return to the People's Park Annex for music and a festival of life.

Saturday: Activities are being planned and will be announced by Friday.

Housing: People's Park Annex is being turned into INSURRECTION CITY so
if you want to sleep outdoors we have tents. Otherwisea come to
1703 Grove or call 841-6794 and 8416480.

Information: The Free Church has lots of information at 549-0649. Otherwise
call 549-0563.

JOIN THE STRUGGLE FOR THE PEOPLE'S PARK
COME TO BERKELEY FRIDAY MAY 30, MEMORIAL DAY
WE WILL MARCH TO OUR PARK --TO THE PEOPLE'S PARK
WE WILL DEMAND THAT THE FENCE COME DOWN

We built a Park. Heyns, Reagan, and Madigan put up a fence. The Park was
beautiful and free so they killed to destroy it.
Private property in America is a God and the pigs are its armed priests. The
University was satisfied with a swamp; the people of Berkeley built a beautiful
park. Helicopters, bayonets, and shotguns were brought in to tear up the grass and
rebuild Heyns' private swamp.
We are fighting to return our park to the control of the people in the community,
the people who built it. Reagan and Madigan fear people who fight back. The black
movement, the student movement, the anti-war movement have begun to ressuerct the
great American tradition of fighting back. Our fight is spreading and we will continue
it.

COME TO THE MARCH

The people of Berkeley are outraged and demand an end to the incredible terrorism
of the reckless professional politicians who control state and police power.
We are marching to demand:

1. The fence must come down.
2. The police must be disarmed.
3. The national guard must go home.
4. All charges against demonstrators must be dropped.
5. Reparations must be paid to the injured.
6. The police criminals and their generals must be brought to justice.

The San Francisco Mime Troupe. Gorilla Band, 1976.

Photo by Tom Copi, San Francisco.

The San Francisco Mime Troupe. Great Air Robbery, 1974.

Photo by Tom Copi, San Francisco.

The San Francisco Mime Troupe. Hotel Universe, 1977.

Photo by Tom Copi, San Francisco.

The San Francisco Mime Troupe. Longshoremen's Hall, 1972.

Photo by Tom Copi, San Francisco.

The San Francisco Mime Troupe. Seize the Time, 1971.

Photo by Tom Copi, San Francisco.

The San Francisco Mime Troupe. The Mother, 1973.

Photo by Tom Copi, San Francisco.

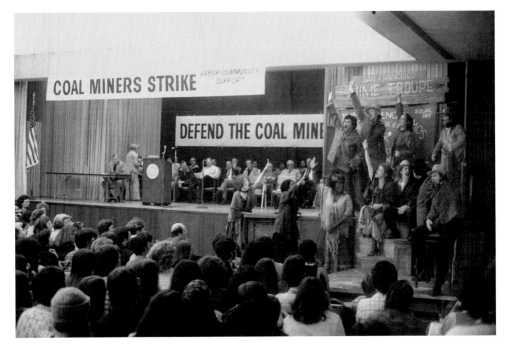

The San Francisco Mime Troupe. Union Hall, 1978.

Photo by Tom Copi, San Francisco.

Nineteen-month occupation of Alcatraz by Indians of All Tribes (IAT), 1969.

Photo by Michelle Vignes, San Francisco.

Illegal structures, 1969.

Morning Star Commune (a.k.a. Morning Star Ranch and Digger Farm), Occidental, California.

Morning Star images reprinted with permission of Ramón Sender from *The Morning Star Scrapbook*, by Unohoo, Coyote, Rick and the Mighty Avengers, (http://badabamama.com/morningstar-scrapbook.html), 1966–69.

Thanksgiving, 1967. Morning Star Commune (a.k.a. Morning Star Ranch and Digger Farm), Occidental, California.

"Absolutely nothing to fear, my friends!"

Confrontation with Deputies, 1969. Morning Star Commune (a.k.a. Morning Star Ranch and Digger Farm), Occidental, California.

"The world is a commune in confusion. We the children of a new age must use our money and leadership power to bring about change. Now is the time for learning how to live in harmony with our natural environment, a time for sharing our earth and loving each other."

Aerial view of Morning Star Ranch, Upper House and Egg Shed upper center, barn to the right, road to the orchard bottom center.

Wheeler's Ranch's first Thanksgiving, 1968.

Communards at Morning Star Ranch.

Bedroom in redwoods.

Black Survival Conference, Free Food Give-away, Community Survival Program, Bobby Hutton Memorial Park, Oakland, May 13, 1972.

Photos by Stephen Shames/Polaris.

Images provided by Dr. Huey P. Newton Foundation Inc. Collection. M0864. Courtesy of Department of Special Collections and University Archives, Stanford University Libraries. Stanford, CA

Birthday party at the Whale School, c. 1978. Photo by Gary Moraga.

Logging road occupied, Albion Ridge, c. 1990. Photo by Gary Moraga.

Birthday gathering, East Caspar, January 1977. Photo by Gary Moraga.

Stump foundation, c. 1978. Courtesy of Tom Wodetzki.

Albion Ridge, c. 1965. Courtesy of Tom Wodetzki.

Loyes and Janferie,
Bigfoot, c. 1983.
Courtesy of Dick
Whetstone.

Corners of the Mouth
collective, c. 1982. Photo
by Gary Moraga.

An "Albion Peasant Tradition," n.d. Courtesy of Tom Wodetzki.

Hoe-down Tonight!
⋆Saturday, Oct. 18.
OLD-TIME
COUNTRY DANCE
& FIESTA! ⋆
Featuring The Internationally-Renowned
New Albion
String Band
Favored by the Crowned Heads of Europe
⋆Luscious Victuals By World-Famous
Salmon Creek Farm
In the Well-Known Albion Peasant Tradition
Jigs, Reels, Fresh Garden Vegetables,
Squares, Soups, Nuts, Zuzus, Pickin'
& Fiddling, Hot Bread & Butter!
ADMISSION $1.50.   At The Door.
COMPLETE DINNER $2.00
Dinners from 7 pm, Dancing from 9 pm
CROWN HALL
Ukiah Street   Mendocino

Salmon Creek Farm printing, c. 1980. Courtesy of Tom Wodetzki.

Building a "Bender," c. 1980. Courtesy of Tom Wodetzki.

Albion girls, c. 1982. Courtesy of Tom Wodetzki.

Table Mountain boys, c. 1982. Courtesy of Tom Wodetzki.

Part III. The Country

"The researches into the lives of the communards of Albion Ridge offer an illuminating account of one central, specifically rural, aspect of the counterculture of the '60s and '70s. The history of this movement has not been told, even though the legacy of Californian communes of that period permeates the wider culture in ways that are mostly unacknowledged and urgently demand documentation and analysis."

The Albion Nation: Communes on the Mendocino Coast

Cal Winslow

> "It is still in so many places a beautiful country, and many of us can work, in different ways, to keep and enhance it. I have had the luck to thin a wood and watch the cowslips and bluebells and foxgloves come back..."
>
> —Raymond Williams, *The Country and the City*[1]

The '60s communards came to Albion Ridge as settlers looking for land. The Ranch at Table Mountain was seen first from the air; Walter Schneider, formerly a Navy Pilot, more recently of Timothy Leary's Millbrook Estate in upstate New York, found it. Together with his friend Duncan Ray, also of Millbrook, they bought it—120 acres for $50,000, paid for with Ray family money. They invited friends up from Haight-Ashbury in San Francisco, including Zo Abell and her young daughter and Allen Cohen, poet and editor of the San Francisco *Oracle*. In 1968, the commune at Table Mountain Ranch became the first of many on Albion Ridge. In the decade following, hundreds of young people would join them on the Ridge, sometimes permanently, more often not; thousands would pass through.

This is the story of the Albion "nation"—a community of communards and back-to-the-landers, as well as a miscellany of antinomians who made their homes here. It begins a little known but important chapter in the history of utopia in Northern California, one that focuses not on media

---

1   Raymond Williams, *The Country and the City* (Oxford: Oxford University Press, 1973), 320.

stars, nor on the most bizarre and outlandish but on the experience of groups of ordinary young people who came to the Mendocino coast in the '60s and '70s, many of whom continue to reside here. The Albion story is significant in its own right but also because it raises important questions about communal life as well as the values widely shared in the counterculture of these years. Just what was the experience? More work needs to be done, though it is already clear that there is much to be learned from this history. What, if anything, can this experience contribute to the discussion of what we would like for the future? What constitutes a genuine *alternative* to our own patterns of work, consumption and life and our twenty-first-century afflictions, primarily permanent war, driven in an era of austerity and imperial decline by neoliberalism and its armies? This implies reflection on the nature and purpose of alternative visions and the tension between realism, desire, and imagination. Is such a conversation wanted? Can it be useful, even possible, in view of contracting time-lines and approaching ecological disaster? This remains to be seen. What follows is intended as a contribution. It examines the experience of some hundreds of people, who "dropped out" in the language of the times, and "left it all behind" for Mendocino, to live a life in common. It examines this "from the bottom up" and suggests elements of their legacies.[2]

We begin with what we have already lost. The '60s settlers were not the first to migrate to the Mendocino coast. Albion Ridge sits above the village of Albion, where the Albion River, South of Mendocino, empties into the sea. This land was home to Northern Pomo people, inheritors of thousands of years of habitation. The site of the village had been claimed by the Spanish, seeking souls; raided by Russian fur traders; then, in 1822, taken by Mexico until 1850, when it was passed on to an English sea captain who, in the imperial spirit of that age, gave the site and its river the ancient name of England—Albion. Settlers followed, first Americans, both citizens and soldiers. Anglos overwhelmed the Pomo homelands. In a pattern typical of the American West, these newcomers came as conquerors and colonizers. In cruel campaigns, they made "a bad situation worse."[3] In 1850 alone, two hundred Pomo were murdered,

---

2   Two accounts (one academic, one fictional) should be mentioned here: Bennett M. Berger, *The Survival of a Counterculture* (New Brunswick, NJ: Transaction, 2004) and Ernest Callenbach, *Ecotopia: A Novel* (New York: Bantam, 1975).

3   Barry M. Pritzker, *A Native American Encyclopedia* (Oxford: Oxford University Press, 2000), 138.

their villages ransacked, their lands stolen. In 1856, they were imprisoned in Mendocino, eleven years later, turned out, "homeless, landless, without legal rights."[4] The horrors of these wars stain memory here; the Anglos succeeded in driving out the Pomo, though not entirely. Survivors regrouped, then regrouped again; they continued summer treks through the coastal mountains to the sea to harvest and dry abalone, mussels, clams, seaweed and salt. They still do.

The Anglo settlers failed as miners and agriculturalists; timber was another story. Albion sits at the coastal edge of the once great Redwood forest—two million acres of giant, ancient trees, a forest that stretched from the Oregon border to Big Sur. The first mill on the Mendocino coast was built on the Albion estuary in 1853. The onslaught unleashed was unforgiving: nature was spared no more than her peoples, each victims of civilization. The California Indian Wars of the 1850s, then, coincided with the beginnings of the ravaging of Mendocino's coastal mountain ranges and the destruction of this forest. The timber men came along with investors, speculators, thieves, and swindlers, wheeling and dealing; they gathered up the land, consolidated it into massive tracts, then lured in the loggers and itinerant laborers—mostly men, though some with families. They came from Maine, Michigan, and Minnesota, as well as from much farther: Sweden, Finland, Italy, Portugal, and China. The workers felled the giant trees, often three hundred feet and more in height, trees impossible to move in one piece. The loggers cut the huge logs into sections, forced them down streams and rivers, and then hauled one section at a time first by mules, then by rail, to Albion and the mill—one of dozens built along the Mendocino coast. The mouth of just about every river and creek became a center of heavy industry. This came with a cost. The loggers took down every tree within reach. A mass of rubble was left behind: slash that was burned, limbs, bark, other trees, undergrowth, birds and animals, beds of Redwood Sorrel, the ferns and flowers, everything that could not escape. Entire (mini) ecosystems were destroyed, leaving the ridges charred, streams unrecognizable. The loggers themselves often emerged from these fires blackened as coal miners, lungs ravished, bodies bent, sometimes broken. Conditions were dangerous in the hills and brutal in the mills. The mill sites festered like open sores along this wild shoreline, producing deafening noise, fire and

---

4   Ibid.

smoke; they were surrounded by a bleak hodgepodge of outbuildings and wooden shacks—instant, temporary slums, together forming a coastal necklace of distress stretching the length of the County and beyond. This was no "golden age."[5]

I am not certain just when this vast section of Northern California came to be called "the Redwood Empire," but the name is apt. This empire of timber and mills became a source of great wealth, extracting profits and power, in this case for the San Francisco robber barons who operated them. But empires seem inclined to dig their own graves: they come and go; they kill the goose; the robbers move on. The Albion Mill was shut down in 1929; Fort Bragg and Southeastern Railroad ceased operations two years later, leaving behind a savagely wounded earth. By 1937, a *San Francisco News* reporter produced a series on Mendocino coastal "ghost" towns, where "no trace of earlier habitations remained...except...some blackened ruin, a few rusty chains hanging from a rocky coast...weather beaten and lichen covered shacks stand gaping open."[6] No mention of surviving Pomo. No mention of ghostly stumps and barren hills. There was "recovery" in the 1950s: chainsaws, bulldozers, ribbons of roads, and trucks took the industry into each and every last enclave of standing timber, but, by the end of the century, little more than one hundred years on, only the giant Union Lumber Company mill in Fort Bragg remained on Mendocino's coast. It, too, is now closed. Perhaps 3 percent of old growth survives, probably less.

The new settlers were not, strictly speaking, environmentalists, though few were unaware of this movement. The first Earth Day was celebrated in San Francisco in March 1970. They were quickly converted, however, by the discovery that big trees were few and far between; by the sight of sparkling streams turned chocolate brown following the first autumn rain; and by the muddy plumes of the Navarro, Albion, and Big Rivers carrying the soil of clear-cut canyons far out into the sea. Salmon, since time immemorial the direct and indirect staple of almost all coastal creatures and peoples from Alaska to the Monterey Bay, were already few and rapidly disappearing.

The settlers came, rather, as revolutionaries eager to live free and in common, while enlarging these spaces, countercultural zones built in defi-

---

5   See Cal Winslow, "The Redwood Lumber and Sawmill Workers' Strike," in *The Encyclopedia of Strikes in American History*, eds. Aaron Brenner, Benjamin Day, and Immanuel Ness (Armonk, NY: M.E. Sharpe, 2009), 438–43.

6   *San Francisco News*, October 18, 1937.

ance of industrial capital; capitalism remained, even in the best of times, transparently cruel and destructive, even when only young eyes could see this. And they were almost entirely youth; some were "small-c" communists, others refugees, escapees fleeing an embattled nation, war in Vietnam, rebellion at home, bitter battles in the mean streets of San Francisco, Oakland, and Berkeley. In the Haight, homelessness, hunger, drug problems, and crime had become endemic; "L'il" Bobby Hutton, the youngest Panther, was gunned down by Oakland police. In Berkeley, at People's Park, snipers and armored vehicles were deployed. James Rector was shot and killed. "The mood of the movement was heavy, violent." (Helen)[7] Otherswere simply desirous of a life with nature. All were in search of freedom and a garden in which they might find it. They discovered, incredibly, that the land remained beautiful. Not entirely, to be sure: huge stumps endure, standing sometimes in formation, reminders of past forests, testaments to what can never completely be restored. But it was recovering.

Property on the steep hillsides of Albion Ridge, Middle Ridge, and Navarro Ridge, was cheap, very cheap: $50,000 seems like a lot; it was, nevertheless, within the range of a modest inheritance, the latter not so unusual in a largely white, middle-class movement. It was also, apparently, in keeping with budgets of new "hip" entrepreneurs, as well as successful dealers. So were abandoned homesteads. Inhabitants were few: "only a handful of residents, 'old timers,' could be counted along the entire Middle Ridge," (Moonlight). Some were friendly, others not. More than a few rescued stranded visitors, picked up hitchhikers, and shared rides to town. The Hamm brothers, two old men who lived in a barn, were the most welcoming. Their home, once their mother's house, had burned down. They were old Leftists, probably Wobblies; they shared country skills and a library of tattered volumes and pamphlets, the stories of earlier generations of revolutionaries.[8] They owned one of the few TVs on the Ridge and so hosted Saturday morning cartoons for the communes' kids.

The climate was mild: fog along the sea, a long rainy winter, cool, dry summers; the panoramic prospect that opens as one descends the

---

7   I have used first names as reference not to disguise identities but to simplify the text and abide by a tradition of first names.
8   Wobblies: members of the revolutionary Industrial Workers of the World (IWW), a workers organization strongest in the first two decades of the twentieth century, with significant numbers in the Western woods.

Albion Ridge is as glorious as any on this spectacular coast—the sea seems as vast and inexhaustible as the forests once must have. Up the coast, Mendocino then housed a small art colony. Fort Bragg, ten miles farther North, a lumber mill town, seemed quite far; it was blue collar, redneck, but in its own way.[9] There had been Finnish collectives in the woods just to the East; there were still communists in the mills. Fort Bragg was another world; nevertheless, it was the only source within reach of all those things that towns can provide.

The late '60s were "gypsy years" in California—kids in cars, hitch-hikers, draft-dodgers, runaways, outlaws, wanderers; the communards and back-to-the-landers sought property. Historians of immigration have revealed the creation of chains of migration—chains composed of humans and their settlements, colonies, and networks. The first to appear are the "pioneers," followed by the "birds of passage," itinerants going back and forth, and then the settlers.[10] This pattern fits Northern California migrants who disregarded boundaries, spatial as well mental and cultural, migrating North, creating an archipelago of communal set-tlements, most of them in the coastal counties North of the Bay Area. Berkeley and San Francisco were both destinations and points of depar-ture, sometimes just stop-over spots. The counterculture traveled north through Marin, then Sonoma, then Mendocino and Humboldt Counties and on to Oregon and back again. Communards found outposts along the way: Morning Star at Occidental and nearby Wheeler's Ranch; Olompali in Sonoma; Rainbow near Philo; Table Mountain, Big Foot on the Noyo; and Black Bear in Humboldt. In these years, the '60s and '70s, Timothy Miller has identified scores of such places, "a wave of new communes...of tsunami proportions."[11] Of the "thousands upon thousands" of new com-munes founded, Miller suggests, "the largest number" were found in the coastal counties North from San Francisco to the Canadian border.[12]

---

9   The term redneck is not intended here as a pejorative, but as an often proudly self-proclaimed term for a rural, white, often socially marginal population when the use of no other term seems adequate. "Local" does not work in its place: there are various "locals." Neither does "loggers," or "ranchers," as not everyone was employed as such.

10 See, for example, Donna R. Gabaccia and Fraser M. Ottanelli, eds., *Italian Workers of the World* (Urbana: University of Illinois Press, 2001).

11 Timothy Miller, "The Sixties-Era Communes," in *Imagine Nation: The American Counterculture of the 1960s & '70s*, eds. Peter Braunstein and Michael Doyle (New York: Routledge, 2002), 334.

12 Timothy Miller, *The 60s Communes: Hippies and Beyond* (Syracuse: Syracuse University Press, 1999), xx, 69.

In contrast to Morning Star, Table Mountain Ranch was remote, seven and a half miles up the ridge on a county road, then a mile of unpaved road. This was easily three or four hours from the Golden Gate Bridge, including two hours on the narrow, winding road from Highway 101 at Cloverdale to the coast. By the end of the first winter, there were perhaps a dozen or so settlers at Table Mountain, including a child. But this figure is misleading. It was clear from the start that the commune was not for everyone; there were people who made it obvious they didn't want to be there. They left, though this seems to have strengthened a core group. More problematically, the visitors were relentless, "in just January 1970 alone, more than a hundred passed through the Ranch." (Bill)

The land at Table Mountain was cut over—it may once have been a dude ranch, or perhaps a hunting lodge. There was a ramshackle ranch house left behind, a "dump" built on stumps with lots of small rooms and a central patio. There were sheep on the grounds, kept by an elderly couple. The first summer, many camped out, some in teepees. Chicken shacks were converted into bedrooms. In 1971, Robert Greenway, a Sonoma State professor and Sally Shook, formerly a suburban Washington, DC, house-wife, and their collective seven children settled at nearby Salmon Creek Farm on Middle Ridge and invited others to join them. Closer to Albion, Carmen Goodyear and her partner Jeannie Tetrault established Thai Farm, a "women's land" and a small collective/commune. Trillium, also a women's commune, was settled just down the road. It was not so inten-tional. "We were just trying to get to more of a country scene. I didn't move up here to be a commune. I didn't move up here because of the women. I just saw the beauty, the Mendocino coast," (Weed). Sabina's Land was on the Navarro Ridge—later it became Lord's Land. Bo's Land was not really a commune; it was closer to "open land," purchased by Bo Romes, a San Francisco artist. "Bo bought twenty acres on Albion ridge... an old house, outbuildings, big plans, little money...people started asking if they could stay the night, then the week, the month, the year...all anar-chists, life in the moment." (Janferie) Bo offered Peter Matlin room and board in exchange for building a sauna. Bo's land is still shared, today called Spring Grove. Azalea Acres hosted fairs. In between, there were rusticators of all sorts, back-to-the-landers as well young people who "just wanted to share some land"—four such simply called their place "The Mune." Big River Ranch was established near Mendocino; just up the coast there was the Compound at Caspar and Big Foot. Visitors camped in Little River Park and Jackson State Forest—to the dismay, of course, of the authorities. One estimate is that by the mid-'70s, the communards/ back-to-the-landers, that is, "'permanent' settlers on Albion Ridge may have numbered 500 or more." (Moonlight)

In its first year, the Ranch was all but overrun: the elementary projects of settling in, physically constructing the commune, establishing an economy, the very basics of survival were all overwhelmed by the scale of visitation. "Things just got out of hand. So many people were coming and going in the spring of 1970 that we had to do something." (Bill) Half the original settlers had left. So Bill, Marshall, and Zo met and essentially closed the gate—"anyone who wasn't here at the last Thanksgiving had to leave." (Bill). This was the end of free land and the beginning of rules— others would follow. At Salmon Creek Farm, later on, a six-week trial period was established for membership.

The house at Table Mountain had to be rebuilt, sleeping quarters constructed—they were scattered around the house in woods connected by paths. Gardens were begun, animals—goats, sheep, geese, a pony, and chickens—gathered and tended in a process that became the norm and was followed at Salmon Creek Farm and at the women's communes down the ridge. The sleeping houses were built sometimes from the rag-tag outbuildings that abounded on such homesteads, sometimes from scratch by hand. The "big" house was communal, with a kitchen and a place for important gatherings; the sleeping houses were more or less private. The communards sought to avoid "the economic system," favoring barter; they helped demolish an abandoned hotel in Fort Bragg in exchange for the scrap. The owner of a Philo mill "paid" for labor with lumber. They sought out salvageable, recyclable, building materials—finding a trove of these in the legendary radical chicken farms of Petaluma.[13] The harvest of gardens was supplemented by traveling as far as to the Central Valley to glean in orchards and fields, then pickle and can.

Conditions on the communes were primitive; they remained so for years. There was no electricity, no phone, no indoor plumbing; the winters were wet, sometimes cold. There was one vehicle at Table Mountain, shared, and, at first, one chainsaw. There was a little store in Albion, the site of the nearest pay phone. There were doctors in Mendocino, but the nearest emergency room was in Fort Bragg. If life was good, it was also

---

13 See Kenneth Kann, *Comrades and Chicken Farmers: The Story of a California Jewish Community* (Ithaca: Cornell University Press, 1993).

difficult; there were obstacles, beginning with staying dry, keeping warm, staying fed. "Everything was pretty loose at first. Everyone had to eat, they needed shelter, and sanitation was a big issue." (Zo) Very few were experienced, let alone skilled in the tasks they set themselves; they were ill prepared for the realities of "living off the land." Soon enough, *Country Women*, the magazine produced by a collective of Albion women, set out to rectify this, at least for women: in each issue, articles on women's liberation were accompanied by practical material—"how-to-do-its" on "country survival skills," carpentry, husbandry, mechanics, gardening, childbirth, child rearing.

From the beginning, there was the problem of "boundaries"—of the world of barriers, rules, and restrictions a whole generation had seemed intent on demolishing. Now there were new questions. How do you stay open hearted and still have boundaries? Rules began to come back, now as new necessities. "We had to make some rules. It wasn't ever clear just who was, and who was not part of the commune. Guests polices were developed. Who can stay and who can't and why?" (Bill) This issue was especially perplexing when it came to lovers, central as this was in the lives of young people seeking sexual freedom, avoiding marriage, and monogamist fidelities. It was well known that the open communes were already failing. The issues of responsibility and trust were made all the more intense by belief in consensus.

"We basically had love affairs, raised food, and raised kids." (Anon.) The Albion communards, so unlike other utopians, past and contemporary, shared no grand vision, no religion, no structures; they were not the followers of a particular leader, there were no gurus. "It's not that we were willfully ignorant; we knew the history of the communal movement. We wanted something different," (Moonlight) "We did not kowtow to /any/ authority...we were non-religious, in terms of formal religion, so there were no religious leaders, and we had to develop these systems as gently as we could, without using the techniques that are usually used— the authority of religion and the authority of politics and the authority of money, the power of money." (Allen)[14] No plans, no high ideals, living one day at a time.

They held, however, some very basic ideas—they wanted to share, to work cooperatively, to live in common, and to raise children in common,

---

14   See Allen Cohen, *'60s Communes Project Interview* (Lawrence, KS: University of Kansas, 1996).

in a community—equally, no laws, no rules, not at first anyway. They believed in experimentation and spontaneity, rejected the idea of limits and sought life without inhibitions. The question was "how far can we go?" and inevitably this involved risks and tensions, but these were turbulent times. They argued that "no one owns the earth"; they were interested in alternative education and philosophies. They became deep environmentalists, quickly turned to organic gardening and made tofu from scratch. At Table Mountain and Trillium, they shared money. Meals were communal in the big house. A day might begin with nursing the baby, going up to big house, building the fire, cooking breakfast, then "who's going to town, who's taking the kids to school?" Work in the garden, get the kids, care for the animals. Cooking and kitchen chores were shared—making granola, baking bread, cooking pots of beans, preparing evening meals. "Walks in the country, lots of visiting, smoking pot, it was totally nice a lot of the time." (Helen)

They spent much time getting and keeping the sleeping houses together. In general, building was utilitarian, do-it-as-you-go work in progress. Dawn "built a small cabin with plans from a U.S. government pamphlet called 'low-cost building.'" There would be few domes on Albion Ridge—instead, the "imperfected pragmatism," as Simon Sadler suggests, of "self-built ex-urban shacks." There were stump houses (dwellings built into the burnt-out hollows of giant redwood stumps, near nature to be sure), fantasy houses, stained glass and flowers, quaint outhouses, compost toilets and pits as well as very crude shelters. At Salmon Creek Farm, communards constructed a sweat lodge.

There were code wars in Mendocino County but nothing as brutish as in Sonoma.[15] In Mendocino County, a disgruntled developer attacked the communes (as well as other sites where there was group living) for violations of the housing codes, a conflict that lasted into the 1980s, when, with new friends on the Board of Supervisors, the authorities allowed for a "clean slate." Various cabins, out buildings and houses were then grandfathered in under "Class K," a relaxed construction standard available for owner-built rural dwellings. In this, the back-to-the-landers were joined by "old-timers" who themselves had built without permits. There seems not to have been, as Felicity Scott argues in the case of Morning Star and Wheeler's Ranch, "symptomatic attempts to loosen the grip of, or even to

---

15   See Felicity Scott and Ramón Sender's accounts in this volume.

sponsor a mass exit from the regulatory and administrative functioning" of the authorities.[16] "Many of us didn't even know such codes existed. We were just living our lives." (Weed) This common cause produced, interestingly, a peculiar convergence, counterculture and rural anarchism, which is still widespread here.

What money the communards had often came from welfare. There was also occasional working for money plus sometimes a gift from home. Some took jobs in town: waitressing, gardening, carpentry, mostly part-time and temporary. There would be one or two trips to Fort Bragg each week to do laundry and similar tasks, but these were shared so that an individual might pass months without being in town in a self-imposed separation from the city. There was a lot of free time, idle time—time valued and seen in sharp contrast to schedule-driven cultural norms.

At the dinner table, all first joined hands and chanted; a hippy religiosity developed, sometimes with "an Indian flavor like using the Indian method of circle readings, one person talking at a time...things we picked up from the American Indian culture." (Allen) There was also spirituality with an Eastern edge and a Jewish tint, but this was never universal nor particularly deep. After dinner, there was hanging out, playing music, smoking dope, drifting in and out. On special occasions, there were drug rituals, sometimes peyote circles. Today, the attraction of hippy spirituality seems elusive; nevertheless, at the time, it was near universally seen then as the "glue" that held these bands together. The "business" of the commune was conducted at Sunday morning circles. All this seemed the antithesis of the celebrated loneliness of rural life; on the contrary, communards remember the intimacy of life on the commune and the power of the group identity.

There were implicit if not intentional social structures in Albion—hence "the Albion Nation." It was an informal structure that tied inhabitants of the Ridge together, with links, tenuous to be sure, to communes and back-to-the-landers as near as Rainbow in Philo and as far as Black Bear in the Trinity Siskiyou's. A Community Center was established in Albion; it hosted events, offered meals, and was a sort of way station. "You could get a good meal for a dollar." (Weed) There was a natural food store, now "Corners of the Mouth" ("a workers'" collective since 1975) in Mendocino; also Down Home Foods and Thanksgiving Coffee in Fort

---

16 See Felicity Scott's essay in this volume.

Bragg. They continue. There was a weaving co-op. There was music; there were routine festivals, including the "Albion People's Fair," though some felt that it "got too big, too many drugs." (Helen) There were craft fairs and outdoor dances on Navarro Ridge. The *Country Women* collective engaged in national/international feminist movements; the magazine was widely read, and its staff participated in national and regional conferences and hosted women's retreats and festivals at the Woodlands, a nearby lodge and campgrounds built in the 1930s by the WPA. Times Change Press at Salmon Creek Farm published accounts of communal life (*January Thaw*), as well as, among other things, Emma Goldman's feminist writings.

In many ways, Albion's crowning achievement was the establishment of the Whale School at Table Mountain in 1971. Created first for the commune's children, it soon opened its doors to other nearby children, becoming an alternative community school up to high school grades. Ultimately as many as fifty children attended, taught usually by four or five full-time teachers and an array of volunteers. Zo Abell managed the Whale School. A sexual division of labor prevailed: men contributed to building the schoolhouse and the bus driver was a man, but most (though not all) teaching was done by women. The Whale School practiced methods of progressive education popular at the time when public education was under fire from the Left, not the Right. "The IRS saw us as a private school, they wanted taxes. I just told them we weren't private, we were just a school. In the end, we affiliated with the Mendocino Unified School District, as a center of 'Independent Study.' In that way we were accredited." (Zo)

There was sex, drugs, and rock and roll. "Yes, it was your mother's worst nightmare." (RW) On one hand, it all seems rather innocent in light of later developments. Partners were often shared. There was promiscuity and experimentation, though more at first than later. There were couples, some longstanding. There were indeed times when the hippies would stream into town and line up at the Clinic in Fort Bragg for penicillin shots. Was there more sex here? Was sex better than elsewhere, on college campuses, during political campaigns, in the collectives, cults and sects, in the suburban bedroom? It was, after all, an era of contradictions, of the sexual revolution, the pill, the porn craze; it was a time before HIV. For better or worse, we live with its results today. Compared to the 1950s, there seem to have been advances, yet there was so much room for improvement. There were frustrations and there were predators, though the latter not always in guru form. There was exploitation, people were taken advantage of; there was one well-known case of pedophilia. There were real dangers—including the perils of country lanes, archetypically in the form of young rednecks in a pick-up. Some deny this: "It was never dangerous—or stressful." (Peter) But others remember "tales of rape, near rape, and then bodies...a girl from Toronto on Big River beach...then there were the Azalea Acres bad boys." (Janferie) These were young locals rumored to be terrorizing hippie newcomers.

Sexual tensions could be pervasive in morning meetings, as could sexual jealousies, leading to excruciating feuding that eroded the collective. The results, then, of sexual experimentation, remain mixed. These will, in the negative, be said to reveal a fixed "human nature" and youthful naiveté, but this seems unlikely to be true. "Conventional wisdom" continues to inform us that male/female conflict—the "battle of the sexes"—is a given. The communards at Albion rejected this; their inability to achieve sexual freedom in any lasting sense speaks as much to the weight of the past, culture and tradition, as it does to their "failures." Moreover, visions of "free love" persist, while acceptable twenty-first-century practices seem to have little positive on offer.

The drugs of choice at Albion appear to have been marijuana above all, followed by hallucinogens including peyote. Interestingly, none of the communes I know turned to the commercial production of marijuana even as so many neighbors, including back-to-the-landers, did, often at great profit. The communes were, after all, anticapitalist; by and large they were nonviolent. Hence, they managed to get by the ultimately destructive developments in the marijuana industry—the industry, involving another curious convergence, the children of both the counterculture and the rednecks that dominates the Mendocino economy to this day. There seem to have been people who smoked too much, but that is not so unusual or remarkable.

In regards to music, the story is much the same: what seemed so radical then and what was shocking to many, is ordinary now; alas, it can all too often be heard riding elevators. There was plenty of music on the communes: there were regular festivals, a tradition that persists though more commercially. Acid rock came and went, but music was and remains a vital part of Mendocino life and culture; importantly, local people compose, play, sing and dance seemingly more than in most places. But tastes now seem rather frozen: white rock persists, though it has lost its edge with the passing years; country music has its limitations, if we want to consider music as liberating. The fare here invariably strikes one as rather tame, all the more so in comparison to the music revolution that was so much a part of the '60s. On radio stations there is nostalgia, but not for the Southern blues, Motown, or rhythm and blues. Hip hop seems to be enjoyed privately, if at all.

How, then, are we to assess this experience and what went wrong? This is often the first question—failure is taken as given. True, these communes did not last forever. Yet, it's not so clear to me that the communes failed, except insofar as they were part of the more general defeat of the '60s movements and the retreat of the remnants. Critical analysis is, of course, essential—this report, after all, is not intended as one more chapter of the "greatest generation." And it is not the end of the story. History proceeds; we can learn from what has passed.

In 1980, the counterrevolution was enthroned and the results of Reagan's election began to weigh heavily upon us, far more than we would have suspected at the time. Beneath this, on the ground level, severe difficulties rose inside the communes themselves. First and foremost, the internal relations were intense and ultimately paradoxical—these were, after all, very small societies. Survival, the tasks of day-to-day life were difficult enough. Whatever structural weaknesses underlay communal existence, interpersonal conflict persisted, thwarting consensus and threatening the entire project. It is indisputable that the '60s "movement" was badly in need of behavioral remediation and attending to the personal, surely in gender relations. But elevating the personal brought its own difficulties; there were limits to individual improvement. The gap between external change and inner spiritual transformation seems never to have been truly bridged.

Sexual issues, jealousies, concerns of exclusion, conflicts over parenting, conflicts concerning whether to have children at all, participation—these never went away. They were not the only sources of tension; for some, the Sunday morning meetings became endless sessions of disputes and conflicts. Over rights and rules—should we hunt deer? No, we can't have guns. And chores, was everyone involved? There seems always to have been those who were not, those who didn't do their share. But it is widely believed that male/female tensions exacerbated conflicts; the question "what's *really* happening here" lurked behind every dispute. This was perhaps inevitable, given the age of the participants. It was a widespread phenomenon throughout the '60s movements. But it may well have been ubiquitous on the communes. It was "as if there were an area where everything was peachy and wonderful and spiritual, getting high, and in tune with nature, and then this other area of whenever crunch came to crunch, there were these tremendous internal turmoils. There was a male-female split, there was an inability for the males to cooperate in the way the females were learning how to do, the women were learning." (Allen) Concurrently, it seems that personal relations were less strained on the women's communes.

This, too, perhaps was/is to be expected. Communal life was overwhelmingly a domestic life. John Gillis, a historian of the family, suggests that women do better in small societies which they enter better equipped to deal with the rhythms, routines, challenges and rewards of the new life and with some training and skills in domesticity, most notably childbearing and raising, and in cooperation.[17] Were these new societies families? It remains unclear. While the stereotypical suburban nuclear family was often rejected, it was not clear what was being put in its place. Was it the "family we never had?" (Weed)

The idea that one could live simply and ecologically itself became troublesome—where was the line between simplicity and poverty? Between necessity and desire? "I didn't come to Mendocino to live in a chicken shack." (Weed) Scarcity, both material and cultural, compromised the communal project. As the years passed, then as children grew, individuals' desires were transformed (though rarely, it should be said, entirely). And, as this happened, the communes, so small to begin with, came to feel increasingly confining and inflexible, restricting rather than facilitating personal growth and development. The communes, in fact, became isolated in a way that had not existed at first, and just at the time when the social terrain was becoming increasingly inhospitable following the decisive political shift against radical activity in the '80s. What had once been seen as a world to win, now seemed more a wilderness into which the flock had been scattered. The communes rather than "the wave of the future" (River) were more likely a haven, toiling in defensive isolation in a hostile world. Survival now demanded rules and fences, all

---

17 John R. Gillis, conversation with author. Gillis is author of *A World of Their Own Making: Myth, Ritual, and the Quest for Family Values* (Cambridge: Harvard University Press, 1996).

self-imposed. And it demanded accommodation. Then, too, sources of new blood disappeared, precipitously in the sudden crash and death of the youth and student rebellion, and there seemed little in place for the next generation. There were other problems, of course, but continuing this laundry list is of limited use, certainly in the face of the Herculean tasks that the communards had set for themselves.

Consensus, as a method, has its limitations, indeed its own tyrannies, all the more so, it seems, when the issues are personal. The personal issues, of course, were often political; this made solutions, however, no less deceptive, no less intractable, and no less problematic as keys to sorting out behaviors and perspectives. Majorities can be oppressive. So can endless debate. There are times when consensus cannot be reached. Talk cannot continue when things need to be done, when structurelessness implies the "the last man standing" rule and is not useful. This seems self-evident. "I just didn't want to sit for four hours every Sunday." (Peter) In the stories of the communes, this sentiment often echoes in every discussion of the experience. "I had this feeling of relief whenever I left for any length of time." (River)

Those who wished to change world had not succeeded, while those who wanted only escape had not been able to do so either. In fact, as years passed, things steadily became rather worse. The communards were not indifferent to all this. Their intention had not been to confront authority, but they did so whenever they were forced to, and fared not so badly as critics might think. The counterculture survives in a variety of forms today; Albion remains a center of feminism and this is all the more impressive in light of the chauvinisms of country culture. There was little support here for war and empire, nor for Reagan's Central American adventures in the 1980s, nor the Bush/Clinton/Bush/Obama crusades in the Middle East.

In terms of issues of race and racism, the legacy of slavery, the despoliation of conquest, the persistence of segregation and race hatred have been undoubtedly simultaneously both an engine of social change in the United States and its greatest stumbling block. The communards did often flee before confronting such issues, or failed to relate to them, or at best felt themselves helpless in face of it all. "The problem of the twentieth century" continues to be the problem of the twenty first, as historian and Pan-Africanist W.E.B. Du Bois stated in *The Souls of Black Folk*. The American "color line" is as complex as ever today and the United States is more segregated than ever. This includes Mendocino County, where, as in the rest of California, two worlds exist: one "white" or Anglo, the other Latino, the latter rapidly outpacing the former. Moreover, the Latino population is young, growing, and energetic but unrepresented in government, in law enforcement, in education, and in the providers of healthcare—this twenty-first-century reincarnation of segregation by definition undermines whatever visions of community have guided coastal inhabitations, including those of the counterculture. This, in turn, is connected to the communards either ignoring or being confounded by both the problem of race and the issues of agency. In this, they were, and are, not alone.

The history of communes thus needs to be seen in the larger context of the generational exhaustion of the social movements and the implosion of the New Left. The demographic sources of these movements were all but the same; indeed some time-lines are virtually identical. It is also striking to me that there seems to be a common trajectory in individual lives as the life patterns of communards fit so easily with those of the entire rebellious generation: the explosion of the movement in 1967 and its collapse; the dispersal into communes, collectives, sects and cults in a diaspora of sorts; "digging in" in the 1970s, industrial colonizing, community organizing, back-to-the-land. Some of these projects evaporated immediately; some lasted just a year or two. But others carried on in cities, in communities, in the country. Salmon Creek Farm lasted ten years, Trillium twelve, Table Mountain nearly twenty, and the latter's land continues to be owned in common.

The 1980s were a fundamentally different time. The world did change, but for the worse. I think the communards, like the counterculture and most of the Left, retreated in the face of this; they had run out of steam, things were just too hard, the rewards were not so great, and so individuals looked for alternatives. They returned to school, took jobs, started families, found new homes, and tended private gardens. "What seemed appropriate at twenty-eight didn't work at forty-five." (Peter) Yet, the radical spirit persists here in Albion, however eccentric: nonconformist, contentious, prone to conspiracy theory and catastrophism, aging, permanently dissatisfied, peaceful, intolerant of rules and regulations. Few say they wouldn't do it all again (mostly).

The most interesting and most revolutionary aspect of this all, it seems to me, was not so much the drugs, the sex and the rock and roll, or any particulars of life on the commune (though all important in their own right), but the whole notion of creating another world—of turning the world upside down, of creating a world outside slavish devotion to the market and the shopping mall, free from economic and culturally imposed patterns of personal oppression and economic exploitation. There are some who will deny this characterization as romantic, an exaggeration; others will contend that it imposes the political on projects that were not intended as such. There is some truth in this, though it is also true that the unconscious precedes the conscious. What stands out to me is how thoroughly these young people—and the much wider movement with which they were associated (like it or not)—rejected bourgeois life in industrial capitalism and attempted to a live a life that was its antithesis. Consciously or not, they rejected the materialism of postwar United States at the height of its prosperity; they rejected its consumerism. They rejected war and refused to fight in Vietnam. They despised the empire; they opposed organized religion. They abandoned the family. "Abolition of the family! Even the most radical flare up at this infamous proposal of the Communists": that's Marx and Engels in 1848.[18] They attempted to do all this through practice: "I left Brown University. I wanted to move beyond the talk of revolution; I wanted to live it." (RW)

Many of us are already familiar with the critique of this project, "the realist" response to the Utopians, particularly severe in the language of Marx and Engels: What about the state? What about the working class? What about power? Still the founders of modern socialism themselves were not without some very kind words for the utopians; after all, they "attack every principle of existing society...they are full of the most valuable materials for the enlightenment of the working class. The practical measures proposed...such as abolition of the distinction between town and country, of the family, of the carrying on of industries for the account of private individuals, and of the wage system, the proclamation of social harmony, the conversion of the functions of the state into a mere superintendence of production." All this was recognized as invaluable by Marx and Engels.[19]

But a critique from the Left persists, characterizing the counterculture as apolitical if not reactionary, and communes as "islands in a sea of capitalism" or worse, "little workshops of capitalism."[20] Certainly some

---

18   Karl Marx and Frederick Engels, *The Communist Manifesto* (London: Verso Books, 1998), 56.
19   Ibid., 74.
20   See Christopher Hill, *The Experience of Defeat: Milton and Some Contemporaries* (New York: Viking, 1984), 290–94.

were all of the above. But compared to what? Albion was never a true utopia. How could it have been? But it was also not so apolitical as might be imagined. They battled with the County in the Code Wards and won. In 1975, there was a campaign against offshore drilling, followed by confrontations with Japanese whalers in 1976. A successful campaign was waged to elect a progressive candidate for County Supervisor to represent the coast. The Abalone Alliance opposed nuclear power. In 2006, Albion residents voted by a margin of four to one in favor of a county resolution, Measure Y, calling for the immediate withdrawal of troops from Iraq. In Bear Gulch, a remote hippie enclave that persists in Northern Mendocino County, the vote was 100 percent against the war. There have been continuous battles with the timber companies in attempts to protect old growth redwoods in Mendocino and Humboldt Counties. Communards anticipated the current environmental crisis as well as positive trends in health and food politics, though they never reached self-sufficiency or food security in the 1970s and '80s.

In conclusion, I would like to follow up on Kate Soper's highly germane contribution to the Socialist Register volume, *Necessary and Unnecessary Utopias* (2000), in which she proposes a "defense of the emancipatory role of utopian visions," the need for "an ongoing and democratic 'conversation' on the quality of the good life," and assurances that life's "pleasures" will not come "only at the cost of human misery and ecological degradation."[21] "Socialists," she writes, "may diverge considerably on the details for what makes for pleasure and right living, but they will agree that all the more subtle, refined and complex pleasures will be grounded in the simpler satisfaction that comes through the elimination of suffering and exploitation."[22] The idea that such thinking is elitist, that it involves imposing our values on the future seems trivial in contrast to the presumptuousness of asking others to follow us "who knows where"?[23] So does the idea that it is unnecessary: "I do not write cookbooks for the kitchens of the future," claimed Marx. In refusing to offer us a vision of

---

21 Kate Soper, "Other Pleasures: The Attractions of Post-Consumerism," in *Necessary and Unnecessary Utopias,* eds. Leo Panitch and Colin Leys (Rendlesham, Near Woodbridge: Merlin Press, 1999), 130.

22 Ibid., 124.

23 I can't help but think of the editorial in the *Seattle Union Record,* announcing the general strike, written February 4, 1919, by Anna Louise Strong, "And that is why we say that we are starting on the road that leads—NO ONE KNOWS WHERE." See Harvey O'Conner, *Revolution in Seattle* (New York: Monthly Review Press, 1964), 133.

the future, Marx and Engels "left open a dangerous vacuum in the theory of communism that in the event came to be filled by a totalitarian form of politics."[24] More, as Iain Boal writes in the prologue to this volume, "In the United States, antiutopianism is linked to fear and contempt of anything that smacks...of communism." We live in turbulent times again. All the more important, then, that conversations within Marxism and anarchism proceed; they are, as Soper suggests, entirely appropriate, even necessary. And such conversations can surely be enriched by recognition of the actual "utopian" experiences of the 1960s and '70s, by the dreams and desires of the communards as well as their illusions. If the past is like a foreign country, the future is unknown territory, a new world. Surely, some speculation, then, is justified; the "what would you put in its place" question still haunts us and we need some answers.

---

24 Soper, "Other Pleasures," 124.

Pathways

Dawn Hofberg—"We 'long-hairs' inhabited a certain patch at lunchtime"

In the 1970s, there was much to reject. The Vietnam War was the wake-up call for understanding U.S. foreign involvement. We identified against the rat race and chose voluntary poverty and land stewardship. We explored the politics and rhetoric of personal change. We thought that by dropping out and raising children in alternative ways we could affect change in the world. Politics was lifestyle, the morals, and not worrying too much about failure. "Being" was itself the point. There was day-to-day sharing of work, music, food, gardening, communal bathing. I learned practical do-it-yourself skills and how to work in a group, creating confidence, and competence in country living.

In Los Angeles in the '60s, my parents had their own modest exploration of the zeitgeist. We attended "cooperative" nursery schools, where we sang folk songs and learned to "hit balls, not people." We attended folk concerts, went to cultural events: Indonesian gamelan concerts and the Teatro Campesino of César Chávez's United Farm Workers. My father, a dentist, and my mom volunteered at the Delano Farm Workers Mobile Dental Clinic. They participated in consciousness-raising groups with Synanon's Chuck Dietrich. My uncle Bill exposed us to the colorful world of gay society and love of the arts.

By high school, I had gravitated toward the outré kids, not the athletic/cheerleader types. We "longhairs" inhabited a certain patch of lawn at lunchtime, eschewed haircuts and polyester, in favor of our own "uniform" ethnic clothing. We listened to Dylan, convinced that "The Times They Are A-Changing."

On one family outing, through the car window, I caught a scene on the steps of the Topanga Canyon Post Office. A young woman with long tresses, in colorful clothing, was sitting on the ground under a tree, openly breastfeeding her baby. In that moment I knew that was something I would do.

I attended UC Berkeley. Sproul Plaza was a forum for political education, for witnessing the abrogation of First Amendment rights by the UC

Regents, Berkeley police, and the National Guard. These events were catalysts to move me away from the city, to pursue my dream of living closer to the earth, to find a more peaceful and simple existence.

While still a student, I bought into a group-owned piece of property in the Anderson Valley, earning land payments by working weekends as a dancer in a bar. My high school sweetheart, Paul Dresher, a musician, and I built a small cabin with plans from a U.S. government pamphlet called "low-cost housing." We spent less than $100.00 on building supplies (tar paper and nails) and scavenged the rest of our lumber and materials from tear-downs around Berkeley. When we separated, I moved to Cotati to get my teaching credential at Sonoma State. I spent time on the land, but the other owners weren't ready to live near Boonville full time, and I hadn't met many locals.

While visiting the coast to buy wool fleece, I met Robert Greenway. He lent his name and teaching credential to the Albion Whale School at Table Mountain. I was looking for a school, and some like-minded people. Robert invited me to visit his commune. He was a professor of psychology at Sonoma State University, divorced, with four children. He partnered with River (Sally Shook) who had three children. Robert purchased land in Albion near the end of Middle Ridge Road and continued to teach at Sonoma State. As he and River traveled, they invited compatible people to share the land, eventually working out a system by which committed individuals could buy into collective ownership and responsibilities for Salmon Creek Farm. I had found my community and land.

Max Efroym (an artist and musician) and I connected at a communal effort taking down an old chicken barn in Petaluma, transporting the wood for the farm's building projects. Max and his partner Leona were breaking up at the time, and I moved in with Max to the cabin that they had built. When I was five months pregnant, we had a wedding celebration in the redwood trees under a silk parachute, complete with a Peace Pipe and prayer circle. My grandmother later referred to this as the "Indian Rain Dance wedding."

We all came to the commune for different reasons and had no stated unifying principles. We did not share a religious belief, follow a guru, and had no enunciated intentions about intimate relationships or "free love." Robert and River were exploring "open relationships," which sounded good, but seemed to be a source of stress for their family. For young parents and teenage children, such facile justifications of desire caused spates of jealousy. The pain was seen as part of the growth process, of breaking away from the proprieties of one's family of origin and other suburban embodiments.

Sexual undercurrents were evident at our meetings, ostensibly for evolving group consciousness and division of labor. In these half-day meetings, we hassled out mundane aspects of communal living as well as those about our philosophy, our shared purpose, our bylaws. We did learn to resolve some conflicts. We explored our rejection of the dominant culture, the ways in which we were its products. We hassled about interpersonal issues, gender politics, and "Who the hell is not doing their chores?"

We discussed how best to use and respect the land and its denizens, thirty-four acres of south-facing second-growth redwood forest, sloping steeply from the top of Middle Ridge to Salmon Creek.

Hours were spent deciding who could become a member of the commune, and then what constituted a crime egregious enough to warrant expulsion. We agreed to make decisions by consensus, giving just one person, adamantly opposed to the group, a loud voice. We eventually conceded not everything could be a consensus decision and anyone who acted in a way that physically hurt someone or threatened harm could be voted out by consensus, save one.

Our weekly meetings borrowed from Robert's Rules, from the holistic and transpersonal psychology movements, and from our knowledge of Native American rituals. We used a power object, a conch shell or a staff, to signify the power to speak and hold the attention of the group. We had a "chief" who directed the agenda and a "vibes-watcher," to observe the mood and emotional tone and to intervene when it was off; a timekeeper monitored how long one person could speak; a scribe took notes. Who knows what happened to all those minutes?

To deepen our personal growth and connections to the land, we held solstice and equinox ceremonies, loosely based on Native American rituals, whose beauty and seriousness moved us. We acknowledged that we changed something sacred to Native Americans into our own version of prayer, song, and catharsis. We used the peyote cactus, which we obtained from Native friends who were willing to trust us to keep it "on the sacred path." They gifted us with a woven blanket, taught us how to properly tie a water drum, build a fire whose morning ashes resemble a bird with outstretched wings, smoke a pipe, and the seriousness of the "peyote way." Sometimes the peyote we used was so old and desiccated we could not be sure that the door that opened was due to its psychotropic properties, or if the force of the ritual itself carried us through the portal. Marijuana was fairly habitual for some on the farm, and there was a visit that I missed from Stanislav Grof, transpersonal psychologist and LSD proponent. Peyote was our main teaching, and I believed (as many do about other "natural" substances) that it was "medicine" as our Native American teachers taught. Ingesting foreign substances to change consciousness was not my primary interest. Growing a completely organic and healthy baby, born at home, was as high a goal as I could imagine.

I gave birth to my first child, Oona, in our cabin with eleven people present. Home-birthing was transformational for my own mother who attended and for others who had been born or given birth under amnesiac hospital conditions. I had turned to the women of Table Mountain commune who had home-birthed children, and to a midwife, Sheila Kearns. My family was the first at the Farm to be, in some sense, a nuclear household; all the others were single parent or blended families.

The Bunk House was our shared kitchen, gathering place, and dining room. Our "openness" to wanderers meant that many mornings I would walk in and cautiously ask a stranger how they had arrived there. The cabins on the land, known by the county building code as "detached bedrooms," were our private spaces, by agreement not to be in sight of one another. Even the teenagers had their own cabins that they built themselves with some adult assistance. Each night, River and Robert's young sons, with "Albion Evereadys" (a candle inside a punctured tin can) in hand, headed off into the forest to their own separate cabins.

I remember my disappointment when my milking partner announced disinterest in the dairy project, leaving me solely responsible for twice a day milking and bottle-feeding all the eleven goats. I remember our half-day long meetings. Endless. And vividly, I remember my two-year-old taking a swig from a clear mason jar left open near a woodstove. It was kerosene.

My family became more separate and "nuclear" after Oona's stomach was pumped. In meetings, others showed little interest in safety and the shared child-raising that I had assumed would exist for my baby. This could endanger her. I brought up issues at meetings such as hanging up the axe, only to find it loose again in the woodpile. There was no commitment to child-raising in common, only a series of loose alliances between children and adults that functioned to provide some care. Maternal instincts aroused, I retreated to my own cabin. My disappointment concerning lack of concern for my child's safety smoldered. Years later, it emerged that the "autonomy" of the older children had come at a grave cost; some had been molested by one adult male who offered them company and shelter.

At its zenith, the commune numbered nineteen members, nine of whom were children. Learning to grow things, to build, to fish, and to hunt, were all deemed as important as formal education. Older children went briefly to school in Caspar, then to Table Mountain's Whale School. Having completed my teacher training and credential, I was thrilled to work at a school where parents, teachers, and students shared a philosophy. In retrospect, I feel the school lacked some academic rigor but imbued a sense of individuality and independence in learning that was often recognized by their teachers in Mendocino High School and then in college.

Having my home at the Farm and my community for support alleviated the sadness of seeing my "nuclear" family fall apart. I moved with Oona into an empty cabin and became a foster parent to Erica P. Martin, a fourteen-year-old girl whose militant-gypsy-lesbian mother would not to live anywhere long enough for her to attend school. I eventually met my life-mate, now my husband, Bob Schlosser. We had our son at Salmon Creek farm, and our daughter in our new home on land next to the commune.

Weed—"We did become a commune, eventually decided to share everything"

I moved up here to Albion from San Diego. I originally grew up in L.A. I went to San Diego State for my undergraduate education. I was there because of the beach and when I was in school it was fine. But I wanted to leave the area.

Once I graduated, I was very clear I was going to move to Northern California. The reason was that in 1969 or 1970, I took a trip around the country with a friend and we ended up camping at Navarro Beach. I said, I have to come back here.

At that time, there was an antiwar demonstration and I met a friend, Bill Seekins, who also wanted to come up here. So we drove up together looking for land together for a group. I think it was because he wanted to move up North himself. It was probably to get out of an urban area and to move up to a rural area.

For me it was trying to get to more of a country scene. It wasn't because I wanted to move up here to be a commune. I didn't move up here to be, you know, because there are women up here. I just saw the beauty, the Mendocino coast. I was a surfer all my life. I saw this coastline and I was tired of urban reality.

At the same time, the SLA, that whole thing was going on. Things were really fractionalizing in the movement. I guess it was when Nixon was in power. I think people were a little disillusioned. The antiwar movement was falling apart. So that's another piece of it.

I moved up here in '71 or '72. I had a friend who was looking for land. I told her where to look. I told her to go along the coast between Navarro and Fort Bragg, there are some nice areas up there. She came up and she bought this land, twenty acres on her first visit. She just saw it in Albion and she said, "Oh, I'd heard there were women up there and I just liked the land and I have some other friends and, you know, maybe we'll all move there." Her parents were deceased and she had an inheritance.

I was a lesbian since I was twenty-one. We did women's studies at San Diego State. I was involved with working and setting up the Women's Studies Programs and I taught labor history. I was a leftist, but not my family. My undergraduate minor was in history and my major was psychology. So we were very much into class analysis.

Julie, who was my girlfriend at the time, was also part of the Women's Studies, and that's how we met, through the Rape Crisis Center starting, the first rape crisis center in San Diego. We moved up here together. Marion had bought the land but didn't move up so I said, "You're not going to move there, how about if I go homestead it?" She said, "Great." So Julie and I moved up here.

We started living here, there were several funky buildings; there was the bunkhouse, a goat shed, and a chicken coop and the barn. No house. It had burned down earlier. I'm sure that this land was all clearcut at some point. This was all probably redwoods here. So it was reasonably inexpensive the land; it cost Marion $39,000 for twenty acres. We thought that was kind of expensive.

I had unemployment because I had been working and was eligible. And I had savings. My friend Bill helped us get our woodstove in and kind of set us up because he was getting himself set up. We had to get our cabin setup so we could winter in it.

There was an old bunkhouse. We cleaned it out, put a door on it, windows and a woodstove. Then Julie and I shared that and then we fixed up a goat shed, put a floor in it, and made that into a cabin, and she moved into that one because in that process, remember free love, it was a wild time. We lived here for about six months before anybody else came up.

Some of our friends or people we met wanted to move up here. And we said, "Sure, we'll just have to fix up one of these out-buildings, right?" It ended up, let's say in like a year and a half, we had four people, four women living on this land and then in another year and a half there might have been six of us living on this land and that's pretty much how it maintained for a number of years.

We weren't a commune, but a group or a collective. In the late '60s and '70s, people were flocking here from urban areas. There were literally thousands. In the summer, sometimes, we would see a carload, a van, a truckload of people coming to live back-to-the-land and they were trying to locate places they could just be. There were these people we'd call the "gypsies," people were really moving around and traveling from place to place and staying on the good graces of whoever the land owners were.

Sometimes we would get a truckload of women and we would send them off to another collective like Thai Farm or if somebody saw men we'd send them up to Table Mountain. That's what was happening. This was a period of probably five years or more. Sometimes people would want to stay, most people were pretty respectful but then there were people who didn't quite get it that it's work, and it was a problem to try and house people and some people were real freeloaders.

Group-living was just several people living on a piece of land without any cohesive bylaws or cohesive understandings, whether they were written or not, right? But then there were people who met every week, say like Table Mountain, who met every Sunday. We met once every couple of weeks as a group. We each had our own cabin. We did become a commune, eventually decided to share everything. We even shared money. The second year we built a main house. That was a lot of fun because a lot of women had never lifted a hammer in their lives. We all built it ourselves.

When I moved here, I went out and bought a bunch of tools, like hand tools, carpentry tools and realized, "Oh, I have to fix up the cabins and stuff" and we just started doing it. I had a couple of books on how to do construction and I would read those.

A couple of us were really athletic. So we were coordinated or comfortable working with tools. When I was a kid, I'd built forts with my brothers. I had that. Some women didn't have that at all and it was a real challenge. It was a period of time that women believed we could do anything so we had to show the guys that we could be mechanics, we could be carpenters, we could be electricians, and we could be plumbers.

So it was really conscious that we, women, in the '70s, that we were taking on the trades and breaking into the trades. It was a real political kind of movement because women were pretty much out of the trades and what we saw was that some of us, being lesbians, saw that it was harder to get into some of the trades if you weren't sleeping with the guys.

My friends who were heterosexual, as women, had an easier time getting on a job or on a crew because they were sleeping with the builder. This month it's the roofer. We'd say, "you're hanging with so and so, ask him if we could use his shop. Doesn't he have a boom? We need a boom over here." The men didn't really quite get it.

I think one of the big problems with communes was how you added new members. Consensus kept it safe for the people you're living with, but to bring new members on, it became very difficult and I think that was problematic over time.

I don't know what the answer would be on that. I'm glad it was consensus and not, like our vote now, the group I still live with. We had other people live on the land but kind of not necessarily to build their own place on the land or whatever. That's kind of a problem. It was a problem across the board even if you weren't sharing money. Salmon Creek had those issues. They had problems of how to expand, how to contract.

I still think the first thing is to be with nature. I liked the beauty in nature and living close to the land. I like that it made people feel safe and friendly so that when you see somebody at the post office there was a friendly exchange. I like the small town community. I grew up in a suburb and knew from a young age I was either going to live in a city or in a something more rural. But I really didn't want to live in an urban area. You have a sense of more control over your life in the country.

It all changed in the '80s, with Reagan and all that. It was a no-brainer for me in the mid-'80s that I'm not going to be a contractor in a male dominated industry; I'm not going to do that. I could, but that's just hardship. I'm going to become the architect so that I can design; it happened that I liked design but that I could have a better reality of pleasure in my work. I went back to school at Berkeley and got my masters in the '80s.

Bill Heil—"Hippies from Alabama headed for the Promised Land"

I was born in 1940 in Elberta, Alabama, a small town in the very deep South on the Gulf Coast near the Florida border. My parents were the children of German immigrants who homesteaded in that part of Alabama as part of a land development scheme, promoted by a Chicago land company in the early twentieth century.

I spent my first twenty-five years on a farm there, living in a nuclear family very isolated from the world. My father raised chickens for eggs. My grandfather was a peddler and he sold the eggs in the nearest cities, sometimes as far away as Pensacola. My father also liked pigs and he raised corn for the pigs and pigs for the market. After World War II, we grew soybeans.

My family was religious, my parents—my mother was the oldest of seventeen children—belonged to a church that believed that Jesus was returning soon and that the job of Christians was to evangelize the world. I grew up thinking I was expected either to be a farmer or perhaps a preacher or, most likely, a missionary.

I worked on the farm until 1962, when I decided that I wanted to go to bible school so I went to the Toccoa Falls College in Georgia. I went there for two years and in the second year I met a teacher who taught theology and anthropology—I guess they thought the missionaries might need this— and I realized how limited my world view really was. He was fired at the end of the year. I realized, thanks to him, that theology as taught there was not going to answer any of the questions that I was dealing with.

So I got out, and then enrolled in Mississippi College, a Southern Baptist liberal arts school in Clinton. It was the oldest college in the state. It was more advanced than Toccoa Falls, but it was still completely segregated in the '60s.

There, I got the chance to go to Europe on a scholarship as an exchange student. I went to the University at Mainz in Germany on the Rhine. I was in Germany for about ten months and this really opened my eyes. I also traveled by motorcycle around Europe before I returned to finish up at Mississippi College.

I can't say I was very aware politically, but I remember once going to East Berlin. And seeing a newspaper with a headline scrolled across the front page—"Civil War in Alabama." That was about Selma, Alabama, and "Bloody Sunday" there in 1965. I realized it was true, there was a civil war there. I thought about getting involved but by the time I got back things were winding down.

The Vietnam War was really heating up then and I realized I would have to stay in school or I would lose my draft deferment, so I decided to go to the University of Alabama at Tuscaloosa as a graduate student in philosophy, though I continued all through these years to work on the farm for money. I spent three semesters there, but my heart wasn't in it. I was part of a small group of students there and we began turning on and thinking about dropping out. And in the Spring of 1967 we went up to New York City and stayed in a commune on the Lower East Side for part of the summer.

When I got home, I met some people who said, "Hey, we're going to caravan to California. Why don't you come along?" And I said, "Yippee!" I joined up with them and in two cars—there were five or six of us and a child—we caravanned to California. Hippies from Alabama going to the promised land!

I had copies of the *Berkeley Barb* and the San Francisco *Oracle* and I realized they were talking about what I wanted to do. We drove day and night to get out there, but when I got to California I ended up in LA not realizing it was different from San Francisco. But I got up to Berkeley—it would have been the late summer of 1967.

I traveled a lot. I spent a couple of months in Humboldt County, way out in the country east of Garberville, but I realized I didn't want to spend a winter there. I went back and forth to Alabama. When I got back to Berkeley the next time, I met a guy I knew from Alabama who had been hanging out in the Haight and he said he knew these people who bought some land up in Mendocino Country and they wanted to do a commune but none of them had any country experience. He thought it would be good if I wanted to go there and it was the kind of thing I'd been wanting to do for a really long time. So I did.

I moved to Albion January 1, 1969. They were already up there, when I arrived, Zo, Duncan and Walter and Allen Cohen, the editor of the *Oracle*. I spent the next almost twenty years at Table Mountain, from 1969 until the late 1980s.

The land at Table Mountain Ranch had been cut over in the '50s so it was growing back, young timber, so it was forested. The house was unique, a great big building built around a central veranda—it must have been built as a guesthouse, I think early on in the 1900s. It was inhabited but structurally unsound. It had stumps for a foundation but the roof was going down in the middle and pushing the sides out.

We weren't kids. I turned thirty in 1970 and several of the others were older than me, though there were some younger people. Still, it took some time to work out what we were going to do. And while we were doing this—in the summer of 1970—there were hundreds of people who came through the ranch. There were twenty or so people who said they lived there but we weren't sure what was going on. We finally called a retreat and got together to figure out what to do.

We had to have something if we were going to live together and we wanted to structure ourselves after the American Indians as best we could, but we didn't quite understand what we were doing. We did some experimenting with drugs, some with LSD, a powerful medicine that was just too strong. We ended up finding peyote and did these rituals for a number of years on the solstice and equinox.

At the same time, we came up with the idea of the Aum Family—we decided we were going to be a family. We named our kids, last name Aum. My son Willow still goes by Willow Aum. Zo's son Ishvi goes by Ishvi Aum.

I think our mission was to be an experiment in group consciousness, that's what we were going to explore. That was our mission and it certainly became the focus for me—what does it mean to be a group and how to function in one but also how to be an individual. We wanted to maintain our individuality; we did not want to lose it. And I don't think any of us did!

What stands out for me, after the first winter, is "By god, we've got to get some housing together!" We didn't want to live all together in the house and we came up with the idea of building some cabins that functioned mainly as bedrooms so we could each have a space.

We had this big house, but most of us wanted private space as well, so we put the cabins in the woods so that the authorities couldn't see them. That was probably a mistake. It would have been better to have all the separate houses quite close by the big house or even a dorm with rooms for younger people, but not have the isolated cabins. It was kind of a romantic idea and was nice in some ways but in the winter time it got to be drag trying to walk home in the rain and mud and finding your house cold and trying to warm it up.

I was always interested in the political scene, but not that much. Especially not early on. It was for me, really, "tune in, turn on and drop out."

On a given day, I would get up get up to the big house start a fire, make coffee, make something for breakfast then go down to my shop and hang out. People would come by. We had a whole schedule. There was at least one day a week when I was expected to be in the house, cooking, cleaning, doing childcare as that came along.

I repaired cars. I had a big junkyard junk ("Chevy Heaven") plus I was teaching at the school. I was the Mechanics teacher. I had a forge and started with six-year-old kids blacksmithing, cutting metal, trying to turn on young people to how the world worked.

Our community focus was the school and most of that was with people coming to us. That's how we really connected with Albion. We went to the city but not often, only occasionally to hang out with people, more often to shop. I never went too much.

I did like going to the Valley. We did that for the first number of years. We got connected through Berkeley with some people in Winters in Yolo County who were very early on organic farmers—this was the '70s. We went over and met them and discovered that lots were left behind after harvesting. There were still the remnants of drying sheds there and we got access to the sheds and we went over and we would pick vast amounts of apricots. We had a big old GM one-ton panel truck. It was great fun, we would camp out and dry apricots for a few days.

There were also abandoned hillside orchards of almonds nearby, but they were still producing almonds and we could go over in the fall and get almonds. We had a flatbed truck, too. There was a farmer in Winters who grew alfalfa and we traded firewood for his alfalfa for our goats. We also discovered that there were fields of Honeydew melons that were growing there and that they would only pick these twice and then turn the sheep on them. But we could go over and get permission to go out and pick Honeydews before they turned out the sheep and we got hundreds of pounds of melons and brought them back and traded them to people in Albion.

My life was pretty much consumed by the Ranch at Table Mountain until it fell apart. I was happy there.

Carmen Goodyear—
"We met in Berkeley...
that heady summer of
love"

Jeanne Tetrault and I were classmates at Vassar in 1963. I have always felt that JFK's assassination early in our freshman year had a profound effect on us. The American Dream was shattered with that event. We both dropped out of school after our sophomore year.

I joined the newly created VISTA program and hoped to help on the Chippewa reservation in Northern Michigan (a disillusioning story). Jeanne went off to live at Millbrook, Timothy Leary's commune.

We met up again in Berkeley and became lovers in that heady Summer of Love, 1967. But once again, we were chased out of the dream by tanks in the streets during the People's Park protests.

I never was much of a gypsy. In the late '60s, Jeanne and I traveled across Canada in our Landrover looking for a farm and an alternative community. Because we were ahead of our time, we were met with suspicion for our tie-dyed clothes and god's-eye decorations. We ended up back in California and soon found what we were looking for in Mendocino County.

We decided we had to get back to the land because the cities were no longer livable. We rented in Philo for a year, acquiring sheep and goats and chickens and some rudimentary knowledge of gardening. It was all new to us, very exciting, but we made a lot of mistakes, too.

Anderson Valley was pretty red-necked in those days and we didn't feel welcome or safe there as two hippie lesbians. The Coast, with its art community, was more inviting. Jeanne had friends there from Millbrook days living at Table Mountain in Albion. I had a small life insurance policy, a tragic payoff after the deaths of both my parents in a car accident (I was twenty at the time). I bought an old homestead in Albion: a two story, redwood farmhouse from 1908, redwood barn, cleared forestland for pastures and gardens. A few years later, the coast was discovered and these kinds of bargains disappeared.

Jeanne and I enthusiastically set out to farm with the help of various Vassar classmates and their male partners. The men were threatened by our power as landowners and it soon became clear that we would need to be women's land only.

Jeanne started a consciousness-raising group (this is around 1971) and more and more "earth mothers," living in the local communes came to attend and share their stories of oppression growing up female in America. And their current oppression as the house slaves of hippie men.

Soon the magazine, *Country Women*, was born. We also started a weaving co-op and an annual festival for women to learn skills and share music at the Woodlands.

The magazine became a national publication with a large subscription base and submissions from all over the country. Half the content was back-to-the-land skills and half was consciousness-raising with themes such as Children, Older Women, Women as Artists, Sexuality, etc.

Country Women magazine was a collective from its inception to the last issue. We had an issue collective composed of women who were interested in each issue's particular subject (children, land, animals, sexuality) and they met weekly to review material and put together the issue. Then there was the editorial collective, a group responsible for the running of the magazine (subscriptions, distribution, printing, etc.). This format worked well for the ten or so years we published.

We had a lot of fun putting the issues together and formed a tight-knit supportive community. We helped each other on our lands with plumbing, livestock, and gardening. Some of the bonds formed are still strong today, forty years later.

More and more women came to the Mendocino coast to see what was going on here and many stayed. There is a large percentage of independent women living here, running their own businesses and tending their lands. The days of "hippie chicks" doing the bidding of their "old men" is long gone.

There is a resurgence of strong young women here whom we have found in researching for our film. Young people have the same feeling that we had—the mainstream culture is doomed and they need to band together and create a viable alternative. I hope they realize how much knowledge we oldsters preserved that was nearly lost after the corporate takeover in the '50s.

I have lived pretty much continuously on this farm all these forty years, because that is what it takes to farm. You must tend the land and animals season after season.

I am amazed now how little I did keep up with larger news. Having grown up abroad, it would seem that I would have followed world events, but there was no source for that. Our public radio station, KZYX, didn't come on air until 1990. We had no television and no daily newspaper. And, of course, no Internet. So life was more land and community based. I have recently turned off my Internet (or at least limited it severely) and find myself living in that same world.

This is a world where I can actually make a difference and one where I am not pushed and pulled by the fears and obsessions of the other seven billion of us.

Our Bodies, Our Communal Selves

Janferie Stone

This is a project of memory. Perhaps all generations have felt that the intense experiences of youth have been drained of importance, that the recital of "the times when" is only the mumbling of veterans. I suspect that for those who once staked a claim in the counterculture, this self-doubt marks the workings of ideology in society at large, subsuming waves of accomplishment, as if they left no tide lines on the beach of history. While self-doubt grows, the world has spiraled back into an eerie and painful déjà vu. Our country is still at war. And if the '60s were the years of the silent spring, now we are in the drought summer, where the toxic chemicals and resource guzzlers of progress manifest in widening oscillations of storm, spill, and fire. At every border, people clad in their "isms" of difference are on the move because there is no choice.

How does understanding the movements of forty years ago affect how we view the world today? Does describing "what was" illuminate other paths in the shadows that darken this century? Narrating the past against social movements whose outlines can now be discerned opens up the space of now to possibility, and to a sense of the self as an actor in changing what shall be. But perhaps we have had this sense before. Then we were young; now surely we are seasoned.

How to convey the momentum, perhaps some of the reasons, for the back-to-the-land movement? Forty years ago, in a utopian pulse that was embodied rather than thought through, some of a generation spun out from urban desk jobs, university cooperatives, and communal houses to the ridgelines and watersheds of a beckoning land. This was land we wished to know more intimately, certainly more slowly, than that seen through the windows of a car on a superhighway that has grown ever wider, engulfing more and more lanes of being.

This movement did not go entirely unchronicled at the time, or since. There were the reporters, the sociologists, the assorted academicians, the historians. Several documenters of the communal movement suggest that the reason many communards gave for having joined a commune, urban or rural, was the idea of a consensual community, a community of and by choice. Having polled my friends, I would suggest additional phases of communal formation that recurred as individuals found common ground with others. The first phase was the impulse to physicality. As one friend put it, "I'm not sure that there was reason or rationale...I was so much into my body and discovering what I could do, how I could manifest in real ways in the physical world, that I was on the move until I found a group of people, until I found a place where I could start to build a house, where I could acquire the skills to take care of myself." Taking care of oneself, the body and the soul, with the mind perhaps reaching for control, but as often as not letting go, to see what would emerge. We moved from one communal situation to the next until the fit between individual and group became proximate and conscious. We learned what was possible through a practice that shifted and flowed, a flight from and a flight toward.

The communal movement must be posed against our sense of the world as a dangerous place. Our dreams were reft by images of nuclear holocaust; some were young enough to be of the generation asked to hide under desks during the Cuban Missile Crisis. We had bomb shelter visions of a world that, if poisoned, might begin anew. Humanity, cleansed by "limited nuclear engagement," tutored by destruction, might make better choices in such a future. With the bodies of young men on line for the morass of the Vietnam War, with American cities setting fire breaks against racial conflagration, we were bodies, almost without volition, moving away from the flames of intensifying societal alienation. Our eyes opened through the mind-bends of drugs (from marijuana to LSD), we saw the world as disintegrating. We thought that in a community of scale, we could pick up the pieces, we could create if not a new society then an *On the Beach* fulfillment of each day that we had yet to live. We could take care of ourselves. We could read how to do it. The books on our shelves as college students including utopian visions, Thoreau, and the wash of eastern spiritualism from Krishnamurti to D.T. Suzuki, inspired the movement to practice, inspired a rejection of man over nature and the embrace of the human within the natural world. Writers such as N. Scott Momaday took up the cause of the buried heart of Native American cultures, the land itself. The way to knowing seemed to be rooted in the spaces we crossed into, as we left the asphalt jungles, sliding along the happenstance road of the thumb, catching glimpses of places we might "be in" from the rear seats of VW buses.

My memories of urban communes are fragmented and sketchy at best. Once I had left the tree-lined suburbs where I was raised and turned from the communal kitchens of urban student housing as being too tame, I pursued roads where the line runs out, the dotted line of the highway stuttering down to the ruts of old logging roads and the barely compressed trails left by deer in forests that leaned and talked.

It is not that I did not pass through cities on my journeys, but that when I did, I scraped by uneasy patches of peoples' parks, the hardscrabble areas around downtown bus zones. I encountered young black entrepreneurs of sex and revolution, heard them shouting after me, "You... You're all the same..." as I exited halls of blighted concrete. Always I was moving out, one of the gantlet of sign holders along Berkeley's University Avenue, or Van Ness in San Francisco, as we thumbed rides across the bridges, through the tunnels into the flood widened valleys and upthrusts of Northern California.

The majority of those who moved to rural communes came from middle-class backgrounds, the mom-dad-and-siblings nuclear family. While one might posit that communards came from loving family environments that gave them the ability to trust and develop in novel solutions, a "not quite!" would be in order here. While some came from working-class, socially conscious families, others came from the unit where Dad sold his soul each day in the greysuit world, where Mom coffee-clatched the hours away and perhaps they met for the cocktail hour; we certainly dreamt of any other way of doing intimacy. Perhaps we had read Margaret Mead, perhaps we heard that other societies had different approaches to sexuality, to love, and we could too, these were our bodies. If we did not hear it, then we felt it as we moved in a heady mix of drugs and rock 'n' roll. Woodstock, New York artists' lofts, desert dwellings in Santa Fe, Summer of Love, San Francisco. Drugs initiated a discontinuity from the strictures of straight American culture. We curved. A period of experimentations was on and one did not go it alone. As for young women? We had the Pill; we had time. While some women would take the freedom of being able to plan for reproduction to begin the ascent of corporate, professional, and academic ladders, others took the opportunity to grasp simpler tools and know their bodies in different ways. Life had to go back, it had to unwind the double helix of industrialization and capitalism; it had to be simple and on the land. We were North Americans out to retrace our history, ironically replicating all the impulses and misperceptions of European ancestors when they came to this land. Like them, we thought that the lands we came to homestead were "empty." Finding that place was the next phase of communal formation.

Back-to-the-landers moved into spaces vacated by family-farms made obsolete by industrial agriculture, to properties with one canted house, the whistling barns that had housed one horse, some cows, the lean-tos for meat cattle, the folds for sheep and the rickety sheds of chicken enterprises. Acres planted to Christmas trees, choked on lost harvest opportunities. This was land farmed while men earned as they could: logging, fishing, or at the mill. Old-timers were ready to let the acres slip, tired of living upon land underfinanced both in money and in nutrients after the ravages of industrial logging. For a few years, back-to-the-landers would be able to make a living by cleaning up logged-over land, or running a fishing boat along the rivers to the open seas. But soon, salmon bearing rivers silted up as the land washed to the sea with the second, third, fourth cuts of forested slopes.

We could not entirely submerge ourselves in the practices of the earth. There were the tenuous ties. We thought of the cities as the counterpoint to our daily reality. Many of us had been in the Bay Area as students. Some had confronted riot police in Oakland, or the turtled-Roman squads on Sproul Plaza, or had skirted clouds of tear gas at San Francisco State. Some were refugees from the law after such actions, in hiding from draft boards, or even AWOL from deployment in 'Nam. Some carried the broken bodies of return from that war, the lesions on soul and body. Everything neared the edge. Free speech, free love, spiritual streams from afar, drugs that broke the conditioning of the labor-all-the-day world, and then because we could, because we had not known want, we followed into a dream of country where our bodies worked.

As I moved from commune to commune on the coast, those who surrounded me mirrored back pale skin, darkening in sun and dirt. We were sliding into voluntary poverty, paring down need until it could be filled by direct application of our hands. We spoke in the words of a finished or abandoned university rhetoric, expressing desires to do, to build, to experience in the sinews of arms and the cracks of skins, enter the elements, water and fire, feel wood and dirt. Our hands thickened as we laid down pens and took up hammers and hoes. Yet this impulse to work the body did not answer the question, "Why a (hippy) commune?" asked by many of our parents (the hippy adjective gulped upon or omitted). The impulse to physical experience was the first phase; working out the project and where, was the second stage, although often simultaneous, perhaps preceded by the phase "with whom"?

Perhaps like-minded individuals formed a commune for an expressed purpose, whether spiritual or ideological or economic. Some communes formed around a charismatic individual. The Farm in Tennessee met these standards of a conscious decision, arrived at through Stephen Gaskin's Monday Night Class at San Francisco State. We who were less organized in thought and deed read their narratives with a little envy and yes, a little suspicion too of the rhetoric and the "guru." Reasons to join a commune could be framed as ideological reactions against mainstream corporate America, or within relational spheres, seeking answers to social challenges, or for personal reasons such as love of a partner or family, or sometimes simply for convenience. A place to rest one's head on rainy nights could be economically decisive. At first, happenstance figured large in the restless movements that eddied and coalesced at any moment in any place, the crashpad culture. The more serious attempts at radical reformation of ownership and social roles arose in response to such drop-in situations and subsequent attempts to organize joint labor on a piece of land.

The discontinuity experience of drugs opened a way into communities in Northern California where the "high" experience was shared among the grouped individuals. Jentri Anders, writing of the Mateel region, calls this a feedback loop in which "the changes in worldview deepened and broadened and were reinforced by the experience of living in [isolated communities] and interacting principally with others undergoing similar changes."[1] Anders locates a crucial element of the shift in worldview within the relationship of self to nonself, the placement of human within nature rather than in domination of it. The steep forested

1   Jentri Anders, *Beyond Counterculture: The Community of Mateel* (Pullman, WA: Washington State University Press, 1990), 71.

lands of Northern California taught the body simply by scale that human tool making was not always enough to control fire and flood. Another aspect of the self and nonself entailed relations with other creatures: the cow swinging her head through the corn patch, deer in the peas, the bear in the compost pile, the mountain lion on the riding trail, the raven gurgling derision from the high tree. But relations with other humans were what took the time. Communes formed as works in progress, applying tension to the strands of personal autonomy and social order, designs of the family and re/production.

The notion of "family" had to expand in range, beyond the knotted units from whence we came, to include arrangements such as singlehood, coupled (legally sanctioned or not), gay or bisexual, single parenting, parenting by couples (straight or gay), serial monogamy, and multi-adult households. In processes of self-discovery, no individual position was fixed. In a culture that encouraged the movement toward desire, working through the emotion and pain inherent in shifting relationships came to be seen as positive for growth. "Family" was to be consciously chosen as a qualitative relationship rather than mere biology or replication of dysfunctional kin networks. This family was a sense of the word to be sought for. Examining family was part of the third phase of communal involvement.

The impulse for many groups that either bought or moved onto a piece of land was to set up childrearing situations where children had access to more than the two adult roles (as in a nuclear family template). Many of the communal cohort sought to untangle their emotional formations around alienation experienced in their childhood; this impulse toward personal growth expanded into a consideration of family structures and the work ethos, taking on the age old issues of reproduction and production. The fourth phase of communal life. An old fashioned sense of economics. Householding, within the circle.

Many communes recognized that enterprises requiring hours spent working off the land base were counterproductive to cohesion within the community. This was especially true in rural areas where most jobs were traditionally filled by males: bucking hay for the old-timer neighbors, logging, undertaking large scale building projects. Such working "out" replicated gender roles absorbed in nuclear-family childhoods about the female domestic vs. the male public labor division. Women who chose not to postpone childbearing (after all it was the ultimate in-body experience) found themselves caught between progress on equality in labor roles and the seductions of childbearing.

Not least of the labors we undertook as women was that of conscious pregnancy, childbirth, and mothering, assisted by partners who wished more connections with their children than they had known with their fathers. Home-birthing was not incidental to the richness of community formation. Presence in the first moments of a child's life could act as a bonding mechanism. How many times did a woman say that "anyone" could be at the birth, until the day when hormonal and emotional tides dictated otherwise? One's fellow communards were only theoretically equal for a mother in the reality of such deeply felt birth energy. And childbearing itself, the dedication to home-birth, to unmedicated experience, was a practice played out against a technological model of birth in which the mother was alienated from her own body and her child. Several women, labeled "unwed mothers," had experienced the humiliation of going into labor in the common wards of large city hospitals. After hours stretching into nights and days of pain-filled endurance, doctors administered drugs to numb and alienate mothers psychically from their bodies in the final hours of bearing their child. Our response was that birth should never be that way again. Women and their partners widened their reading to La Maze, Frederic Le Boyer, and the how-to manuals of Ella Mae Gaskin. They prepared for, wrote, and photographed the raw birth experience. They worked the supposed pain, past fear, to sublime experience. Moving to the country did not solve the problems of getting help with childbirth, but it did pose the problem at a smaller scale, more amenable to individual and group campaigns for change. This was one way the communal circle moved experiential learning out into the wider local community, the fifth phase of the communal enterprise. Such movement hoped to fulfill the needs of the inner communal group but also to change the local mindset.

Women had to mobilize as consumers within a "birth" market to create birth centers within hospitals or to recruit trained midwives to the area, lest they take on the risks of homebirth and the possible injury or death of a child. One of the first exploratory birth centers was at the Mendocino Coast Hospital. Until such support systems were in place, a few communal groups experienced first hand the pain of child-loss at birth or soon after. Advice from elders was a rarity, for neighboring women had experienced pregnancy as pathology, an experience they had endured and forgotten as soon as possible. Attuned to our bodies, from a generation with little experience with death, we had few emotional defenses. Healing from child-loss was slow, a process grounded in physical labor and group support. And if we supported each other as best we could in loss, it was more joyful to cohere around ideas of nurture and life.

We had to contend with the labor dichotomies that arose in childrearing. Experiencing the body meant a dedication to nursing the baby and, moreover, continuing to nurse children for (years) longer than met approval in society at large. Women could and did care for and nurse other women's children. But it was impossible for males to attend to infants for long until mothers were freed from direct nursing by the widespread importation (from Europe) of simple suction breast pumps. But this was not until the late '70s. These pumps met the demand of women who desired both more autonomy and the best nurture (that is, breast milk) for their child. Until that time, breastfeeding often meant that mothers were more routinely tied to the domestic spheres, for we soon discovered that the childcare of young infants or adventurous toddlers did not always mesh safely with building or mechanical projects. Women could and did try to learn these traditionally male domains, but the demands of childcare curtailed the length of their work shifts.

Disciplining children was always a make or break issue in the lived reality of the Big House or Land. In my experience, while discipline was often a subject at the weekly meetings, it remained one of the thorniest issues, provoking high emotions and firing deeply implanted circuits from past family lives. Children had a spectacular ability to project the unresolved issues (emotional and social) of their parents. Moreover, within their own cohorts, they participated in games of hierarchy and dominance that always challenged the apparently orderly surface of adult interactions. A searing kind of jealousy and resentment could rear its head. Such issues required research in child rearing literature and consultation within and outside the community. But raising children was ultimately about raising oneself. The best model that many of us could tap was an imagined one—we were attempting to reestablish the extended family kin networks of an agrarian past. Where the industrial revolution posed the nuclear family as the mobile labor unit, we looked for our children to become cousin-brothers and sisters, and we worked to bind those relationships with land and place. As the children grew, such issues of group formation and discipline evolved into discussions of education and toward the formation of schools, either within the land base (as with the Whale School at Table Mountain) or in nearby communities. Parental groups recruited Montessori or Waldorf teachers to the area in an active engagement of modes of teaching and evolving curricula to integrate all the senses in the education of children.

Many secular communes were set up on quasi-economic bases to devote individual selves to communal living for its own sake as a way of institutionalizing within and around a chosen domestic place. Secular communes, with a cohesive, narrated group identity, emerged and existed for certain amounts of time. They expected to work as house-holding, landholding families, and that these holdings could function as the world in which the majority of their social interactions took place. How long such a group could last hinged on land base, scale, and loca-tion. The reality of the external economy meant that ultimately small communities could not function autonomously. The degree of auton-omy they could maintain was directly related to the distance from urban centers, their isolation from neighbors, and the viability of the agricul-tural or economic enterprise. In Northern California, these same factors, in conjunction with personal predilection, influenced the choice to grow cannabis, which theoretically would allow the communal situation to be released from daily economic interaction with mainstream society. Ironically, illegal cultivation entailed inherent drives to secrecy and indi-vidual endeavor, even paranoia, which divided rather than promoted the coherence of the communal enterprise. At least three communes on the Mendocino coast ruled against any large-scale cultivation for these reasons.

I elide many issues that were crucial in the evolution or devolution of other communes. Economic issues, "who puts what and how much into the pot?" created resentment in the long term. While I have cited anger on the interface of child-adult relations, I have not discussed the more volatile emotions of jealousy and anger in adult relations. Jealousy could spread within a community, linked to the pasts of individuals and their unmet emotional needs, on soap-operatic scales that consumed them and splintered groups. The most common reasons for individuals to leave communes were sexual involvements and relationship fallouts that could not be resolved. While we might try for a greater openness and honesty in relationship, there were many times when it seemed we could do no more than replicate what we most abhorred in the previous generation. Our own mode of partner swapping could drain the sex and family of loving intention. Falling in love could be addictive. Moreover, women within the open sex equation found their bodies carrying the load of STDs, with long-term consequences for health and fertility. There was no such thing as free love; women paid for it. Our bodies were the petri dishes that fed a new medical understanding of the number and reach of sexual disease cultures. Women became herbalists and healers of necessity and in rueful acknowledgment of the warnings of their foremothers. The deepest scars came as the first wave of AIDS in the '80s carried off children, first an androgynous teenager, then a daughter, and then women with grown children and grandchildren, who (unknowing) had chosen bisexual lovers.

This overview has touched on issues of communal formation, the lived bodies moving beyond the discontinuity break of consciousness initiated by drugs, the desire for artisanal competence, family formation on chosen land, the role of birth and breastfeeding in gender roles and work, and the difficult/joyful process of raising children in a group; it has barely touched on the mechanisms of conflict resolution, group work parties, and interaction with the neighbors. I have suggested a series of phases: first, the individual impulse to physical experience; second, the formation of the land project; third, with whom and in what family formation; fourth, economics and labor (developing competence in both physical and social interactions); fifth, expansion to the outer community to provide for group needs and effect change in a wider arena. The next (but one on-going from the first) phase might be labeled therapy: how to resolve ongoing tensions, amassed over years, between individual and group desires or investments. Group meetings addressed these, yet concessions and buried resentments piled up incrementally, until the impulse to do something, rather than talk it out one more time, moved individuals to say to themselves "Leave Now." In leaving, the next phase of communal interaction comes into being: assessment. What did, does, it all mean?

How is the success of a commune to be measured...by its longevity or by the quality of interactions described by participants? While some communes formed with a specific purpose, a particular utopian narrative, the back-to-the-land movement might be better characterized as one of "developmental communalism." At the second and third phases, did the community have goals that were set out in some kind of charter, verbal or written? What were the original and long-range goals? Did the community fulfill its goals or does success sometimes lie in unintended qualities arising from the relationships, especially among the children? How have people inside and outside the community benefited? Tracing the long-term societal results of even short time commitments to communal living is to feel one's way along a web of interconnections. While rural communes did sometimes structure themselves for accepting new members from the networks of travelers, they were not always concerned with boundary maintenance (other than keeping good fences and the animals in) for they found themselves relying on the knowledge of older neighbors who had been working the land over a lifetime or even generations. Moreover, with backgrounds in social activism and a growing commitment to resource conservation (forests and ocean harvest) and concern with providing a range of options for natural food, health care, and schools, communal offshoots often formed the core of organizing groups in the wider communities. They wrote and published small newsletters and magazines to communicate with like-minded groups, to influence the wider world. They came to initiate networks for organic food cultivation and distribution within health food collectives. They participated in action circles for causes as diverse as local elections, community health and dental clinics, alternative healing and massage centers, elder care, and community-based schools from the preschool to high school levels, in models ultimately taken up by the charter school movement. The work on schools was instrumental in expanding the fictive kin networks and social cohesion for the children. The connection with the land base meant that the work moved into forestry activism and land acquisition campaigns for watersheds. Over life courses, the original drop-out impulse, tutored by the land and communal interactions, expanded into networks between small-scale communities and dynamic ventures in a society construed as open to change.

People moved onto land forming groups, and off the land as individuals or in nuclear families. Commune experiences gave them a hard won knowledge of the embodied enculturation that they had brought to the spaces and a respect for processes of negotiation that had allowed them to change within them. As they navigated educational and professional paths, these modes of relating influenced the structural organization of a growing technology revolution and of contrary politics in arenas as local as county government and as international as support networks for beleaguered peoples in Central and South America. If we had to some extent dropped out, our government had never ceased being at war. From Guatemala to Rwanda, conflicts and fallouts of military/industrial strategies grew to genocidal proportions, By the '90s, the U.S. government moved toward the free trade agreements that advanced corporate expansion, masked covert wars with an apparent peace, and belied continued environmental degradation in every part of a globalizing economy.

On the North Coast, land once managed by the Pomo speakers, then communities of Italian, Portuguese and Finnish immigrants, and then the '60s counterculture generation, now experienced waves of migration from Mexico and Central America. Given historical interactions, how could one untangle the twined strands of politics and economics in the creation of refugees and their legal or illegal status? Any sensations of having once created a counter to the dominant culture, islands within the global stream, were counterevidenced by changing faces on the streets and in our own schools, churches, and businesses.

The challenges of the widening circles of interaction may nevertheless be addressed by the very processes learned within such active communal experiments, now examined against the background of decades of war and peace. Communities of scale, neighborhoods, aware of their land and resources, may be able to address step-by-step seemingly endless waves of crisis. The impulse to action is now seasoned. On what issues? For which place? With whom? Now there are more generations to engage, but the words and dialogue must be linked to daily practices of conscious change.

Acknowledgments

In writing about the communes of the Mendocino coast, I acknowledge all the former communards who attended conferences, gave interviews and long hours of thought and writing that are only reflected in these pages. I especially mention Andrea Luna for all her work, which shall bear fruit elsewhere. I thank Bruce and Rosalind Moore and others from The Farm; my family from the Caspar Compound: Andrea, Annie, D.J., Carl, Joel, Davis...and my family from Bigfoot: Mac, Loyes, Sylvia, Dick, Margie, Jeff, Sheridan, Walter, Sara, Terry, and all the now grown children who have their own relationships and thoughts about what it all means.

Part IV. Legacies

"This cautionary observation seems to give priority to the rural moment of the city/country dialectic as somehow more 'basic,' but it contained a truth that the rusticating back-to-the-landers grasped, however naively at times. The cities of the future will have to minimize their parasitism on the hinterland. Experiments in cooperative living and urban farming that burgeoned in the '60s are beginning to flourish once again, prefiguring a very different social and ecological order... West of Eden."

Green Gold and the American Way[1]

Ray Raphael

The back-to-the-land movement of the late 1960s and early '70s was the creation of a rebellious subculture, a reaction against the materialistic excesses and the spiritual complacency of mainstream America. Consciously and purposely, the new pioneers wanted to recreate a new society on the outer edges of the old.

It was no mere accident that such a vision found its fullest expression here in the backcountry of California, at the very edge of the North American continent. The original pioneers had always headed west, and now the new pioneers hoped to find their own new beginnings and the farthest reaches of our country's westward leanings.

It was an outcast community that settled in these hills, even if the exile had been voluntary. And then the outcasts discovered an outcast industry: the production of marijuana. As their economy became ever more deeply rooted in illegality, one might have expected the outcasts to be driven even farther away from mainstream society. In some respects, this happened. The marijuana industry served to highlight and accentuate the cultural differences that already existed. And yet, strangely, it has also had the reverse effect of bringing out some of the shared values of apparently disparate cultures. Ironically, this illegal industry has been a catalyst for the inadvertent movement of the radical new pioneers back toward mainstream America. Marijuana has brought the back-to-the-landers out of seclusion and onto the front pages of the newspapers and magazines; it has also brought them closer to the traditional American mores they once seemed to reject.

---

1   This essay is drawn from the author's *Cash Crop: An American Dream* (Mendocino: Ridge Times Press, 1985).

The increasing Americanization of the back-to-the-land subculture takes many forms. Most obviously, there has been more of an acceptance of standard American materialism. Conspicuous poverty, in the early days of the back-to-the-land movement, was something of a status symbol. Money was seen as directly related to the spiritual bankruptcy of Mammon; money in any significant quantities was therefore morally suspect. This, no doubt, was a reaction against the conspicuous consumption of mainstream America in the postwar, post-Depression era. The rampant materialism of the 1950s and '60s was one of the motivation forces that drove the young idealists out of the American Metropolis and into the woods.

At first, the production of marijuana fit well into this ascetic mystique. Marijuana was a small cottage industry, providing just enough extra money to insure the survival of the homesteads. Yet since the money form marijuana was necessarily secret, the public aura of poverty could still be maintained. During a brief period of transition in the mid-'70s, the new pioneers were able to play both sides of the money game with apparent equanimity; money was flowing in, the lean years were over, yet the money remained well concealed and the ascetic stance was untainted. Before long, however, the public posture of poverty became untenable. The cat was out of the bag; too many homesteaders had too much money and everyone began to suspect where it came from. The transformation from apparent poverty to obvious prosperity necessitated at least a partial revision of the ascetic mystique. Affluence could no longer in good conscience be regarded as a sin.

Today, popular folklore has substituted the image of the affluent dope grower for that of the impoverished hippie. The growers are now supposedly blessed with solar-powered hot tubs, new trucks, electronic gadgets—all the things that were beyond their purchasing power in the old days. When compared with the old lifestyle—cars that would rarely work, cold-water showers (or no running water), no TV or telephone or electricity—the new lifestyle appears as the height of decadence. And yet, in truth, the alleged decadence of marijuana growers is nothing more than a sharing of normal American materialism. The luxuries now enjoyed by the folks off in the hills are luxuries which most mainstream Americans have long since taken for granted. Marijuana has provided the means for the former hirsute to reenter the consumer society.

As a rags-to-riches story, the marijuana boom goes straight to the heart of American mythology. There is nothing that titillates our fancy more than a get-rich-quick scheme with its promise of instant fortune for anyone who is willing to take a little risk. Of course, this particular rags-to-riches story is told with a different slant, for the riches were not being actively sought by the people in rags. The riches arrived almost inadvertently, and yet, once there, they were certainly hard to refuse.

The acceptance of money provides the most obvious example of how marijuana has brought the rebels back toward the mainstream. But there are many other ways in which this illegal industry has accentuated traditional American values and steered the outlaws closer to the heart of what this country is all about.

A heightened sense of individualism—that definitive ideal of Americanism, the theoretical hub of our social philosophy—is central to the ideology of marijuana growers. The flamboyant and free-spirited "do you own thing" of the original back-to-the-land movement has evolved quite effortlessly into more traditional manifestations of American individualism: an obsession with private property and a conservative reaction against governmental intrusions into private affairs. Many marijuana growers who once extended their energies outward toward social reform now secure themselves behind their gates—just as the local rednecks have been doing all along. Hippies and rednecks alike, a staunch conservatism based on the conception of privacy pervades the local philosophy: "Ain't no gov'ment can tell me what to do and what not to do on the privacy of my own property—or to the privacy of my own body." The spirit of frontier America is alive and well here in the marijuana hinterlands, where smoking weed or chewing tobacco are seen as basic rights of the individual, inalienable personal liberties that form the cornerstone of a free and democratic society.

A crucial element of rural conservatism, a corollary to the basic belief in property rights and personal freedoms, is the willingness to use force, if necessary, to protect those rights and freedoms. A Humboldt grower proclaims he is willing to best into the home of the government inspector and have it out with him "on a one-to-one basis." Uncle Sam proudly boasts that he's "gonna be the first one to fire at some son of a bitch that's spraying Paraquat over my property." Both the grower and Uncle Sam believe it is the right, and even the responsibility, of the individual to protect himself physically against the tyranny of abusive governmental intrusions into private affairs. That's what the Second Amendment to the Constitution was all about: the right of the people to bear arms for self-defense. The Second Amendment figures prominently in rural ideology, perhaps even more prominently than the First Amendment. Humboldt County recently voted three-to-one against a gun-control initiative that appeared on a statewide ballot; the margin of defeat in the outlying districts of the county was of course even higher. Signs displayed by local landowners to keep people off their property reveal a strong belief in the right of the individual to protect himself with force; "No Trespassing. Survivors Will Be Prosecuted"; "This land insured by Smith & Wesson." Once upon a time, such humor might have offended the peace-loving, nonviolent, back-to-the-land idealists. Now, with many of the homes of marijuana growers protected by guns, the redneck propensity for a public display of weaponry doesn't always appear to be quite so outlandish.

The presence of guns as tools for self-defense is meaningless unless accompanied by a willingness to use the guns when necessary. The introduction of firearms into the homes of many new homesteaders therefore implies that some form of latent (and, in some cases, actual) violence has entered their lives. This, too, marks a return to more traditional American values. Their original nonviolence was a sign of deviance from the mainstream culture; now the violence on TV or on the streets of the cities seems closer to their own reality.

Of course, the extent of the local violence has been greatly exaggerated: the lesson to be learned is not that we have more violence than normal here in the backcountry, but only that violence does exist—just as it exists in the rest of the United States. A nonviolent utopia has not been fully realized.

Violence is hardly new to this area. From 1860 to 1865, the Indians were systematically and ruthlessly massacred. The white folks moved in, but because the homesteaders were so far from any center of civil authority, most disputes among them were settled quickly, physically, and right on the spot. Frontier justice remained the law of the land for the better part of a century. Curing the logging boom of the 1940s and '50s, lumberjacks lubricated with alcohol were prone to getting into fights almost as a matter of sport. Old-time residents, veterans of the logging era and even before, still talk with ill-concealed pride about the fights of yesteryear. And when the urban émigrés first moved here in the late '60s and early '70s, it was common sport of the good old boys to ride into the night, shooting up the water tanks of the newcomers. In sum, the marijuana-related violence seems to fit right in with the local ethic, and the overall American ethic, of violence.

Vigilantes form an integral part of frontier violence, both past and present. There are some circumstances in which good, decent citizens seem to have no choice but to take the law into their own hands. In the old days, the settlers were simply too isolated to rely exclusively on official law enforcement, so they felt compelled to administer justice themselves. Today, communities which are based on marijuana farming, likewise find themselves unable to rely on the official administration of justice. When a rip-off comes, will the grower call the sheriff? Unlikely—unless he wants to get himself arrested. Instead, the grower is more likely to get together with his neighbors in an attempt to protect the life and property of the community. From the standpoint of the growers, community vigilante groups might be the only means of preserving the peace and administering justice; from and official point of view, they represent mob action and cannot be condoned. The rip-offs, on this particular issue, tend to side with the official power of the state: what right do the growers have to protect their illegal crop? And so it is that some robbers, having been shot and injured by growers, are now suing the growers for personal damages. The administration of true justice under conditions such as these takes on the air of black humor. Frontier bandits, vigilantes, and now lawsuits—it might seem brash, uncouth, and selfish, but it is also very American.

Frontier violence has been revitalized by the marijuana industry, but so have more positive aspects of the American frontier. The Jeffersonian ideal of small, independent farmers is alive and well here in the heart of marijuana country. Marijuana has provided the first truly populist form of agriculture since homesteading the original frontier. If forty acres and a mule were all you needed to survive in the old days, twenty acres and a patch are all you need today. And anyone can do it; all you need is a small grubstake for a down payment on some land, a willingness to take a risk, and some raw guts. Isn't this what the frontier spirit was all about?

Indeed, marijuana farming is the perfect embodiment of a people's capitalism. With little capital investment required, it offers an ease of entry to entrepreneurship—a rarity in our modern world. In many respects, it's a conservative's delight: no permits required, no zoning regulations, no environmental impact statements to endure. It's free enterprise all the way, with the promise of prosperity for anyone who's willing to work for it. And, of course, there are no taxes. One grower tells the story of taking his father, a respectable business executive, on a tour of his patch. The father stood there for several minutes, gazing in utter astonishment at the thirty mature plants ready for harvest. He was speechless. Finally, he burst out in uncontrolled excitement: "All this, and no taxes!" It's an American dream come true.

From a democratic point of view, perhaps the biggest failure of the traditional capitalist system is its tendency for consolidation. Small businesses continually go under, either driven out or swallowed up by their larger competitors. Even in agriculture, the family farm is no longer a viable unit; high-tech agribusiness drives prices down to where small, labor-intensive farmers can no longer compete. Apparently, consolidation is an inevitable feature of capitalism—except in the case of marijuana farming. In the marijuana industry, there are structural forces that counteract the natural tendency toward centralization. The combination of illegality and geographic isolation provide built-in guarantees against consolidation. The larger the operation, the higher the risk—so there's a strong incentive to stay small and decentralized. As the government eradicates the larger, more visible plantations, the less visible and safer enterprises might enjoy a greater share of the market. Governmental eradication of marijuana agribusiness therefore can serve as a sort of protective subsidy for small, independent growers, doing as much for the cause of democratic capitalism as the Small Business Administration could ever hope to do.

And so, unexpectedly an illegal industry becomes one of the last bastions of Jeffersonian agriculture and independent, entrepreneurial capitalism. Perhaps the patriotism of the growers is inadvertent, but it is worth noting nonetheless. And the unsuspecting patriotism continues: the domestic production of marijuana is one of our biggest allies in trying to offset the nation's balance of payment deficits. Many billions of American dollars (no one can say exactly how much, but everyone knows it's a lot) are sent abroad each year to support the collective drug habits of American citizens; the more marijuana that is produced in this country, the less money will be lost in international trade.

And there are still other ways in which marijuana farming can be seen as a true embodiment of American culture. The rapid development of *sinsemilla* marijuana is a classic example of applied Yankee ingenuity. In a decade of production, the yield form a typical plant has increased approximately fourfold, from a quarter of a pound to around a pound. From soil preparation to seen selection to guerrilla gardening, he growers have developed a new technology to suit the idiosyncratic needs of the industry. With commendable American style, they have found the tools to tackle the job at hand.

Even the job itself is appropriately American: the production of a drug used for leisure and relaxation. The United States is the leisure capital of the world, and the production of the instruments of leisure accounts for a significant chunk of our commercial enterprise; movies, television, sporting goods, spectator sports—and drugs. The drug habits of American citizens are notorious: the ubiquitous use of caffeine and nicotine and aspirin and alcohol; the overuse of diet pills and sleeping pills and waking pills; the heavy dependence on prescription drugs and chemical treatments by the medical establishment. In this context, supplying marijuana for the recreational use of tens of millions of users throughout the country does not appear as counter to American culture—it *is* American culture.

In this particular community in the coastal hills of California, drugs serve as a catalyst for yet another phenomenon that is common to the American experience: the melting-pot syndrome. Recreational drugs have formed a common bond between the youthful members of disparate subcultures. Hippies or rednecks, growers or nongrowers—the younger generation has shared both its booze and its pot. It's not just the schools that have brought the young folks together—it's also the taverns and the parking lots outside the dances.

In all these ways, the marijuana industry can be viewed as a reflection, not a contradiction, of dominant American culture. Consequently, I believe the deviance of marijuana growers has been greatly exaggerated. True, it is still an illegal industry, but there is plenty of precedence even for illegality within central currents of American culture: Prohibition, the western frontier, and the widespread income tax evasion practiced by ordinary citizens today. On balance, it would seem that the marijuana industry is the best understood as a manifestation of American society, not just a reaction against it.

Even before the marijuana industry blossomed, the seeds to some of these aspects of the American Way had been firmly implanted in the back-to-the-land subculture: the Jeffersonian ideal of independent farmers, the resistance against governmental interference in private affairs, a compelling belief in personal freedom, and the use of recreational drugs. Marijuana farming naturally accentuated each of these themes: the solvency of the small farms became a reality instead of just a dream; the fear of governmental interference was heightened into collective paranoia; the belief in a person's freedom to grow and use a recreational drug formed the ideological support which rationalized an illegal enterprise. Marijuana served to reinforce and exaggerate these preexisting cultural tendencies. It also introduced some other aspects of traditional American culture that had been notably absent (or at least well hidden) in the counterculture rebellion: a visible consumerism, the quest after money, and the element of violence. Whether or not the genesis of all these cultural traits preceded the marijuana industry, one thing is certain: such standard manifestations of the American Way are a lot more common than they used to be on the back-to-the-land homesteads in the hills of California.

How much of this cultural transformation might have occurred anyway, irrespective of the marijuana industry? Could some of the changes have been caused merely by the simple passage of time and the natural progression of history? Is the increasing Americanization of the growers attributable only to marijuana, or was it an inevitable result of the psychological and sociological development of the new pioneers?

Such questions are impossible to answer. Causality is always hard to pin down, and it is even harder in the case of an idiosyncratic historical quirk such as this. There are no comparable control groups to test our theories and hypotheses. All we can really do is tell the story as it occurs, and follow its development over time. And now, ten years into the marijuana boom, the broad outlines of that development are beginning to emerge. The back-to-the-land folks flocked to the hills with the idealistic dream of recreating society from scratch. They wanted to watch it grow from a solid foundation and to avoid the mistakes of the past. Their new society proceeded to grow more quickly than they might have hoped or imagined—and it has turned out to bear an unexpected resemblance to the society they once tried to reject. Even a rebellious subculture cannot easily deny its own cultural roots. In many respects, the new pioneers have paralleled the historical development of the original pioneers who slowly moved toward the mainstream of a modern world; a century of historical development seems to have been foreshortened into a decade. Perhaps a similar process would eventually have occurred without marijuana, but it appears that the marijuana industry has acted, at the very least, as a catalyst in speeding up the pace of history.

It might be worth noting that cultural transformations have worked both ways: the American mainstream has itself been affected by the back-to-the-land subculture in form if not in substance. Foods that claim to be "100 percent natural" are marketed in earth-tone packages and sold in giant grocery chains across the nation. Environmental concerns are at least given lip-service in centers of power. Recycling and solar energy, once dismissed as the fantasies of wide-eyed idealist, are now afforded official recognition (although not much official support). And finally there is *sinsemilla*—now grown by rural rednecks on their farms, by suburban housewives in their backyards, and by young urban professionals in their closets. The horticultural advances of the new pioneers in the California backcountry have made it possible for people everywhere to "grow their own," and for people in some places—whether hardened criminals or seemingly respectable citizens—to make lots of money by producing marijuana.

It is also worth nothing here that the increasing Americanization of the back-to-the-land subculture is only a tendency, not an accomplished fact. There are competing tendencies that seem to pull in opposite directions. The underground economy, for example, presents a significant obstacle to the incorporation of the growers into the mainstream of workday America. What does a marijuana farmer put down for "recent history of employment" on a conventional job application? How does he explain to the IRS how he's made a living for the past ten years? The difficulties of reintegration into the legal economy are likely to be formidable. Because of this difficulty in adjusting to legal employment, a grower today might feel condemned in perpetuity to a life on the illegal fringe of the mainstream economy. On this one crucial level, marijuana serves to keep the growers as a class apart, a subculture that might never be totally incorporated into the American middle class.

Indeed, mainstream society has not been quick to welcome the growers back into the fold. Aside from questions of morality and legality, there's that underlying sense of jealousy: why should the growers have been allowed to get away with it? All that easy money—and no taxes! The cultural prejudice that was once directed against bare feet and welfare checks is now directed against hundred-dollar bills that were acquired illegally.

Even the government itself has singled out this particular subculture for special treatment, and government agents are admittedly trying to destroy some to its values. The acceptance of illegality is seen as a threat to established political authority, causing the enforcers of authority to confront the subculture head-on. And the growers, conditioned to a seemingly perpetual state of paranoia, must certainly wonder whether it is only the marijuana—or are they attacking the lifestyle itself?

There are still plenty of distinguishing characteristics of this subculture, despite the new prosperity and despite the passage of time. Certain matters of style, taste, and belief continue to define the back-to-the-land growers as a people apart. In their own minds, these folks still see themselves as Gypsies and Indians, a special tribe of spiritual seekers who refuse to conform to the boredom of a synthetic society. An eclectic interest in international culture is reflected in colorful attire and creative activities that have little or nothing to do with drip-dry clothes or network TV. Their environmental awareness is keen, and so is their interest in alternative technology; they might seek more comforts than in the old days, but they are trying to satisfy those comforts with ecological and decentralized methods. Economically, they are now middle-class but their political preferences remain on the fringe; they are far more likely to vote for Leftist Democrats or third-party candidates than for solid, conservative Republicans who appeal to their economic peers within the mainstream culture. These political preferences are founded upon some very basic beliefs in alternative social structures. Their beliefs might have been partially neglected or even slightly tarnished by the peculiar events of the past decade, but in the minds of many, they have not been totally shattered.

Thus, there are plenty of attributes that still defined the back-to-the-land culture as a unique social unit. Even if it is not quite so special as it once hoped to be, it is a subculture that is presently in the process of writing its own chapter in American history. The first few sections of that chapter are now in the past: the emigration from the cities, the early struggles on the homesteads, and then the transformation that accompanied an unexpected prosperity. The question now is: How will the new pioneers react as prosperity starts to erode? Will the Ecotopian vision be helped or hindered by a possible return to poverty? Indeed, how will the entire local community react as it swings into a downward phase of the familiar boom-bust cycle? Or will that happen? Is the bust for real, or will the people finally figure out some way of developing a balanced, diversified, and stable local economy?

From where we sit in the middle of this particular chapter in history, the events that envelop us often appear as weird and bizarre, strange contortions of ordinary life. Is it really normal to hear the incessant and heavy whoop-whoop-whoop of helicopters from dawn to dusk for three solid months every year? Is it really normal for a small town in the middle of nowhere to be descended upon by an annual pilgrimage of reporters who write up the local events in distant metropolitan journals? Is it really normal for a local economy of a rural community to be based on the production of a plant that has been declared illegal?

It's not exactly normal, but neither is it quite so strange as it seems. Both the culture and the economy, as we have just seen, are quite in keeping with many aspects of traditional Americana. They also fit in with the tradition of rural anarchy which seems endemic to the disjointed coastal hills of California. In a couple of decades, the whole bizarre spectacle will probably be reduced to an amusing little footnote in the ongoing saga of human endeavor.

Certainly, that's what has happened with Prohibition. To judge from popular folklore, the major legacy of Prohibition is to make us giggle as we watch TV comedies or quaint, period-piece movies. The complex human drama that was once played out for real has been reduced to becoming the subject of amusing stories. Listen, for instance, to the tale of my old friend, the late Glen Strawn:

> We used to fish out of Shelter Cove. I fished two years for the market during Prohibition, so I hauled whiskey most of the time. Made lots of money hauling whiskey. Three or four boats laying out there twenty-five miles—you just go out, get a load, and bring her in. They had big stills working on the boat. Label it Canadian Whiskey. They had labels for everything—any kind you want. When I was gonna go out an get a load of whiskey, I'd fish all day with no hooks on the line—just go round and round. Finally I was the last boat, I'd go out to the mother ship, get a load of whiskey, and come on in. Wouldn't even tell my brother when I was gonna do it. Them hijackers was pretty bad. They get you and knock you in the head and take your load of whiskey and scuttle your boat and sink it. They was dangerous. I wasn't scared of the Revenue—it's them hijackers I was scared of, 'cause they kill you for a load of whiskey. We had a Lewis machine gun—when we'd get a load, we'd always set her up. We never had to use it, but we always had it set up.

How do we react to this story? Conditioned as we are by popular culture, we probably find it somewhat cute—like the folk image of grandpa blasting away with a shotgun at the hindquarters of his granddaughter's suitor. In actual fact, the suitor who got hit in the tail probably didn't think it was a quaint little story at all, and Glen Strawn, at the time, saw nothing very cute about setting up his Lewis machine gun and possibly doing battle with a hijacker who would gladly take his life. No, Glen's story is not cute; it's a sad tale of paranoia in the extreme, as the whiskey runner would not even trust his own brother.

And so it is with marijuana. Once the uproar has subsided, this little chapter in history has all the elements for some lively and entertaining stories. But when you're right in the middle of it all, fear and hate and paranoia do not appear as merely amusing. The events of the present are vivid and real—and not always very pleasant. There is a nasty undercurrent that otherwise might be more joyful. In the words of a grower who once got ripped off, "What boom? How can you call it prosperity when you have to dodge the helicopters or when you're tied up on the floor at gunpoint? Is this really why I came here?"

Yes, the fear is for real—but so are the dreams. Here in the once-promised land, it has been an up-and-down path toward the realization of a utopian vision. The joy of fulfillment, the frustration of failure, these too are very real—and so is the uncertainty of being in between.

Counterculture, Cyberculture, and the Third Culture: Reinventing Civilization, Then and Now

Lee Worden

Reinventing Civilization

Stewart Brand was raised in Rockford, Illinois, an industrial town specializing in heavy machinery, machine tools, and metal toys. He learned early to fear the Communists. "In the early '50s somebody compiled a list of prime targets for Soviet nuclear attack, and we were seven, because of the machine tools," Brand recalls.[1] Like many children of his generation, he was awoken at night by nightmares about nuclear Armageddon. His diary from 1957, his freshman year at Stanford, records his continuing worries about Soviet invasion:

> That my life would necessarily become small, a gear with its place on
> a certain axle of the Communist machine...
> That my mind would no longer be my own...
> That I would lose my will.[2]

After his education at Phillips Exeter and Stanford, and a few years as an Army parachutist and photographer, Brand joined the emerging counterculture of the 1960s as a multimedia performance artist, producing experimental public events and mingling with the New York art scene. An intelligent,

---

1   Fred Turner, *From Counterculture to Cyberculture: Stewart Brand, the Whole Earth Network, and the Rise of Digital Utopianism* (Chicago: University of Chicago Press, 2006), 41.
2   Ibid., 42.

ambitious young man concerned with making sense of the postwar world, the gathering intimations of social change, and the perplexing questions of how to resist the pressures of bureaucracy and conformity, he turned to the writing of Marshall McLuhan, Buckminster Fuller, and the cybernetic theorists such as Norbert Weiner and Heinz von Foerster. Inspired by Fuller's *Operating Manual for Spaceship Earth*, Brand launched an ambitious project to expose the public to NASA's new photographs of the whole planet, to catalyze awareness of humanity's role as stewards of the planet.

In the late '60s, Brand inherited a sum of money and developed his Earth photographs project into a business purveying tangible and conceptual tools to commune dwellers. After an extended tour of visionary communes in the Southwest (Drop City, Libre, the Lama Foundation, and others), he introduced the first *Whole Earth Catalog* in fall 1968, with NASA's Earth pictures on the covers. The *Whole Earth Catalog* is an eclectic compilation of resources, mostly available by mail order from various distributors around the country. Wood stoves, well-digging equipment and instructions, and home medicine manuals appear side by side with books on teaching, Taoism, electronic music, and the theory of cybernetics and feedback processes. The book opens with a page on Fuller—"The insights of Buckminster Fuller initiated this catalog"—and with a manifesto:

> We *are* as gods and might as well get used to it. So far, remotely done power and glory—as via government, big business, formal education, church—has succeeded to the point where gross defects obscure actual gains. In response to this dilemma and to these gains a realm of intimate, personal power is developing—power of the individual to conduct his own education, find his own inspiration, shape his own environment, and share his adventure with whoever is interested. Tools that aid this process are sought and promoted by the *WHOLE EARTH CATALOG*.[3]

Indeed these are the major themes of the *Whole Earth Catalog*: provision of "Access to Tools" as the means to positive social change, but also a deep rejection of the existing system, and a fundamental faith in the individual. Brand describes his mission in this way: "Fuller, like McLuhan, was one of the people we were paying attention to. And Wiener was in there, Cage was a little bit in there. But the initial audience in my mind

---

3   *Whole Earth Catalog* (Spring 1970).

was communes, was people who were trying to reinvent civilization, and I was just trying to provide the tools with which to reinvent civilization."[4]

The *Catalog* was republished yearly for a while, with more or less quarterly supplements full of corrections and suggestions from readers. In 1974, the supplement became a separate magazine in the same vein, called *CoEvolution Quarterly*. Its title drawn from the work of Brand's Stanford mentor, evolution expert and population-control advocate Paul Ehrlich, this magazine focused more on sustainability, on forecasting the future of the planet, and on appropriate technology. Cybernetics visionary Gregory Bateson became a major influence during this period, sharing the honor with Fuller.

CoEvolution Quarterly was the first to report on James Lovelock and Lynn Margulis's Gaia hypothesis, and then scooped science journals by presenting the first scientific critique of the hypothesis in a 1982 article by biologist W. Ford Doolittle. (In his introduction to a 1980 Lynn Margulis interview by an admiring woman student, Brand takes the opportunity to comment indirectly on contemporary social movements: "Lynn's rampant non-feminist style in male-dominated science reminds me somewhat of Margaret Mead—she never slights someone for being male, only for being stupid.")[5]

Brand had a long interest in computer technology. He was brought in as cameraman for Alan Kay and Douglas Engelbart's famous 1968 demo of the first computer pointing device. He wrote a *Rolling Stone* profile of Stanford computer game pioneers in 1972, stating, "Ready or not, computers are coming to the people. That's good news, maybe the best since psychedelics." But computers were a minor player in his publications until 1983, when, his publishing ventures failing, he took his literary agent's suggestion to create a *Whole Earth Software Catalog*. Despite a $1.3 million deal to produce the *Software Catalog*, a larger sum than ever before for a paperback, the catalog and its accompanying magazine, the *Whole Earth Software Review*, failed miserably. Nonetheless, it was a watershed in the history of the Whole Earth project.

The *Software Review* and *CoEvolution Quarterly* became the *Whole Earth Review*, focusing far less on ecology and far more on flexible business management, scientific ideas about complex systems and self-organization, and computer software and networking. This period also saw the launch of the WELL, the "Whole Earth 'Lectronic Link," a computer

---

4   Lutz Dammbeck, *The Net: The Unabomber, LSD and the Internet* (San Francisco: Other Cinema, 2006), DVD. Released in Germany as *Das Netz*.
5   *CoEvolution Quarterly* 25 (Spring 1980): 31.

bulletin board for Bay Area folks to talk and network with each other. The WELL was staffed predominantly by former residents of the Farm, the rural community headed by Stephen Gaskin in Tennessee.

In the '90s, Brand became primarily involved with the Global Business Network, a think tank he founded together with executives and business consultants from Shell and the Stanford Research Institute, whose purpose was to advise corporate executives about new ideas and help them embrace flexible management strategies, network forms, and self-organizing processes.

In 1992, the *Whole Earth Review*'s managing editor, Kevin Kelly, was hired away to run a new magazine called *Wired*. He brought with him a whole network of Whole Earth contributors, including Brand, cyberspace civil-liberties promoter John Perry Barlow, virtual reality entrepreneur Jaron Lanier, and *Catalog* editor and cyberfuturist author Howard Rheingold. *Wired* was the primary print organ of the '90s dot-com boom. During Kelly's tenure as managing editor, the cover of *Wired* featured right-wing heroes Newt Gingrich and George Gilder, the latter in an enthusiastic promotion of telecommunication deregulation.

The Whole Earth catalogs and magazines have gone out of business; *Wired* still appears monthly. In the last few years, Brand has begun to promote nuclear power and genetic engineering as the best response to global energy and climate crises (and he has reaffirmed his pronuclear position, unchanged, just after the Fukushima disaster).[6]

Brand now dismisses the back-to-the-land tradition that his *Catalog* originally served, and says that technology is the real legacy of the '60s:

> The communes that tried to go back to basics and just farm made a real good try at doing that, and some of them even learned a fair amount of basic farming. A book that we purveyed in the *Whole Earth Catalog* called *Goat Husbandry* was a very popular book—and it's a good book! You know, you can get the book, get a goat, and you can do it. Milk and everything. But it didn't play out very far. It was basically a different kind of dead end from what drugs were, whereas some of the technology, some of the alternative energy technology showed real promise. Solar energy basically took off gradually and takes off to this day. Computer technology obviously. And because the counterculture, hippie frame of reference was there for outlaws of all kinds, it basically swept right through the outlaw computer people, the hackers, and became their

---

6   Charles Homans, "Nuclear Winner," *Foreign Policy*, March 22, 2011.

frame of reference, and a kind of a gift-economy, optimistic approach became then the basis for personal computers, personal computer software, then the Internet, and the web, and on and on. And that's the main legacy from the '60s as far as I'm concerned, is the open system approach to everything having to do with computers.[7]

Brand's publications were an inspiration to more than one generation of social innovators and free thinkers. They were compelling and exciting. One long-time contributor describes the power of the *Catalog*: "Soon after I moved to Prague, I showed the *Last Whole Earth Catalog* to a friend in Bulgaria. She was fascinated but perplexed. 'Who is this for?' she asked. It took me a few moments to reply, as my first impulse was to say, 'everyone.' But instead I answered, 'It's for practical intellectuals.' She continued browsing through the *Catalog* with her eyes starting to moisten. Eventually she said, 'How I wish we had such people.'"[8]

I read the *CoEvolution Quarterly* and *Whole Earth Review* whenever I could get my hands on them, from the age of ten or so onward, in my hippie childhood in rural Northern California. I thought they were great. When I was a college student in computer science, I was still an avid reader and dreamed of being part of a community of such kind people doing exciting, good work. I was in computer science partly because of those magazines' features on the liberatory potential of personal computing and digital communication. I was very slow to recognize that what I was reading there wasn't really congruent with things I deeply value, and that it was probably steering me astray as a guide to creative, ethical living.

As we have seen, the *Whole Earth Catalog* project began as a tool for the '60s counterculture, helping people work out how to create a new society, and ended up promoting computers, business and the dot-com boom, which has been a disaster not only for the people who lost their investments in the '90s but for electronics sweatshop workers, people living in areas poisoned by the fabrication and disposal of computer chips, people evicted in the Northern California real-estate bubble, and everyone on the bottom end of the widening gap in wealth it induced. Brand now promotes deeply antienvironmental technologies with the argument that they're the best alternative we have because a truly better world isn't possible.

---

7 Dammbeck, *The Net.*
8 Robert Horvitz, "Whole Earth Culture," http://www.wholeearth.com/history-whole-earth-culture.php.

Plenty of '60s figures turned conservative in the Reagan years, so it's natural to think that Brand was one of them, and his magazine changed with him. However, I don't think that's the case. There may not seem to be much connection between '60s idealism and '90s high-tech innovation, but there are deep continuities. In this essay I argue that the market libertarian Brand of the '90s is the same Brand who was widely respected as a leader of the '60s counterculture and the '70s environmental movement; that his ally John Brockman similarly exemplifies a counterintuitive continuity between '60s hip and '90s techno-capitalist cultures; and that there is a strong contemporary social movement that traces directly back to the technophilic, futuristic experimental intellectual movements of the '60s that gave rise to these men. I suggest that anyone who wants to make a better world today must recognize the dangerous and powerful draw of this movement, not because it is deeply committed to individual freedom but because it values freedom at the expense of justice. I believe that it is possible, however, to create a new image of the "practical intellectual," one who does deeply satisfying, meaningful rebellious work to create a new world, guided by justice and solidarity as well as freedom and creative self-expression.

The original *Whole Earth Catalog*s begin with Buckminster Fuller, its patron saint and inspiration. Fuller's central position is that the modern world has such an abundance of know-how that if we choose, we can eliminate scarcity and depletion of resources by the intelligent application of design. When people understand that there is no more scarcity, he says, there will be no more war and we will enter a new era of peace and intelligent stewardship.

This ideology of design, with its faith in the power of ideas, and denial of the persistence of inequality and exploitation, is almost identical to the mythology of the dot-com era—that new technology can bring with it a new social order that will set everyone free without hardly trying, and power disparities aren't worth worrying about except where bad governments interfere with free thought and free speech.

The *Whole Earth Catalog* of the late '60s was not friendly to left-wing politics. Consider one Jay Bonner's letter in the January 1970 *WEC* supplement:

> Sometimes I don't care about nothing, but right now I do. It sickens me to think that over 150,000 people are going to pick up the *Whole Earth Catalog* and thoughtlessly think it's great, like I did. The function of the catalog is to provide access of tools for and from the WHOLE Earth. Roughly 80 percent of the peoples of this Whole Earth are being sucked

on by various capitalistic countries of this world. Yet for some reason the problems of these "third world" people are not even mentioned in the catalog. There are books and various publications written by educated and experienced writers on these problems and their solutions. I really don't think the title "Whole Earth" is quite adequate for the catalog at this point. Stewart Brand, the man who originally created and conceived the idea of a *Whole Earth Catalog* and truck store, does not seem to share my feelings that these types of political books and various publications should be in the catalog. Once, while working with him on the catalog, I asked Mr. Brand if he would not carry any of a various number of politically oriented underground newspapers. Upon reply he told me that three of the first restrictions he made for the catalog were no art, no religion, no politics. I would like to point out that, although Mr. Brand apparently does not think so, all of the three basic ground rules he set up for himself at the beginning and told me of little over three months ago, he has broken: To start with art… Then we move on to religion… Lastly we come along to items of political significance. In this we find quite a few.

Handbook for Conscientious Objectors
The Population Bomb
Population Evolution and Birth Control
Birth Control Handbook
Atlas Shrugged
The Wall St. Journal and any number of "future" books.

I can understand why Mr. Brand makes such a distinction between, for example, the *Handbook for Conscientious Objectors*, and a good book on Marxian theory, it's because he's a capitalist. The inclusion of books on such subjects would hinder catalog sales, and after all it's not serving the people he's interested in, it's making money, and believe me he has plenty of it. Besides, it's against all his economic beliefs. Yes, Mr. Brand's personal feelings really show up in what should properly be called the "Stewart Brand Catalog." From all the 128 pages of the *Whole Earth Catalog* there emerges an unmentioned political viewpoint. The whole feeling of escapism which the catalog conveys is to me unfortunate… The idea of the catalog is a good one. The people need a Whole Earth Catalog, but not the one they're getting! If you feel at all the same, write Stewart Brand.[9]

---

9   *Whole Earth Catalog* supplement, January 1970.

Stewart Brand's response appears in the same issue:

> Jay worked with his brother Joe doing layout on the Fall *Catalog* and
> was not rehired for January production, because of too many technical
> mistakes on his pages. Jay is 17. (I'm 31. How old are you? It matters,
> more than any of us like.) Correct I have some money, thanks to
> parents, which I'm putting into work like the *Catalog*. My salary is $5/
> hr. The *Catalog* is non-profit, so our income…can only be spent on
> further educational projects. The capitalism question is interesting. I've
> yet to figure out what capitalism is, but if it's what we're doing, I dig
> it. Oppressed peoples: all I know is I've been radicalized by working
> on the *Catalog* into far more personal involvement with politics than
> I had as an artist. My background is WASP, wife is American Indian.
> Work I did a few years ago with Indians convinced me that any guilt-
> based action toward anyone (personal or institutional) can only make a
> situation worse.
>
> …I'm for power to the people and responsibility to the people.[10]

The original *Catalog* is characterized by much the same libertarian ethos
that we see in *Wired* in the '90s: the domination by white men and silencing of other voices, the embrace of capitalism, the faith in social change
through technological innovation and not through political deliberation
and organizing, and, oddly considering its place as bible of the countercultural communes, a strong advocacy of individualism. (And what happened to "don't trust anyone over thirty"?)

Inventing Reality

These continuities in Stewart Brand's history make it clear that it wasn't
just a case of a community leader losing his commitment to "the movement" at the beginning of the '80s.

Still, there was an important shift in 1983, when Brand and his publishing projects turned from the old focus on rural homesteading and
whole-systems philosophy to the new focus on computer software. That
shift seems to trace back to a conversation between Brand and his agent.
This literary agent and change agent merits a close look in his own right.
His career is curiously parallel to Brand's: an intellectual celebrity of the

---

10 Ibid.

counterculture who transforms seamlessly into an icon of '90s popular technoscience, shifting from "hip" to (not to put a fine point on it) right-wing without any actual perceptible change in his politics.

John Brockman, representative to the nerd stars, actually enters the story well before the first *Whole Earth Catalog*. Brockman and Brand first became friends in the New York multimedia art scene of the early and mid-'60s. Brockman emerged as a producer of "environmental intermedia" events, rejecting the style of Allan Kaprow's participatory Happenings for a more passive process of immersion in sensory stimulation produced by new media technologies such as slide shows, strobe lights, and loud recorded sound. Brand and Brockman were both connected with USCO, a performance collective in upstate New York with a strong interest in new media.

Brockman was introduced to cybernetics by composer John Cage, and the connection led him to multiple major turning points. In the late '60s and early '70s, Brockman produced three ambitious works of philosophy, ultimately anthologized under the collective title of *Afterwords*. Drawing heavily from the ideas of cybernetics scholars like Norbert Wiener and Heinz von Foerster as well as particle physicists and neuroscientists, along with media scholar Marshall McLuhan, Brockman outlines a radical philosophy in which the idea of the individual is a delusion, as are mankind, words, consciousness, opinions, ethics, politics, and Brockman himself. There are only neural networks and the sensory impressions that shape and are shaped by them. As a result, it is very important how we shape our sensory experiences, for instance by the design of the media we use. Brand is one of Brockman's intellectual sources, quoted early in the first book of *Afterwords*. The *Whole Earth Catalog* reviews Brockman's first volume: "His book is an interpretation of recent work in brain-study, information theory, and art. It proposes that man is dead, replaced by a superior being—once he learns this—called invisible."[11]

Also featured in Brand's *Catalog* are the two volumes of Brockman's catalog, *Real Time (A Catalog of Ideas and Information)*. Ed Rosenfeld, *Real Time*'s other editor, recounts, "John Brockman and I were friends in the early 1970s. We both admired the *Whole Earth Catalog*, especially the first section: Understanding Whole Systems. We thought that a 'catalogue' focusing on those kinds of interests would make a great book."[12]

---

11 Stewart Brand, *Whole Earth Catalog* (June 1975): 308.
12 *Lined and Unlined Blog*, http://blog.linedandunlined.com/post/403585976/home-library-2-real-time, July 7, 2009,

Real Time focuses much more on collecting sources of scientific ideas, communication technology, and media theory, and far less on the hippie lifestyle resources.

Meanwhile, Brockman's immersion in the New York artist and intellectual circles spun off a lucrative career for him:

> The circles widened, so there was Heinz von Foerster, who was the dean of the world cyberneticists, there was Gregory Bateson, Stewart Brand. Almost all these people were authors, as I was; I'd read all their books, and no one in New York had a clue that there was something happening, that there was a consciousness or mindset that had evolved, and you could connect all these people...you know, there are ways to put it together and to see a cohesive whole, and they were bestselling authors, and they were getting screwed by the publishing industry. So I was, ah, dragooned into becoming an agent, because I had a business background, and they said, "Why don't you just go back and look after our interests. It'll take you an hour a day," and I thought it would be a nice way to pick up some money while I wrote books, and I found out very quickly that I was sitting on an oil well that I couldn't control, and that was thirty years ago.[13]

In time, Brockman has emerged as the premier representative of science and technology figures who write books. Since the '70s, Brockman has picked up a stellar roster of clients in the sciences, including Richard Dawkins, Jared Diamond, Steven Pinker, Daniel Dennett, and of course, Brand, Rheingold, and Kelly. He more or less invented the field of computer books in the early '80s, the failed *Software Catalog* being only a bump in Brockman's road to success. He invented the word "digerati" to promote his clients, and regularly publishes collected volumes of his clients and friends' contributions to the public sphere.

Brockman's own major public work after his early books is his 1991 essay "The Third Culture." This piece argues that contrary to C. P. Snow's hopes, the famous dichotomy of the two cultures—the sciences and the humanities—is being resolved, not by greater understanding between the two groups, but by the emergence of a new third-culture figure, the scientist who speaks directly to the public. Humanities scholars are dismissed: "Their culture, which dismisses science, is often non-empirical.

---

13 Dammbeck, *The Net*.

It uses its own jargon and washes its own laundry. It is chiefly character-ized by comment on comments, the swelling spiral of commentary even-tually reaching the point where the real world gets lost."[14]

Brand is quoted in this essay, "Science is the only news. When you scan through a newspaper or magazine, all the human interest stuff is the same old he-said-she-said, the politics and economics the same sorry cyclic dramas, the fashions a pathetic illusion of newness, and even the technology is predictable if you know the science. Human nature doesn't change much; science does, and the change accrues, altering the world irreversibly."[15]

In a 2003 follow-up essay titled "The New Humanists," Brockman quotes at length from *National Review* columnist and Joseph McCarthy biographer Arthur Herman, arguing that rejection of the West and of civ-ilization has become "the dominant theme in intellectual discourse":

> This new order might take the shape of the Unabomber's radical environmental utopia. It might also be Nietzsche's Overman, or Hitler's Aryan National Socialism, or Marcuse's utopian union of technology and Eros, or Frantz Fanon's revolutionary fellahin. Its carriers might be the ecologist's "friends of the earth," or the multiculturalist's "persons of color," or the radical feminist's New Amazons, or Robert Bly's New Men. The particular shape of the new order will vary according to taste; however, its most important virtue will be its totally non-, or even anti-Western character. In the end, what matters to the cultural pessimist is less what is going to be created than what is going to be destroyed—namely, our "sick" modern society... [T]he sowing of despair and self doubt has become so pervasive that we accept it as a normal intellectual stance—even when it is directly contradicted by our own reality.[16]

No, the world is not sick or in decline, it is getting better, thanks to science. Jaron Lanier, prophet of virtual reality, applauds this essay: "Bravo, John! You are playing a vital role in moving the sciences beyond a defensive posture in response to turf attacks from the 'postmodernists' and other leeches on the academies."[17]

---

14   John Brockman, *The Third Culture: Beyond the Scientific Revolution* (New York: Simon & Schuster: 1995).
15   Ibid.
16   John Brockman, *The New Humanists: Science at the Edge* (New York: Sterling, 2003).
17   Ibid.

Both Brockman and Brand are subtle, elusive characters whose belief systems can be hard to pin down. Brockman has hardly abandoned his early radical views of reality. He outlines his point of view in a 1987 *Whole Earth Review* interview: "Reality is a process of decreation. It's what people say it is. The world, the world that we know, is not necessarily out there, it's invention—human invention—an invention created by a finite number of people throughout history. I thought it would be interesting to track such people living today and find out what they're thinking about."[18]

Brockman also ran an elite evening salon throughout the '80s called the Reality Club, during the time of these aggressive attacks on post-modernists and science scholars. He says the name of the Reality Club is a pun, and continues to use the closing lines of *Afterwords* as a motto: "Nobody knows, and you can't find out."[19] You might take him for a post-modern relativist or social constructionist. But he simultaneously makes these aggressive arguments for reality and science, against the purported solipsism of the academic establishment.

In Brockman's edited books, he and his contributors keep coming back to this issue—many agree not only that science is the only intel-lectual field that matters, but that it's won, and the humanities are mar-ginal and irrelevant. This line of argument combines the authority of science with a right-wing defense of European heritage, and includes direct attacks on left-wing politics, and the strong assertion that anyone who is in touch with reality must believe that modern society is good and getting better. Both Brand and Brockman argue that science, not politics, is the way to change the world.

They take a side in the academic culture wars of the time, and it seems to be the conservative side, against "political correctness," but if so, there seems to be more than one conservative side: this is not about defending the European literary canon against multiculturalism; in fact, it's not even conservative, in the sense that Brockman and Brand want to change everything, not keep it the same. But they are certainly aligned with the Right in their attacks on Leftism, dismissal of political critique, and vehement embrace of the Enlightenment values of reason, individ-ual initiative, and the grand narrative of progress through scientific dis-covery. This is strangely ironic, since the culture wars tend to be charac-

---

18   *Whole Earth Review* 55 (Summer 1987): 2–5.
19   Hartford Courant, "Edge.org Compiles Rules of the Wise," January 9, 2004, for example.

terized by conservatives attacking the legacy of the '60s, and Brand and Brockman are icons of the '60s counterculture.

In all the public intellectuals' contributions in Brockman's collections, even those who are not scientists or computer specialists, I have seen no engagement with postmodern critiques of science, or with specific postmodernist scholars, or other critiques of science for that matter. The humanities are simply caricatured in the ways we have seen (also ironically, since science is supposed to be superior because it makes claims backed by evidence).

Rebuilding the Living World

The story of Stewart Brand and the Whole Earth publishing projects is analyzed masterfully by Frederick Turner's 2006 book *From Counterculture to Cyberculture: Stewart Brand, the Whole Earth Network, and the Rise of Digital Utopianism*, a major source for this chapter. Turner spotlights the *Catalog's* joining of high-tech research and counterculture ideology. Making this connection, he says, allows the two to legitimate each other, connects disparate communities—cybernetics and computer researchers and commune dwellers—and makes possible what he names a "contact language" that allows ideas to cross over between the two domains. This connection was crucial in redefining the image of the computer from a tool of centralized regimentation and oppression to a tool of personal and political liberation, and this hybrid image was central to the mythology of the dot-com era.

Brand's "New Communalists," as Turner labels them, left the cities for rural communes, but also studied cybernetics and electronics, hoping to use new technologies—not only LSD and guitar amplifiers but also new media and communications technologies—to reintegrate the whole self, create community, and make a new society. These hopeful pioneers became the computing innovators who have, in fact, more or less reinvented civilization by creating the personal computer and the software tools that comprise today's Internet.

Turner identifies a number of ironies in the history of the Whole Earth project, in addition to the shift from opposing centralization and hierarchy to promoting government deregulation and concentration of political and economic power. While espousing equality and focusing heavily on futurism and models of global trends, they ignored trends of increasing wealth disparity from the 1970s to the '90s and "created a rhetoric that masked them"; they consistently obscured existing hierarchies of power, from Stewart Brand's dominance of the publishing projects to the impacts on workers of the "flexible" business practices they promoted. It also pioneered a business model, beginning with the original *Catalog* and continuing with the WELL, that blurs the line between the company and its customers, essentially encouraging customers to create the product, and then selling the customers and their work to each other and keeping the profits. Today, of course, this is how Google, Facebook, and a thousand other online businesses work. I would add to this list of ironies the shift from serving visionary rural communitarian projects to promoting "virtual community," while contributing to the destruction of real communities in the Bay Area and worldwide by the dot-com economy and neoliberal economics.

The *Whole Earth Catalog* contributed to the transformation of the counterculture into a form of consumer identity in obvious ways. It also, of course, promoted economic globalization, at first metaphorically and later literally.

The original *Catalog* fit neatly into a general move away from Vietnam War activism, the New Left, and the rising militancy exemplified by the Black Panthers and the Weather Underground, and toward an emphasis on lifestyle and changes in consciousness. As it developed, it tracked changes in countercultural ambitions through the back-to-the-land shift of the late '60s, through the replacement of systemic critique by self-realization in the '70s, to reabsorption by mainstream business in the '80s, and into the digital utopianism of the '90s and beyond.

The *Whole Earth Catalog* surely had multiple constituencies, from East Coast universities and art scenes to rural Western homesteads. But a crucial one, if not the primary demographic, was technically minded young men, and a smaller number of women, in California, the young explorers who became the creators of personal computers, their software and the networks that connect them.

When the *Catalog* went out of business for the first time in 1971, Brand threw a Demise Party at the Exploratorium in San Francisco, at which the audience (as a whole) received a surprise gift of $20,000 in cash and was left to decide what to do with it. After much discussion most of the money ended up entrusted to a man named Fred Moore, to work out how to spend it later. Fred Moore went on to become a founder of the Homebrew Computer Club, which included future Apple Computer creators Steve Jobs and Steve Wozniak, and among whose ranks were also the first known pirates of Bill Gates and Paul Allen's proprietary software.

Moore and Lee Felsenstein became part of Resource One, a local project funded in part by the Demise Party's money, and aiming (in Fred Turner's words) "to establish public computing terminals at several locations in the Bay area, with an eye toward creating a peer-to-peer information exchange." *Whole Earth Catalog* staffers were involved in the 1972 creation of the People's Computer Center in Menlo Park, California, a place for the public to gain access to the means of computing.

The People's Computer Center and Resource One are alive and well in the form of today's hackerspace movement, which is now creating a global network of physical spaces, like San Francisco's Noisebridge, where people are invited to come together freely to learn about technology and create their own.

It's more accurate to describe the *Whole Earth Catalog* as a document of this early populist technology movement than as a creator of it. Regardless, that movement, which is still alive, growing and changing in multiple forms, was always part and parcel of the "consciousness or mindset" to which Brockman alludes. It includes the older cybernetics theories, ecological concern, Fuller-style architectural iconoclasm, Taoist and Zen nonduality, and commitment to learning, innovating and changing the world for the better—a movement, that is, distinct from "the movement" that opposed the draft, patriarchy and capitalism. Brand's and Brockman's histories illuminate this movement's history in many ways.

The Free Software Movement originates in the nationwide community of idealistic early computer users. Its platform is that software should be freely shared and adapted, not controlled and sold. To date it has given us three of the world's top five web browsers, the software behind most of the websites on the Internet, the powerful Linux operating system, and massive, incontrovertible evidence for the ability of voluntarily cooperating humans to get serious work done in the real world without a profit motive.

The Free Software Movement's offshoot, the Free Culture Movement, extends the same ideals to free circulation of music, literature, journalism, film and video, educational materials, and anything else that is eligible for copyright.

In the early '90s, the Cypherpunks organized to bring unbreakable cryptography from secret agencies to the masses. (Their name derives from science fiction's "cyberpunk," a hybrid of the hacker and punk esthetics.) They imagined (and many still do) an extreme libertarian utopia, in which the flow of money is untraceable, speech is absolutely free, and censorship and taxation are impossible because anyone at a computer has access to complete privacy and anonymity. The "Cypherpunk's Manifesto" spells out their attitude toward changing the world: "We don't much care if you don't approve of the software we write. We know that software can't be destroyed and that a widely dispersed system can't be shut down."[20]

A loose movement that we might call "liberation technology" holds that information technology can help democratic social movements to overcome repressive regimes in their countries. For instance, it was widely claimed after the Tiananmen Square massacre that democracy activists in China were able to get news in and out of the country despite censorship because they had the use of fax machines, an updated version of the Soviet bloc's samizdat. Activists create and provide software to help people in places like China and Iran to circumvent restrictions on access, help citizens to report government abuses while hiding their identity from retribution, and allow opposition movements like Tibetan nationalists and Burmese democracy activists to communicate using private, encrypted email. Some of these efforts, for instance in support of the recent uprisings in Iran, have been partially backed by the U.S. State Department. Meanwhile, WikiLeaks's Julian Assange, a former cypherpunk, is now using his expertise and connections to turn liberation technology against the United States and its allies.

Peer-to-peer filesharing on the internet has effectively brought the music and movie industries to their knees. When people can easily download music, first-run movies, and software for free, using free software like BitTorrent, FrostWire, or SoulSeek, they often choose not to pay for the products.

Oddly, out of all these interlinked movements, it is advocates of illegal file sharing who have made the move into traditional politics, organizing Pirate Parties in several European countries—political parties, that is—and the original Piratpartiet has become Sweden's third largest party in just a few years since its founding, and won two seats in the European Parliament. Their platform includes blanket opposition to copyright and patent law and to laws (antiterror laws, for instance) that infringe personal privacy.

Wikipedia, the online encyclopedia written collectively by its readers, is now about twenty-five times the size of *Encyclopædia Britannica*, and a comparison done by *Nature* found the two to be roughly equal in accuracy. Wikipedia is widely cited as a triumph of "commons-based peer production," meaning creation of a product by an open, self-organizing community of

---

20 Eric Hughes, "A Cypherpunk's Manifesto," 1993, http://www.activism.net/cypherpunk/manifesto.html.

often volunteer workers. Using terms such as "crowdsourcing," "wikinomics" or "p2p," the success of Wikipedia and free software is named by a number of advocates as a model for a new way of organizing labor based on uncoerced creation of commons, possibly even as an alternative to wage labor.

The impact of free culture and peer production movements is now percolating into the sphere of academic research, in the form of the Open Access and Open Science movements. Open access is simply the application of free culture ideas to research, resulting in the position that published research should be accessible to the public and free for reuse. Open Access is a reaction to the current system dominated by corporate publishers, whose expensive journals effectively can't be accessed by anyone without a university position, and whose copyrights prevent researchers from reusing and adapting the figures and text of the articles they draw on.

The open science movement is more multifaceted, encompassing scientists' use of blogs as "open lab notebooks," science wikis for collaborative peer production of research, online sharing of data, and a general ethic of sharing information quickly and freely rather than holding it back in order to establish priority by publishing in a peer-reviewed journal. This is more or less just the ideals of the free software movement translated to the practices of science, or, from another perspective, simply the original ideals of science updated to the era of the Internet by way of the free software movement.

So far in this new decade (I write this in the end of 2010), open science, and the more general idea of "Science 2.0," seem to have found their strongest foothold in the infant field of synthetic biology. Synthetic biology, according to its practitioners, is the practice of "rebuilding the living world" from the bottom up, by designing new organisms' genomes from scratch rather than the comparatively conservative genetic engineering techniques of inserting foreign genes into existing species. Synthetic biology researchers are currently receiving funding from the U.S. Department of Energy and other bodies in the United States and Europe, and from private sources including genome entrepreneur J. Craig Venter. They are working in newly formed departments of Biological Engineering at MIT and Stanford, at UC Berkeley and BP's Energy BioSciences Institute, and in numerous biotech startups.

The synthetic biology community is home of what is probably the most advanced online "Science 2.0" initiative, a very active wiki website called OpenWetWare.org. Many researchers use the wiki daily to share their data, software, and unpublished results with each other and maintain densely updated research logs. OpenWetWare creator Drew Endy is additionally working to create an online Registry of Standard Biological Parts, an online database from which gene experimenters can freely upload and download gene sequences they have found useful. Proponents predict that synthesis of DNA molecules from arbitrary gene sequences will soon become cheap and easy enough that individuals can do it in their garages. At that point, these free software-inspired online databases of "biological parts" will allow private actors to create a broad range of organisms of their own design, unconstrained by precedents or regulations. Endy is a gifted coiner of phrases: he has memorably declared his intentions to "rebuild the living world"[21] and to "reimplement life in a manner of our choosing."[22]

Along with the institutionally supported "synbio" community, an outsider movement has arisen, behind names like "DIYBio," "Biohack," or "Biopunk," to make "garage biotech" a reality. A project called BioCurious has raised, via public microfunding facilitated by online fundraising site Kickstarter.org, its $35,000 target to create a biotech hackerspace in the San Francisco area for homebrew bioengineers. A Biopunk Manifesto has been circulated and presented to the FBI's biosafety experts and academic biotechnicians:

> To paraphrase [cypherpunk] Eric Hughes, "Our work is free for all to
> use, worldwide. We don't much care if you don't approve of our research
> topics." We are building on the work of the Cypherpunks who came
> before us to ensure that a widely dispersed research community cannot
> be shut down...we are acutely aware that our research has the potential
> to affect those around us. But we reject outright the admonishments of
> the precautionary principle, which is nothing more than a paternalistic
> attempt to silence researchers by inspiring fear of the unknown.[23]

Brand's cultural pioneers, leaving the Haight-Ashbury to reinvent civilization on the homestead, became the hacker pioneers, subverting copyright law and using the Internet to create new forms of global commons and to bypass authoritarian governments' restrictions on communication. Brockman's "invisibles" who have learned the truth about reality's

---

21   Endy on Nature molecular systems biology blog, April 12, 2008, http://blog-msb.
     embo.org/blog/2008/03/synthetic_biology_nsabb_and_cr.html.

22   Oliver Morton, "Life, Reinvented," *Wired* 13, no. 1 (January 1, 2005): 168–75.

23   Meredith L. Patterson, "A Biopunk Manifesto," January 30, 2010, http://maradydd.
     livejournal.com/496085.html.

moveable feast became his scientists and inventors who reinvent reality by making new tools for thinking and communicating. Now the "open system approach" to computing is becoming an open approach to science, which will empower everyone who has the time and access to remake reality, not only by studying it or making communication tools, but also by rebuilding the living world itself, without the hindrance of rules and regulations.

This is not empty hype, any more than eccentric predictions about networks of personal information devices were in the 1970s. Scientists will create new microbes that excrete food, medicine, and gasoline substitutes. Some of them will have unforeseen impacts on existing plants and animals' habitats, just as genetically modified organisms have done already, but more so. Unaffiliated individuals will use cheap, empowering biotech tools to make their own experiments and living products, and some will have large-scale impacts. Eventually, there will probably arise a biological analogue of WikiLeaks—an idealistic and populist intervention, and one that is globally disruptive, places innocent people in danger, and is imposed on the world without participation in the decision and without accountability. We can also expect biological counterparts to the personal computer and the Internet—radically disruptive inventions that pull us all into a new world in which we have to adjust to a new texture of daily life whether we like it or not, and we will have no say in whether they are in fact desirable changes. We can be even more confident of biological versions of Google and Facebook, and sooner—proprietary products that centralize power over our daily lives in the hands of a few hyperpowerful corporations on a scale that we can hardly imagine in advance.

A fundamental value is being obscured in these visionary projects, from the People's Computer Company to BioCurious: technological innovations are not an unalloyed good; they can have immense consequences for people and communities not involved in their creation, and it is not liberating to impose massive changes on passive victims without their participation. This is the problem with Brand's sponsorship of Access to Tools, with Brockman's promotion of one-way communication from scientists to the public, and with high-tech visionaries' crusade for open access, freedom, and transparency.

Notably, both Brand and Brockman have made their fortunes portraying communities they are not part of. Brand never lived on a commune, and does not write software (though he deserves recognition as an accomplished practical systems thinker), and Brockman is neither a scientist nor a creator of technology. More to the point, the people and institutions that are creating new science and technology are generally based in the most developed nations, and are not directly affected by the impacts of their work on less powerful communities around the world; those communities tend to have little or no say in the decisions that set the directions of research and technological development.

Justice requires everyone affected to be included in deliberation, or at least to have a voice. Liberation requires accountability, or at least exposure to the consequences of our choices. To live as if we were gods and "used to it" requires we have the strength of character to forgo choices that are clearly bad ones. It includes the responsibilities of stewardship and solidarity.

The social movement that is rising, traceable through these generational shifts and back to Buckminster Fuller's generation of wild-eyed engineers and cyberneticians, is a fundamentally technocratic one that trusts technically smart people to make the best decisions about how and whether to reinvent the world. Technically smart people have created internal combustion and its apocalyptic climatic consequences; X-Rays, Thalidomide and DES; uncounted ubiquitous pollutants, toxins and carcinogens; and, of course, the apocalyptic dangers of the atomic bomb. It doesn't take a specialized education to understand the consequences of social and environmental changes due to new inventions, and to take a position on which changes are desirable. Technocracy has not served us, and it will not serve us better in the future. A fair, wise alternative is difficult to imagine, but this is what we need to do.

In filmmaker Lutz Dammbeck's documentary on technology, networks and opposition, Brockman tells how he first met the computer:

> I got a call from A. K. Solomon. He was head of biophysics at Harvard and...[he said] "a group of us would like to invite a group of artists to come and spend a couple days in a seminar," you know, to talk about mutual interests. So I was invited to put this together, which I did. And then they took us to see the computer. There was a room, and everybody there was wearing white coats, and they were cold, and we were cold, watching the computer. And all these cards and, you know, file cards, and I just stood there like a kid with my nose against the window. And it was so exciting. And I have no idea why.

Why is the computer so exciting? Computers are an immensely powerful platform for scientific exploration and discovery, and of course enable new forms of communication that are inducing intense social change and making new forms of cooperative politics possible. They are also like a drug, at least for some, that can induce an intense trance state and deep dissociation. The seduction of the computer can take precedence over hunger, pain, the presence of other people, daily responsibilities, and at times, over careful weighing of impacts and consequences. Even without the hypnotic effect of the computer, the draw of abstraction can be compelling. It reminds me of J.R. Oppenheimer's famous testimony on the creation of the atomic bomb: "When you see something that is technically sweet, you go ahead and do it and argue about what to do about it only after you've had your technical success. That is the way it was with the atomic bomb."[24]

If the decisions that decide what our world will be like are made without accountability by a few privileged experimenters in Europe and the United States, and they are made by doing whatever is technically sweet and worrying about the consequences later—or by doing what is technically sweet and seems like a good idea to the inventor—we are facing a future of great violence and injustice. (And it would be terribly sad if the greatest legacy of the 1960s turns out to be yet another form of self-destructive, addictive behavior.)

In hacker circles and other Petri dishes for cultural experimentation such as Burning Man, the word "do-ocracy" has become popular. It stands for an ethic of self-organization in which anyone who decides to do something is empowered to do it, and to make the decisions about how to do it. For instance, if I decide to build a temporary plumbing system for the Burning Man desert encampment, anyone who thinks it should be done differently has less say than I do because I'm the one who's putting the work into making it happen. This is a simple, powerful form of practical anarchy that works well for getting things done.

However, it doesn't work well for resolving conflicts between people who want different things to happen; it doesn't protect people who have less ability to do things because of unequal access to time, or to resources, or unequal physical ability; and it is no help to people who believe that certain things just shouldn't be done at all. It also happens to be the way technology is managed in the current world. The decisions whether to create a new technology are in the hands of the creators and their funders; anyone who has the time or resources can create or fund a new invention;

---

24 J.R. Oppenheimer, testifying in his defense in his 1954 security hearings, http://en.wikiquote.org/wiki/Robert_Oppenheimer.

and anyone who thinks it shouldn't happen, for instance because we don't want to give some maladjusted high-school kid the tools to create a renegade bacterium that will eat our entire biosphere, is just out of luck.

Do-ocracy is popular partly because it offers to fulfill the promises of Wikipedia and Linux, that we can make a better world together, all acting as equals, and throw off the chains of oppressive institutions. What is the alternative, anyway? Making laws against things? Making people get permission from some kind of central authority before they can learn things and use their creative spirit to try out new ideas? Social change movements on both the Left and the Right (and in other directions) agree on the need to devolve power downward and create horizontal forms of self-governance. It is important to address these problems in an antiauthoritarian way.

I believe that this is in fact a fundamental challenge of antiauthoritarian social movements. We must be able to offer a plausible way to hold people accountable for the damage they do. We have to have a way for those affected to participate in deliberation about what will be done to their communities. This may be a part of the ongoing project of understanding how communities manage commonly held resources—the biosphere is one of our largest commons—or it may be more usefully seen as simply a fundamental problem of self-governance. Humans are generally agreeable, and these problems may be largely solved by people becoming aware of the issues involved in their decisions, and by their becoming more directly connected to and aware of the communities impacted. We may do well to cultivate a general ethic of responsibility and accountability, so that people who violate the norm have to face the disapproval of their community. Overall, though, the problem is unsolved and must be addressed if we are to responsibly claim to provide a promise of a better world.

The technological social movement that Stewart Brand names as the "main legacy from the '60s" is powerful, liberatory, wildly successful, idealistic, and in some ways astounding, but it is at the same time deeply flawed, incomplete and dangerous. Its good parts are very good, and it can be an invaluable springboard to a much better social movement—one in which we continue to create entirely new forms of collaboration, sharing, democratization and bottom-up empowerment; establish new forms of solidarity and community; discover how to coordinate effectively on a global scale; create powerful, fluid horizontal network structures; and develop reliable processes of accountability that allow us to protect the things that we hold most sacred without surrendering the power of enforcement to an elite class of masters.

Many readers will have noticed by now that we've fallen into a kind of looking-glass world of politics here, in which "conservative" right-wing values include smashing the state, building a new world in the ashes of the old, and championing the liberal ideals of Enlightenment science and democracy. This contrasting, putatively "progressive" alternative is focused on conserving traditional values such as accountability, responsibility, and the integrity of existing communities and places. It's generally only free-market libertarians who insist that "Left" and "Right" are obsolete, but in this context of a clash between competing systems of radical antiauthoritarian values, it seems clear that the traditional dichotomy between rational, progressive Left versus traditional, religious Right is unhelpful at best.

There are many legacies of the '60s, and other generations' experiments in collective liberation. The pro-technoscientific social movements are only a few of the many seeds that were planted in the hippies' creative explosion. Their champions have gained a great deal of power, partly by denying the importance of the crucial work of their contemporaries that also continues: movement organizers, peace advocates, feminists, antiracists, spiritual syncretists, psychotherapists, consciousness expanders, alternative educators, science studies scholars, critics of Enlightenment, and pioneers in collective process.

Those less-exposed traditions are exactly what we need now, to fully embrace the challenges of reinventing the world. We need to turn our creativity and passion from simple techno-lust to the fuller and more satisfying challenges of developing effective ways to thrive together, care for each other, and realize our massive potential in a flourishing natural world and within peaceful, compassionate, fair social relations. Our "practical intellectuals" must not only be technically savvy, but also socially intelligent, humble, and able to listen to and take leadership from others who are different and have different needs and perspectives. We must make it possible for them to work and think within a functioning global community and be accountable to the communities that are affected by their work. The final impact of the '60s movements has yet to be determined, and if we are willing to take on the hard questions about justice and accountability, it can ultimately be much greater, more human, and part of a far more beautiful and livable future than it will be otherwise.

Caught on the Hop of History: Communes and Communards on the Canvas of '68

Michael Watts

> The "official story," whether its emphasis is moral or systemic, would thus present '68 as a plaything of history, a vanishing mediator, a patsy for the cunning of capitalist history.
>
> —Alberto Toscano, *Beginnings and Ends: For, Against and Beyond '68*

> On the one side, there remains the perennial trap of thinking old dilemmas can be out muscled by the luck of youth; on the other, the trap of thinking the future is doomed to be nothing more than the past; between them possibly, the space to invent.
>
> —Todd Gitlin, *The Sixties: Years of Hope, Days of Rage*

Was the commune movement in Northern California at heart nothing more than a flawed utopian gesture, youthful exuberance and middle-class infantilism masquerading as a viable alternative to 1960s consumer capitalism? Has the wider commune movement, from the vantage point of the twenty-first century, been obliterated by the neoliberal grand slam, its collective traces washed away by the riptides of modernity? If one believes in Perry Anderson's forbiddingly bleak assessment at the millennium, American capitalism asserted its primacy in such a fashion that "virtually the entire horizon of the '60s generation has been wiped away."[1] Was back-to-the-land communalism just one other expression of a

---

1   Perry Anderson, "Renewals," *New Left Review* 1 (2000): 10.

decade-long postwar delirium—the language is from Roger Scruton who saw in 1968 nothing more than "an unruly mob of self-indulgent middle-class hooligans...(full of) Marxist gobbledegook. I was disgusted by it, and thought there must be a way back to the defense of western civilization."[2] The '60s were, on this account, no more than a long decade of arrested development that refused to pass over into adulthood. To what extent was the communal and the back-to-the-land movements a chip off the same block? Was communalism part of a grand oedipal revolt destined for the trashcan of history, another in a long line of failed utopian projects?

Osha Neumann, founding member of Up Against the Wall Motherfuckers and famously described by a New York judge hearing his arrest case as "a cross between Rap Brown and Hitler," addresses these questions in his compelling memoir of the 1960s and 1970s.[3] By 1969, the Lower East Side of New York, stomping ground of the Motherfuckers, had begun to turn sour, partly due to violence and the growing presence of hard drugs on the streets, but mostly due to the acrimonious defections and splits within the group itself. The core of the Motherfuckers de-camped to New Mexico to hook up with the Alianza, but this proved short lived and Neumann ended up in 1970 at Black Bear commune where he lived for two years. Neumann's own revolutionary trajectory led him, in other words, to a flirtation with the communal movement. His short description of Black Bear Ranch reads very much as Scruton would have imagined it. Part-time work with the Forest Service helped keep the "col-lective pot" if not full, at least viable ("we had the expectation that we would take from the common pot what we needed, and pour into it what we could").[4] But his account, while "all good," is bleak and unforgiving. The dominant motif is almost entirely physical and bodily, which is to say largely sexual and excremental. Neumann's vivid description reads like the chronicle of a death foretold. The communal family too often bred abandonment, resentments and dissent. Everyone knew that "it wouldn't last forever," that "the white people would go off to claim their privilege" leaving the rest to fend for themselves. He concedes that the wealth—such as it was—was never really shared. Isolated and despon-dent, Neumann and his family left Black Bear in search of a place where

---

2   Roger Scruton, "Dispatches from a Turbulent Decade," *New Statesman* 127 (1998): 49.

3   Osha Neumann, *Up Against the Wall Motherfucker: Memoir of the '60s, with Notes for Next Time* (New York: Seven Stories Press, 2008).

4   Ibid., 136.

love of "motherfuckeresque politics of disruption and confrontation" might be better nurtured.[5] Not surprisingly, this proved to be Berkeley.

West of Eden tries to approach these same questions without condescension. In many cases the responses are from those who helped build and live on the Northern Californian communes themselves. Many of the contributors in the book think about the utopian impulses of communalism in a way that immediately distinguishes them from the anti-'60s ideologues and those for whom utopia connotes the death march of the twentieth century. There are indeed virulent forms of utopianism that afflict the modern age: the attempt to resurrect the Caliphate in the name of revolutionary Islam would be one. The psychotic phantasy that global free markets imposed from within and without could cure global poverty would be another. But the point surely is—to paraphrase Terry Eagleton— that in the same way that no sane person would propose disbanding the Girl Guides because of their failure to resolve problems in quantum physics or suggest that Henry Ford's preposterous attempt to construct Fordlandia in the middle of the Amazon would provide grounds for the total condemnation of capitalism, the record of the California communards cannot constitute grounds for the refutation of communal living.

In this regard, we can learn much from Terry Eagleton's discussions of Marxism's purportedly utopian failings. He returns to the flamboyant call of the 1960s: "Be realistic: demand the impossible!" As he points out, as a slogan its accuracy resides in the fact that what is realistically demanded to repair society is beyond the capabilities of the prevailing system, and in that sense is impossible: "But it is realistic to believe that the world could in principle be greatly improved. Those who scoff at the idea that major social change is possible are full-blown fantasists. The true dreamers are those who deny that anything more than piecemeal change can ever come about... Such types are always in danger of being caught on the hop of history."[6]

Eagleton's invocation of the slogan *par excellence* of Paris in 1968 offers, I think, a different vantage point from which one can assess the commune movement, that is to say to place it within the wider landscape of the 1960s (in all of its utopian complexity), and specifically in relation to the revolutionary moment of 1968. After all, what '68 represented—not simply in Berkeley or Berlin but globally—was a profound sense, to quote Eagleton once more, that "those sad, self-deceived characters who hallucinate that given more

5 Ibid., 139.
6 Terry Eagleton, *Why Marx Was Right* (New Haven: Yale University Press, 2011), 78.

time and greater effort capitalism will deliver a world of abundance for all" were utterly bankrupt, that the hard-headed pragmatism which sees capitalism's failures as regrettable accidents required a radical makeover. The communards caught the pragmatists on the hop of history. This, I believe, is the ground on which we can reflect upon the complex legacy of the great wave of commoning exemplified by the communards who struggled on Albion Ridge.

*

In January 1968, in the early hours of the morning of the third day of Tet (the Vietnamese New Year), Vietnamese liberation forces, across a front six hundred miles long, launched an assault on 140 major cities and provincial towns in South Vietnam. It was an auspicious beginning to the year. 1968 proved to be the *annus mirabilis* as *Time* magazine christened it, a year that defined and, in some ways, signaled the end of the 1960s. To glance through Tariq Ali's coffee-table book, *1968: Marching in the Streets*, is a salutary experience not only because it *is* a coffee-table book, rendered as such by a central figure in the British New Left, but also because it returns us to the twelve months of turmoil and bedlam that was '68. The year 1968 was, like 1848, a world historical moment. To use Ali's vernacular, it was "a year that those who lived through it, on either side of the political divide, will never forget."[7] With his customary bluntness and an ear for the *bon mot*, Abbie Hoffman put it thus: "Living in America I expect to get killed."[8] 1968 was the "year that rocked the world."[9]

In his chronicle of that year, Ronald Fraser noted an antiauthoritarianism that challenged "almost every shibboleth of Western society."[10] Yet for all its great merits, his is a parochial judgment, one which underestimates the global resonance of '68. It felt as if the Tet offensive detonated a series of explosions around the globe, all somehow linked together by some sort of inexorable, and often terrifying logic. The Vietnamese war, said Göran Therborn, has produced a "simultaneous multiplication and radicalization of resistance to it."[11] A final verdict on the legacy of the cataclysmic events of 1968 is surely not in, but nobody questions their gravity and historical significance. A simple, and very partial, historical

---

7   Tariq Ali and Susan Watkins, *1968: Marching in the Streets* (New York: The Free Press, 1998), 7.
8   Cited in Richard Avedon, *The Sixties* (New York: Random House, 1999), 4.
9   Mark Kurlansky, *1968: The Year That Rocked the World* (New York: Ballantine, 2004).
10 Ronald Fraser, *1968: A Student Generation in Revolt* (New York: Pantheon, 1988), 354.
11 Göran Therborn, "1968: From Saigon to Petrograd," *New Left Review* 48 (1999): 10.

inventory of that legendary year still retains its astonishing shock-value: the Tet offensive and the massacre at My Lai; the assassinations of M.L. King Jr. and Robert Kennedy; the May *événements* in Paris (including the strike of ten million French workers); "Socialism with a Human Face" in Prague, Warsaw and Belgrade; the Soviet invasion of Czechoslovakia; the high-tide of the Chinese Cultural Revolution; the Medellin convention that launched Liberation Theology; students' rebellions in Tokyo, Delhi, Berkeley, Rio and Berlin (indeed just about *everywhere*); the massacre of Mexican students in Tlatelolco Square; Regis Debray's imprisonment in Bolivia (and marriage in jail); growing turmoil and civil strife in Ireland and Palestine; the debacle surrounding the Democratic Convention in Chicago; the so-called hot winter in Pakistan (and later in Italy); the early stirrings of feminist protest surrounding the Miss America Contest in Atlantic City; the collapse of the British pound; the first rumblings of a major economic crisis; and, lest we forget, the election of Richard Nixon and the move across Washington, from the Pentagon to the World Bank, of a beleaguered and morally contorted Robert McNamara.

Just to blink was to miss something, said Christopher Hitchens.[12] *Fortune* magazine, surveying the events of spring 1968 judged, with good reason, that American society had been "shaken to its roots."[13]

And then there was the pure spectacle of it all, what James Miller in *Democracy Is in the Streets* called the "carnivalesque atmosphere of confusion."[14] Bakhtinian revelry flooded the streets, calling forth a new politics of display, a desire to do politics differently. Very differently indeed: Abbie Hoffman, Allen Ginsberg and company attempted to levitate the Pentagon; the Yippies caused havoc on Wall Street by throwing money onto the floor of the exchange; the Strasbourg Situationists denounced boredom; the Dutch Provos created pandemonium in Amsterdam by releasing thousands of chickens in rush-hour traffic; the Diggers declared love a commodity; and Ed Sanders and the Fugs marched on Prague to masturbate on the Soviet tanks.

The events of '68 were revolutionary not because governments were, or might have been, overthrown but because a defining characteristic of revolution is that it abruptly *calls into question existing society and presses*

---

12 Christopher Hitchens, "The Children of '68," *Vanity Fair* (June 1998): 101.
13 David Horowitz, "The Fate of Midas," in *All We Are Saying: The Philosophy of the New Left*, ed. Arthur Lothstein (New York: Capricorn Books, 1970), 185.
14 Ali and Watkins, *Streets*, 5.

people into action. Sixty-eight was, to quote Saint-Just, a revolutionary theorist of an earlier epoch, a "public moment," an instance in which the social contract is simultaneously reviewed and reconstituted through action. Walter Benjamin described revolution as the moment—a moment of danger—when the human species traveling in the train of history reaches for the emergency brake. It is a metaphor which retains its allure.

The fact that the jury on '68, indeed the '60s in general, is still out more than forty years on must surely turn to some degree on the enormous complexity, perhaps the incomprehensible diversity, of what was a global insurrection. Some commentators, such as Paul Berman, see the events of 1968 as sufficiently disparate that only their unexpectedness and drama provide a (rather spurious) sense of coherence and unity. In China, students and workers were lodged in the vanguard of the Great Proletarian Cultural Revolution instigated by Mao to block the "capitalist roaders"; in Mexico, students bravely protested the autocratic political monopoly of the Institutional Revolutionary Party (PRI) and were savaged as a consequence; in the United States, the imperialist war in southeast Asia, civil rights struggles and the alienated culture of consumer capitalism supplied fuel for the fire of personal emancipation. Prague, Paris, Tokyo, Addis Ababa, Berlin, Calcutta, and Caracas were different yet again. But everyone, wherever they were, sought alternatives.

The communal movement was one such alternative, and one with a deep history, as contributions to this book make clear. It was a complex space of invention and experiment. Like the '60s in general, communalism stood in a transverse relation to the Left, and its forms of invention and experiment were cultural, musical, architectural, social, agronomic, sexual, and organizational. Communalism was a long march through the institutions of gender, family, and relations of production—in short, modernity itself. The events of the era, and of 1968 in particular, *were* a disruption, a derangement of the complacent bourgeois dream of "unproblematic production, of everyday life as the bureaucratic society."[15] The sweeping *political* challenges posed during the '60s, to say nothing of the innovations of the New Left, constitute a veritable treasury whose present dilapidation impoverishes us.[16] Yet so much of what the radicals and activists rendered

---

15   Sohnya Sayres, Anders Stephanson, Stanley Aronowitz, and Frederic Jameson, eds. *The Sixties, Without Apology* (Minneapolis: University of Minnesota Press, 1984), 2.

16   Richard A. Couto, *Making Democracy Work Better: Mediating Structures, Social Capital, and the Democratic Prospect* (Chapel Hill: University of North Carolina Press, 1999).

as a new politics, an "anti-institutional struggle...which transforms the publics of classical bourgeois society into *critical publics*,"[17] has become so wrapped in cant and the worst sort of revisionism, so clouded by the admitted excesses and confusion of the times, so discredited by the defeats and reversals that followed the turmoil of 1968, and so silenced by the perils of nostalgia (in which the new generation of activists are rightly loathe to participate), that it has become impossibly difficult to reclaim what was, and indeed what remains, so radical and relevant about the '60s.

Revisionist histories of the '60s written in the decades after '68 produced what Julie Stephens calls "the death narrative": a revolutionary and emancipatory project dashed on the shoals of political immaturity and idealism.[18] What little critical writing on the Californian communes exists has often recapitulated this sense of immaturity mixed with failed idealism. The fact that so many of the '60s generation themselves retreated from, or were reticent to return to, the period meant that the territory was unfortunately ceded to the public intellectuals of the New Right—Roger Kimball, David Frum, David Horowitz, Gertude Himmelfarb—and their formidable publishing apparatuses, for whom the '60s was an object of reproach, marking the decline of just about everything.[19] The mere mention of the '60s, and the counterculture and the New Left, still arouses strong emotions on both sides of the Atlantic. No other event in American life—not the 1930s or World War II—has been continually capable of calling leading politicians to account (did you fight, did you flee, did you inhale?). For Allan Bloom, the self-appointed arbiter of American culture and taste, the '60s ideologues were crypto-fascists, as destructive as the Nazis. A countercultural bacillus infected and permeated society with all sorts of new ideas and generated, as a consequence, a culture of confrontation. "Enlightenment in America," Bloom opined, "came close to breathing its last during the '60s."[20] Yet, none of the '60s anxieties and concerns have receded of course (how could they?); the ur-texts of 1968—penned by the likes of Cohn-Bendit, Debord, Oglesby, Fanon—retain their exhilaration, excitement and freshness. Public moments never recede.

---

17 Carlo Donolo, "Politics Redefined," in Lothstein, *All We Are Saying*, 57.

18 Julie Stephens, *Anti-Disciplinary Politics: Sixties Radicalism and Postmodernism* (Cambridge, UK: Cambridge University Press, 1998), 4.

19 Rebecca E. Klatch, *A Generation Divided: The New Left, the New Right, and the 1960s* (Berkeley: University of California Press, 1999).

20 Allan Bloom, *The Closing of the American Mind* (New York: Simon & Schuster, 1988), 56.

The year 1968 marks, then, a sort of condensation of the convulsive transformations incubated between the late 1950s and the oil crisis, the economic recession and the dollar devaluation of the early 1970s. It is a period that achieves a kind of coherence across political philosophy, cultural production, economic cycles, and political practice. Johnson's decision to bomb North Vietnam, Dylan's decision to go electric at Newport and the appearance of Pynchon's *Crying of Lot 49* were somehow all of a piece. Arthur Marwick's bulky encomium of the period, *The Sixties*, provides a shopping list of the distinctive features of the decade: new subcultures; the growing influence of youth; new forms of popular culture (TV/music); massive improvements in material life; racial, class and family upheavals; new forms of self-expression especially through fashion, civil and personal rights; multiculturalism; and the dialectical oscillation, as he sees it, between a liberal "measured judgment" and extreme reaction. The communal experience produced its own subcultural forms and iterations.

From the vantage point of the Euro-Atlantic economies, the '60s movements contained a number of striking paradoxes. First, their anti-materialism emerged at the very apogee of a stunning postwar consumer boom. John Updike's marvelous poem "Superman" captures both the suffocating material abundance and the alienation produced by American Fordism at full throttle:

> I drive my car to the supermarket
> The way I take is superhigh
> A superlot is where I park it
> And Supersuds are what I buy

Secondly, the '60s attack on liberalism occurs at the very zenith of the Great Society. And not least, the shock troops of the insurrection were the professional classes, the intellectuals and students—conspicuously not an insurgent working-class (the national strike in France in 1968 notwithstanding). To put it crudely, one might say that it was the social rather than the economic contradictions of consumer capitalism—what was referred to then as authoritarian or repressive capitalism—which burst into the open.

These paradoxes are part of the indisputable sense of division and rupture that pervades the period. In this sense Maurice Isserman and Michael Kazin in *America Divided* are right to draw a parallel between the 1960s and the 1860s—that is to say, with the American Civil War. Norman Mailer's brilliant "novel," *The Armies of the Night*, based on his participation in the 1967 march on the Pentagon, made the same point.[21] The 1960s plunged Americans "back into anguished scrutiny of the meaning of their most fundamental beliefs and institutions. ...They reacted with varying degrees of wisdom and folly...all those things that make us human."[22] Virtually all of the personal experiences recounted in *West of Eden* engage with the sense of scrutiny—a reexamination of the human—conjured up by Isserman and Kazin.

Ideas, practices, and events of momentous import are always fought over and contested but there is the ever-present danger that they become, as Beatrice Webb once said of Adam Smith's ideas, "the gospel of the employer" (she actually said, "By what silent revolution of events could the scientific expression against class tyranny and oppression of the many by the few be changed into the Employers Gospel of the nineteenth century").[23] The 1960s in particular tend to travel poorly. By what silent revolution, then, could they be transformed into the neoliberal gospel of the 1980s, into Marwick's *apercu* that, from its very inception, 1968 was protocapitalist, "imbued with the entrepreneurial, profit-making ethic,"[24] or into Mazower's judgment in *Dark Continent* that 1968 "created a fragmented and bitterly dogmatic Left, tempted by violence and unwilling to comprehend the scale of capitalism's triumph."[25]

The death narrative achieves its final victory by positing what Carl Boggs called a "total break" as popular struggles purportedly came to an explosive and sudden halt between 1968 and 1970.[26] Perhaps this revisionism explains a particular form of '60s silencing and forgetting. It is as if 1968 is the buried child, to use the title of a Sam Shepard (another '60s man) play, the product of an excess, of a surplus libido best forgotten. When it does reappear it is trivialized. Hollywood offered up its own celluloid analysis of Abbie Hoffman and the '60s in the appalling film by Robert Greenwald entitled *Steal This Movie*. History has not been kind to the 1960s.

---

21 Norman Mailer, *The Armies of the Night: History as a Novel, the Novel as History* (New York: Penguin Books, 1968).

22 Maurice Isserman and Michael Kazin, *America Divided: The Civil War of the Sixties* (New York: Oxford University Press, 2000), 12.

23 Cited in Emma Rothchild, "Adam Smith and Conservative Economics," *Economic History Review* 45 (1992): 88.

24 Arthur Marwick, *The Sixties: Cultural Transformation in Britain, France, Italy and the United States, c. 1958 - c. 1974* (London: Oxford University Press, 1998).

25 Mark Mazower, *Dark Continent* (New York: Knopf, 1998), 319.

26 Carl Boggs, "Rethinking the Sixties Legacy," in *Social Movements : Critiques, Concepts, Case Studies*, ed. Stanford Lyman (New York: New York University Press, 1994).

What characterizes writing on the '60s is a curious combination of defeat, disorder and deviancy.[27] On the one side (the Left) stands a *failed political project* and on the other (the Right) stand the decay and depravity of a *successful cultural revolution*. The '60s hold a special place for the neoconservatives not only because it drove them to the Right (indeed the '60s *launched* the New Right) but also because it marked the loss of civility and the "gradual slouch toward Gomorrah" as Judge Robert Bork described the period.[28]

But even those who identify in some way with Left while recognizing that the 1960s incubated something healthy and politically worthy (feminism, sexual tolerance, environmentalism, civil rights), are also quite disillusioned and sad. Marshall Berman, in his stunning Faustian account of the '60s, saw the street activism as a "mirror image of the hotshot stock operators" on Wall Street: high risk, extravagant and built on flimsy foundations. Michael Kazin in *The Populist Persuasion* (he was a '68er himself) says the 1960s radicals tore off the ideological blinders worn by past friends of the people and "donned some thick ones of their own," and that the movement "discredited the old order without laying the political foundation of a new one."[29] Isserman and Kazin's final verdict resonates with many of the former denizens of the New Left: the '68ers were "flawed but earnest idealists."[30] Even Regis Debray, *the* revolutionary theorist of the Left Bank, the architect of *foco* guerila theory and liberated zones, and someone who might be expected to cast a nostalgic glance toward the *soixante-huitards*, now claims that 1968 stabilized class relations; it was, to use his language, a "giant servo-mechanism" that accomplished "the opposite of what [it] intended."[31] Deluded Maoism produced, in short, the free market.

And for those liberals like Arthur Marwick who can see something good in just about anything, the solution is to forget politics, or at least organized politics, altogether and see the '60s like Himmelfarb and

---

27 Gerard DeGroot, *The Sixties Unplugged: A Kaleidoscopic History of a Disorderly Decade* (Cambridge, MA: Harvard University Press, 2008).

28 Cited in Roger Kimball, *The Long March: How the Cultural Revolution of the 1960s Changed America* (San Francisco: Encounter Books, 2001), 14.

29 Michael Kazin, *The Populist Persuasion: An American History* (New York: Basic Books, 1995), 218.

30 Isserman and Kazin, *America Divided*, 12.

31 Regis Debray, "A Modest Contribution to the Rites and Ceremonies of the Tenth Anniversary." *New Left Review* 113 (1978): 51.

Kimball as a cultural revolution but as a redemptive one, echoing Philip Larkin's great poem "Annus Mirabilis":

> Sexual intercourse began
> In nineteen sixty three
> (Which was rather late for me)—
> Between the end of the Chatterley ban
> And the Beatles' first LP

But here, too, the '60s came up short. Emancipatory rhetoric succumbed to a "preoccupation with every nuance of the private psyche," a culture and politics of consumption, most especially of an encounter culture of "consumption of narcissistic contemplation, personal selfhood and the stroking of the victim role."[32] A diagnosis of failure is, of course, perfectly understandable because 1968 proved to be a sort of climacteric. Within a few years, the bubble of revolutionary rhetoric had burst. All the signs were reversed, said Perry Anderson in *The Origins of Postmodernity*, "all the political dreams of the '60s were snuffed out."[33] The May revolt was absorbed without trace as political identities splintered, the Czech spring and socialist reformism were smashed, the luster of the guerrilla movements tarnished, and the flashes of labor unrest in Europe dimmed by the late 1970s. Soon enough, the vitality of the students' movements had either soured or drifted into violence and terror signaled by the Weathermen, the Red Army Faction, Front Line, and the Red Brigades. It is to be expected that the guerrillas fared no better despite the continued roar of revolutionary overthrow during the 1970s in Nicaragua, Iran, and elsewhere.

But what of the alternative notion that 1968 was a harbinger, a great "rehearsal"? The explosions of 1968 and their aftermath can be interpreted as symptom of the fact that the system is approaching its historical asymptote. The year 1968, with its successes and failures, was thus a prelude, better a rehearsal, of things to come.[34] The year 1968 almost looks as though it had been designed, noted Eric Hobsbawm in his tenth anniversary remarks, "to serve as some sort of *signpost*" (emphasis added).[35] If

---

32 David Burner, *Making Peace with the Sixties* (Princeton, NJ: Princeton University Press, 1995), 222–23.

33 Perry Anderson, *The Origins of Postmodernity* (London: Verso, 1998), 91.

34 Giovanni Arrighi, Terence K. Hopkins, and Immanuel Wallerstein, *Antisystemic Movements* (London: Verso, 1989), 110–11. See also Daniel Singer, *Prelude to Revolution: France in May 1968* (New York: Hill & Wang, 1970).

35 Eric Hobsbawm, "1968: A Retrospective," *Marxism Today* (May 1978): 130.

1968 was indeed a rehearsal or a signpost of things to come, what exactly was it a rehearsal for, what was it signaling? Was the student unrest anything more than the mere reflection of a postwar generation coming of age? To what extent did it prepare the ground for the antistate neoliberalism of the 1980s, or postmodern political disengagement?[36] Did this rebelliousness achieve anything more, as Donald Sassoon suggests in his magisterial history of socialism, than the weakening of the traditional Left without leading to any alternative?[37] Or do we conclude, with Paul Berman, that the "insurrection in middle-class customs" was a prelude for liberal democracy's finest hour?[38] Suddenly it was obvious that the authentic political revolution of our era was now, not then. For Berman, the '60s were a way station for the real revolution that came later: the revolutionary exhilaration in 1989 and the end of history.

Berman's account is, I think, at once too easily fooled by the powers of hindsight, and too inattentive to the labyrinthine reverberations, and the long-term accommodations and disruptions of revolutionary change.[39] What such accounts studiously ignore is a sense of what was *built*, what German New leftist Rudi Dutschke, echoing Gramsci, called "the long march through the institutions."[40] The year 1968 bequeathed a "working against the established institutions while working within them," a project to build counterinstitutions and liberated zones, as Dutschke put it in his electrifying address to the International Congress on Vietnam in West Berlin in 1968.[41] It is to the politics (and not to culture narrowly construed) of this long march that one must necessarily turn to grasp the complex meanings of the political repertory that was to follow "the great rehearsal." There are good reasons for seeing the communal movement as part and parcel of building counterinstitutions.

How then might the history of 1968 inform a reading of the communal movement of the period? In the first place, it must be understood

---

36 Alex Callinicos, *Against Postmodernism: A Marxist Critique* (Cambridge: Polity Press, 1989).
37 Donald Sassoon, *One Hundred Years of Socialism: The West European Left in the Twentieth Century* (New York: New Press. 1996), 406.
38 Paul Berman, *A Tale of Two Utopias: The Political Journey of the Generation of 1968* (New York: W.W. Norton, 1996), 19.
39 Immanuel Wallerstein, "Antisysemtic Movements," in *Transforming the Revolution*, eds. Samir Amin, Giovanni Arrighi, Andre Gunder Frank, and Immanuel Wallerstein (New York: Monthly Review Press, 1990)
40 Cited in Todd Gitlin, *The Sixties: Years of Hope, Days of Rage* (New York: Bantam, 1987), 422.
41 Herbert Marcuse, *Counterrevolution and Revolt* (Boston: Beacon Books, 1972), 55.

as a truly global phenomenon; there was hardly any region of the world, noted Hobsbawm, "which was not marked by the spectacular and dramatic events of 1968."[42] According to a survey in *Le Monde,* over seventy countries had major student actions during that year. Between October 1967 and July 1968, there were over two thousand incidents worldwide of student protest alone; if one were to add the related worker actions and other nonstudent demonstrations each country in the world would, on average, have had over twenty-five "incidents" over the nine-month period.[43] But 1968 was global in another regard, namely, in the committed internationalism of the movements that were indisputably multicultural in orientation and transnational in aspiration. The Parisian communards were internationalist through and through. Parisian *enragé* Daniel Cohn-Bendit was, after all, a German Jew; the Situationists certainly neither knew nor encouraged any national identification; and whatever one may say of the New Left, it was never parochial in outlook. Cross-border networks, transnational alliances and the global traffic in ideas—activists were often reading the same foundational texts by Franz Fanon, Herbert Marcuse, Che Guevara, and Mao Zedong—drew London, Mexico, Prague, Paris, and Delhi into a revolutionary maelstrom. The year 1968 provides a vivid illustration of "activism beyond borders." The American women's movement inspired European counterparts; festivals and protest brought students together across borders; the Polish Commandos were afforded a heroic status by many among the New Left. It is revealing that Vaclav Havel was at Columbia in the heady days of the 1968 occupation. Cross-border traffic in ideas—1968 was without precedent as regards its participants reading and writing books—was matched by a footloose revolutionary vanguard, in tandem generating something like a radical diaspora unprecedented in the twentieth century.[44]

The Vietnam War functioned as a tremendous galvanizing force in the 1960s, a sort of global catalyst. Göran Therborn, writing in the *New Left Review,* noted that "the dialectic of the war has transferred the ideology of the guerillas into the culture of the metropolis."[45] He might well have pointed to how opposition to the war stimulated student movements in, for

---

42 Hobsbawm, "A Retrospective," 131.
43 George Katsiaficas, *The Imagination of the New Left: A Global Analysis of 1968* (Boston: South End Press, 1987).
44 Eric Hobsbawm, *Revolutionaries* (London: Quartet Books, 1977).
45 Therborn, "1968."

example, Belgium, Thailand, and Sweden, and they in turn with the assistance of the mass media ("the whole world is watching"), helped make the events resolutely global. Moreover, the affairs of 1968 unfolded at a crucial juncture in the Cold War that had the effect of linking national and world affairs in radically new ways. As a result of the strategic reverberations within the global geopolitical system, "fundamental shifts on the local, national or global level resonated with and grew out of each other."[46]

The centrality of colonial wars in two of the most important crucibles of '60s radicalism, France and the United States, suggests a fourth sense of '60s globalism, what Jameson calls "politicocultural models" and the resistance to "wars aimed precisely at stemming the new revolutionary forces in the Third World."[47] Third-worldism, for better or worse, put on offer the "heroic guerrilla" (the year of the heroic guerrilla, as Fidel Castro dubbed it in his 1968 New Year speech), a mobile and transnational figure if ever there was one. For revolutionary theorist Regis Debray (1967), the guerrilla *foco* (operation) was so mobile as to be beyond geography narrowly construed, occupying the space between town and country, operating as it were in the wilderness of the Sierra Mestra. Cuba, China, Vietnam, and the postcolonial African states provided the model of radical practice for the New Left and in this way 1968 helped shatter the Eurocentric idea that the advanced proletariat of the West socialism as a "gift" to the "backward" masses of the periphery. The third world was formative for not only the '60s New Left, but also for those of the October tradition and, as Eric Hobsbawm again reminds us, to the entire radical community who needed something more than social security and rising real wages as the pillars of the New Jerusalem.[48] So often it was to the peripheral other—Ho, Mao, Fidel—that the 1968ers turned for their reference points, their heroes, and their hopes. Third-worldism corroborated not only a sense of revolutionary internationalism, but also confirmed that there were models of revolution and liberation outside, and beyond, both the Communist and Social Democratic traditions.

Finally, the 1960s were inextricably part of a long boom that simultaneously transformed and coupled the world in fundamentally new

---

46 Carole Fink, Philipp Gassert, and Detlef Junker, *1968: The World Transformed* (Cambridge, UK: Cambridge University Press, 1998), 2.
47 Frederic Jameson, *The Ideologies of Theory*, vol. 2 (Minneapolis, MN: University of Minnesota Press, 1988), 180.
48 Eric Hobsbawm, *The Age of Extremes* (London: Pantheon, 1994), 437.

ways. The '60s, noted Jameson, was the period when capital was "in full dynamic and innovative expansion."[49] When Eric Hobsbawm in *The Age of Extremes* characterizes the period as "the most rapid and dramatic revolution in human affairs to which history has record," he is of course referring to the extension of capitalist industrialization to large portions of the globe.[50] New clusters of capitalism merged in Latin America, northeast Asia and elsewhere; indeed the defining attributes of the original industrialization in northwest Europe—proletarianization, urbanization, commodification—now became "a global experience."[51] A common ancestry in industrial modernity underlay the "common cause" from which the wellspring of oppositional energies issued forth.[52] Opposition to racial, patriarchal and economic exploitation, deepening the concept of freedom, enlarging the base of radicalism and revolution, the extension of the democratic process, and an emphasis on direct action: these were the defining expressions of a global New Left.[53] Freedom, justice, and self-determination—a complete disaffection with "the system"—resonated deeply between East and West, North, and South.

If '68 was unequivocally global, it was irreducibly local too. A number of commentators have noted national differences but the fact remains that in an array of locations—from Prague to Peking, from Cairo to Cape Town, from Berkeley to Berlin—each movement possessed a distinctive *local* identity within the circumference of a global wave of New Left protest. Articulation, a term I have taken from Stuart Hall that refers to the simultaneous rendering of an identity (say communard or hippie) and the linking of that identity to a political project (commoning, self-management, participatory democracy), lends itself well to the geographical interpolation of multiple 1968s.[54] Precisely how geography and articulation produced local inflections of '68 can be seen by briefly reflecting upon the cases of Japan, India, and the UK.

In Japan, for example, the 1968 student actions grew from *shimin* (citizen) movements of the 1960s. So-called Anpo movements were pre-

---

49 Jameson, *Ideologies*, 186.
50 Hobsbawm, *Age of Extremes*, 286.
51 Alex Callinicos, *Social Theory: A Historical Introduction* (New York: New York University Press, 1999), 258.
52 The language is deployed by Fink, Gassert, and Junker, *1968*, 3.
53 Katsiaficas, *Imagination*, 23–27.
54 Stuart Hall, "When Was the Postcolonial?" in editors, *The Postcolonial Question: Common Skies, Divided Horizons*, eds. Iain Chambers and Lidia Curti (London: Routledge, 1996).

cipitates of the U.S.-Japan Security Treaty which granted to the United States the right to intervene in the event of domestic unrest. A combination of Cold War politics and the dubious legitimacy of U.S. hegemony in the region produced a violent internal struggle between ruling conservative and opposition parties which in turn stimulated a whole raft of new social movements. Anpo simultaneously met up with four other '60s actions: the anti–Vietnam War movement (*Beheiren*), environmentalism (dating back to the Minamata poisoning), farmers' struggles (most notably in relation to the Narita Airport) and the communist and Trotskyist student movements which grew up around the famous Uno Kozo school of Japanese Marxism.

In India, 1968 was ushered in by a riot in Connaught Place in Delhi, part of a growing student mobilization during the 1960s whose high-water marks were 1966 and 1970. Much of this activity was explicitly seen as an attack on "comprador capitalists" and on a deeply institutionalized and bureaucratic Congress Party pursuing its staid Nehruvian socialist path. If Mao and cultural questions figured prominently in these movements, they were nonetheless diverse enough to include anti-English instruction in Rajasthan, and anti-Hindi attacks by Tamil students in Mysore. While the Indian movements were national in scope, they were especially active in Bengal around an increasingly fragmented Communist movement. Yet, in the Indian case, it was peasant insurgents that were to prove decisive, giving rise to the Naxalite guerilla movement (aided by Maoist militants from Calcutta) which drew inspiration from the nineteenth-century Indian *jacqueries*, from the 1940s rural insurgencies, and from the political successes of Marxist parties in Kerala during the 1960s.

In Britain, the New Left, which had its origins in the 1950s in the fallout from the Hungarian invasion and the Campaign for Nuclear Disarmament, encompassed three major political trends: dissident communism based on nineteenth-century native radical traditions, independent socialism, and theoretical Marxism of a continental European persuasion.[55] Each contributed to different strands within the New Left (socialist humanism, Marxist culturalism, workers' control), and intersected with a number of ideas of peculiar British inflection and origin

---

55 Lin Chun, *The British New Left* (Edinburgh: Edinburgh University Press, 1996); M. Kenney, *The First New Left: British Intellectuals After Stalin* (London: Wishart, 1994); Gregory Elliot, *Perry Anderson: The Merciless Laboratory of History* (Minneapolis: University of Minnesota Press, 1998).

(for example, R.D. Laing's psychoanalysis and Hegelian existentialism). The Vietnam War engaged a youthful anti-imperialist movement but the student movement was shallow and in many respects unimportant. The "May Day Manifesto" of 1968, drafted by Raymond Williams, E.P. Thompson and others associated with the *New Left Review*, has a very different tenor from comparable manifestos written in Paris (The "Amnesty of Blinded Eyes") or the United States (the "Port Huron Statement").

One could go on of course. What matters, I believe, is that in each of these places the practice of commoning and back-to-the-land movements were among the many paths taken toward building alternatives. It goes without saying that much of this local history has been ignored, passed over or simply lost (is this any less the case in the United States?). The key point is that Black Bear, Morning Star, the Hog Farm, and New Buffalo had their sister communities around the globe, each colored and shaped by local culture, politics and civil society.

Jean-Paul Sartre asserted that 1968 demanded "the enlargement of the field of the possible." It unleashed a polemical and practical struggle—a wild leap of imagination, as Oglesby put it—around the very constitution of the political. The purpose of the '60s, says French historian Herve Hamon, was "to change life in the social arena, to distrust belonging to the State, including the deadly closures that inevitably issue from professional politics."[56] The '60s addressed issues studiously ignored by the dominant political tradition: the limits of reason, the meanings of personal emancipation, and the unconscious origins of the desire of domination, participatory democracy and self-management.

Insofar as the public sphere was compelled to take account of private lives—to enlarge the space of the political—the 1960s were in some senses deeply individualist and libertarian ("Why don't we do it in the road?"), and it is to be expected that the populist elements within these discourses were articulated in quite disparate forms of political projection. Rebecca Klatch's book *A Generation Divided* shows precisely that these libertarian currents produced in the United States the birth of a New Left *and* a New Right— with similar sorts of trajectories. Young Americans for Freedom (YAF) and Students for a Democratic Society (SDS) were both born in 1960, each harbored a hostility to the Vietnam War and to the state, and both disintegrated in similar ways in 1969. A desire to "control one's own life" contained

---

56 Hervé Hamon and Patrick Rotman, *Génération, Tome 1: Les années de rêve* (Paris: Editions du Seuil, 1987), 11.

a radical individualism susceptible, when circumstances changed, to a neoconservative subversion by the likes of Mrs. Thatcher or Mr. Reagan. Robin Blackburn lamented, in his reflections on Britain, "Instead of controlling your own place of work it became a questioning of owning your own house."[57] Some of the chapters in *West of Eden* point to the sorts of radical individualism which attended the day-to-day operations of some of the communes. Surely we should not be at all surprised by this.

And yet in their inclusiveness, the 1968 movements were a *cri de coeur* against the world system in which Old Left and Old Right had both failed. They gave impetus to new sorts of activism across the political spectrum in which distrust of authority, individual freedom, decentralization, and antistatism were all constitutive of doing politics differently. This was as true for ornery students in North America, whose anticapitalism was suffused with a critique of a suffocating parliamentary politics, as it was for their Eastern European comrades who wished to reform socialism and push the boundaries of human and political rights.

If the '60s inspired, to use Daniel Cohn-Bendit's turn of phrase, "a radical democratic tradition," it immediately has to be said that there was no single mode of political practice corresponding to such a tradition.[58] The communes were of course one expression. But what distinguished the movements were their multiple and hybrid forms. To oversimplify matters greatly, three salient anticapitalist expressions were evident within this radical democratic opening: the *Marxist* (seen, for example, in Trotskyist Parisian *groupuscules*, some of the British New Left organizations and postcolonial guerrilla movements); the *social democratic* (for example, Charter 77, many of the socialist dissidents, the reformist student and feminist movements such as SDS, and some democracy-orientated third world antinationalist movements); and the *anarchist* (the Situationists, the Diggers, Up Against the Wall Motherfuckers). Specific political issues—feminism, the environment, race, disarmament—cut across these broad movements, making for enormously complex political hybrids, crossovers and interconnections. Furthermore they differed, often dramatically, both in their style of politics—the antidisciplinary politics (no leadership, no platform, no organizations) of, say, the Diggers as opposed to the vanguardism of some of the extreme Left *groupuscules*—and in their organizational forms and tactics. Conflicts

57 Cited in Fraser, *1968*, 364.
58 Ibid., 361.

between them, needless to say, could be ferocious (memorably between the Diggers and the mainstream of SDS), and they often fragmented or imploded during the '70s. In ideological terms, the communal movements contained complex hybrids of some or all of these sentiments, and in certain cases represented an alternative to them (for example, a spiritual alternative to what was perceived as the coarse materialism of a Marxist project).

Yet they all took seriously the idea of a democratic deficit, a call for a popular radicalism so to say. Its emancipatory impulses were expressed through forms of direct action, through "antidisciplinary politics," through new social movements and the creation of new community organizations and civic institutions.[59]

Guy Debord, who had little sympathy either for third-worldism or many of the New Left homilies, famously noted that "the problem is not that people live more or less poorly; but that they live in a way that is always beyond their control."[60] And it seems that in seeking to extend control, the movements took up, sometimes in defeat and sometimes by default, Dutschke's call to march through the institutions; to question cultural hegemony; to repeal repressive and authoritarian practices; and to render political those domains that were traditionally seen to be beyond politics. The point, said the Situationists, was to live instead of devising a lingering death—there is a resonant echo here in many of the communards' voices. And it is to the new political practices, to the new organizations created (as much as old institutions they attempted to reform), and to the enlarged role of civil society that the '60s legacy still speaks. Hilary Wainwright puts all this nicely into perspective: "1968 led us to see that power comes through building organizations at the base rather than restricting our political paths to the established institutions... These sorts of transformations need new forms of political power."[61]

We now take this complex mix of civic, popular-participatory and extraparliamentary politics for granted, but perhaps we should not. The '60s were central to this way of doing politics and as such they did not so much stop in defeat as "disappear" underground, working on and through institutions, networks and new organizations, building in their polyp-like activity a veritable reef of oppositional practice. Wini Brienes, for example,

---

59 Stephens, *Anti-Disciplinary Politics.*
60 Cited in Anselm Jappe, *Guy Debord* (Berkeley: University of California Press, 1999), 158.
61 Cited in Fraser, *1968,* 364.

has charted the affinities between the '60s activists and all manner of 1970s and 1980s community organizing in the United States.[62] But the genealogy holds for Latin America where military rule forced former revolutionaries into squatter movements, indigenous peoples' struggles, and rural activism, as much as for the western European autonomist movements that sprung up in the 1970s (and indeed which still flourish today).[63] Neither should we be surprised that the road from personal liberation to community organizing and direct action, the long march from self-determination to associative and deliberative democracy, took the social and cultural sphere *as* politics.[64] These notions were always embedded in communal movements, whether or not they were in any way realized.

How might one summarize the place of the communes and the Californian communards on this larger canvas and in relation to the events of '68? First of all, the communes were utterly inseparable from the turmoil and social-political struggles of the 1960s. Precisely because the '60s contained the birth of both a new Right and a new Left, these tendencies were not surprisingly contained within the communal movement itself. It would be far too reductive to see the call to go commoning or "back to the land" as particular expressions of an emergent new Left, but it is hard to conceive of a Morning Star or Black Bear outside of the emancipatory impulses informing the environmental, feminist, cultural and antiwar movements, and more generally without reference to the deep political frustrations emanating from American Fordism. Second, communes by definition demand the construction of counterinstitutions, new and often untried practices of collective organization, self-management, and deliberative democracy on a small scale. The commune was of course not the only crucible within which these experiments and new politics were tried, yet it remains true that the legacies and lessons of the communal experience have been much less appreciated and attended to than other forms of extraparliamentary politics and civic activism. Finally, placing communes

---

62 Wini Brienes, *Community and Organization in the New Left, 1962-1968: The Great Refusal* (New York: Praeger, 1982).

63 Jorge Castañeda, *Utopia Unarmed*: The Latin American Left After the Cold War (New York: Knopf, 1993); George Katsiaficas, *The Subversion of Politics: European Autonomous Social Movements and the Decolonization of Everyday Life* (Atlantic Heights, NJ: Humanities Press, 1997).

64 Joshua Cohen and Joel Rogers, *Associations and Democracy* (London: Verso, 1995); Paul Hirst, *From Statism to Pluralism: Democracy, Civil Society And Global Politics* (London: University College Press, 1997).

in the ambit of struggles and conflicts within American capitalism drives home the important point that the construction and defense of alternatives, as well as forms of commoning are far from exhausted. This is not simply because there are new generations of communards embarking upon their own paths in Northern California (and elsewhere), but more profoundly because the deadly solicitations of the marketplace and of competitive capitalism constantly replenish the well from which communalism draws its strength and from which it drinks so deeply.

Further Reading

Anderson, Jon Lee. *Che Guevara: A Revolutionary Life*. Boston: Grove Press, 1997.

Arato, Andrew and Jean Cohen. *Civil Society and Political Theory*. Cambridge, MA: MIT Press, 1992.

Benjamin, Walter. *Reflections: Essays, Aphorisms, Autobiographical Writings*. New York: Vintage, 1967.

Berman, Marshall. "Sympathy for the Devil," *American Review* 19 (1974): 34–46.

Brooks, David. *Bobos in Paradise: The New Upper Class and How They Got There*. New York: Simon & Schuster, 2000.

Buck-Morss, Susan. *Dreamworld and Catastrophe: The Passing of Mass Utopia in East and West*. Cambridge, MA: MIT Press, 2000.

Caute, David. *Sixty-Eight: A Year of the Barricades*. London: Hamilton, 1977.

Collins, Robert M. "The Economic Crisis of 1968 and the Waning of the American Century," *American Historical Review* 67 (1996): 396–422.

Daniels, Robert V. *The Year of the Heroic Guerrilla: World Revolution and Counterrevolution in 1968*. Cambridge, MA: Harvard University Press, 1989.

Debray, Regis. *The Revolution in the Revolution?: Armed Struggle And Political Struggle In Latin America*. London: Penguin Books, 1967.

DeKoven, Marianne. *Utopia Limited: The Sixties and the Emergence of the Postmodern*. Durham: Duke University Press, 2004.

Dirlik, Arif. "The Third World." In *1968: The World Transformed*, edited by Carole Fink, Philipp Gassert, and Detlef Junker. Cambridge, UK: Cambridge University Press, 1998.

Fanon, Franz. *The Wretched of the Earth*. London: Penguin Books, 1967.

Farber, David, ed. *The Sixties: From Memory to History*. Chapel Hill: University of North Carolina Press, 1988.

Fraser, Nancy. *Justice Interruptus: Critical Reflections on the "Postsocialist" Condition*. London: Routledge, 1995.

Gilmore, Mikal. *Stories Done: Writings on the 1960s and Its Discontents*. New York: Free Press, 2008.

Gitlin, Todd. *The Twilight of Common Dreams: Why America Is Wracked by Culture Wars*. New York: Metropolitan, 1995.

Gutman, Amy. "Deliberative Democracy and Majority Rule." In *Deliberative Democracy and Human Rights*, edited by Harold Koh and Ronald Slye. New Haven, CT: Yale University Press, 1999.

Habermas, Jürgen. *The Inclusion of the Other: Studies in Political Theory*. Cambridge, MA: MIT Press, 1999.

Himmelfarb, Gertrude. *One Nation, Two Cultures: A Searching Examination of American Society in the Aftermath of Our Cultural Revolution*. New York: Knopf, 1999.

Hobsbawm, Eric. *New Century*. New York: New Press, 2000.

Jacoby, Russell. *The End of Utopia: Politics And Culture In An Age Of Apathy*. New York: Basic Books, 1999.

Johnson, Chalmers. *Blowback: The Costs and Consequences of American Empire*. New York: Henry Holt, 2000.

Khilnani, Sunil. *Arguing Revolution: Arguing Revolution: The Intellectual Left in Postwar France*. New Haven, CT: Yale University Press, 1993.

Lasky, Melvin J. "The Ideas of '68," *Encounter* LXX (1988): 3–18.

Leggewie, Claus. "A Laboratory of Postindustrial society." In *1968: The World Transformed*, edited by Carole Fink, Philipp Gassert, and Detlef Junker. Cambridge, UK: Cambridge University Press, 1998.

Macedo, Stephen, ed. *Reassessing the Sixties: Debating the Political and Cultural Legacy*. New York: New Press, 1997.

Melucci, Alberto. *Challenging Codes: Collective Action in the Information Age*. Cambridge, UK: Cambridge University Press, 1996.

Miller, James. *Democracy Is in the Streets*. New York: Touchstone, 1994.

Oglesby, Carl, ed. *A New Left Reader*. New York: Grove, 1969.

Passerini, Luisa. *Autobiography of a Generation: Italy 1968*. Hanover, NH: University of New Hampshire Press, 1996.

Quattrocchi, Albert and Tom Nairn. *The Beginning of the End: France, May 1968*. London: Verso, 1998.

Readings, Bill. *The University in Ruins*. Princeton, NJ: Princeton University Press, 1997.

Rosen, Ruth. *The World Split Open: How the Modern Women's Movement Changed America*. New York: Viking, 1999.

Rowbotham, Sheila. *Promise of a Dream: Remembering the Sixties*. London: Allen Lane, 2000.

Sartre, Jean-Paul. "The Risk of Spontaneity." In *All We Are Saying: The Philosophy of the New Left*, edited by Arthur Lothstein. New York: Capricorn Books, 1970.

Starr, Peter. *Logics of Failed Revolt: French Theory After May '68*. Stanford, CA: Stanford University Press, 1995.

Statera, Gianni. *Death of a Utopia: The Development and Decline of Student-Movements in Europe*. New York: Oxford University Press, 1975.

Tourraine, Alain. *The May Movement: Revolt and Reform*. New York: Random House, 1970.

Wang, Shaoguang. "'New Trends of Thought' and the Cultural Revolution," *Journal of Contemporary China* 8 (1999): 197–218.

Williams, Raymond, ed. *May Day Manifesto 1968*. London: Penguin Books, 1968.

Epilogue
Cal Winslow

In looking back over *West of Eden*, where in the spectrum of anarchist, socialist, and utopian thinking and experimental living are we to place this experience? I suggest it belongs alongside a tradition not widely known in the United States but one of great interest, especially in light of the crisis of the environment and the reaction to it, namely, the widespread and growing sentiments in favor of simpler living, more variety, richer lives, lives not dependent on war and the exploitation and misery of others and not destructive of the environment.

This is the tradition of William Morris, the late nineteenth-century English socialist, artist, designer, craftsman, environmentalist, the author of *News from Nowhere*—a utopian vision of a society transformed from the industrial squalor of Victorian Britain, with its wretched slums and sterile suburbs, to a pastoral paradise, a place with no government and no laws, a decentralized democracy where beauty is valued. Its peoples are harmonious, polite, and friendly. They love folk festivals, handicrafts, embroidered cloths, and haymaking. They live a "life of repose amidst of energy, of work which is pleasure and pleasure which is work."[1] London, the scene of the story, has regressed to preindustrial culture where meadow and woodland flourish, commerce and money no longer exist, and people gather in workshops to make beautiful objects for everyday use.

Utopian? Yes, but worth thinking about. *News from Nowhere* is relevant in that it rejects the "grand scheme"—it is not the top-down plan of some great man, no matter how enlightened.[2] Moreover, it is historical—it is a vision of the future but one that develops from the here and now;

---

1   William Morris, *News from Nowhere and Other Writings* (London: Penguin, 1993), 222.
2   Thanks to Sasha Lilley for help on this point.

the contrast of past with the present is ubiquitous. It is "this present—that past; it is a never-ending contrast."[3] It is not just a nice story; rather it constantly draws attention to the wretchedness of the present. It is, as Edward Thompson has written, a tale where "the world of the dream and the world of reality are united... We are made to question continually our own society, our own values and lives. This is why the story engages our feelings. We cannot sit back as spectators, looking at a pretty never-never-land."[4]

Morris also offers an historical vision. "Nowhere" develops in the aftermath of a revolution ("How the Change Came"), but develops from the bottom up as a free society, based on complete equality, in sharp contrast both to the "State Socialism" of the utopias of Edward Bellamy and others and the "actually existing socialisms" of the twentieth century.[5] We can add, in sharp contrast also to top-down communes and cults of the '60s, as well as to so much of the Left—with its hierarchical structures, permanent leaders, authoritarian centralism, rules, and discipline.

When Margaret Thatcher said, "There is no alternative," she meant no possible alternative whatsoever to capitalism, and she and her followers have been successful beyond their wildest dreams. But today turbulent times have returned, and the Empire, bankrupt, barbaric and in deep decay, is blindly lashing out—creating "two, three...many Vietnams" though tragically not yet with Che's emancipatory implications, but also, again, yes, alternatives.

We in Mendocino can in fact quite easily imagine a "Nowhere," the world as unspoiled woodlands, meadows and gardens—we can imagine the beauty of renewed redwood forests, though not perhaps in our own lifetimes. We can see streams teeming once again with salmon, the sea again plentiful. These all were, and must be again, recalling Iain Boal's words in the Prologue to this collection, "not 'resources,' but the very ground of our lives."

We can see a place where the Pomo might again be free—where once more they can truly live off the land. We can imagine an end to Empire, internal as well as external—a world where neither the fruits of one's labor nor the wealth of the earth are spoils, to be snared by some far-

---

3   E.P. Thompson, *William Morris: Romantic to Revolutionary* (Oakland: PM Press, 2011), 694.

4   Ibid.

5   Edward Bellamy, *Looking Backward* (Oxford: Oxford University Press, 2009).

away power—or next-door neighbor. No U.S. Empire. No imperial San Francisco. No Redwood Empire. Can our urban comrades do the same, imagine great communes, centers of human creativity, a Paris of 1871 in the future, true coalescences of diversity—democracies on a grand scale? Or can we break down altogether the distinction between town and country? What is not so easy to imagine is how to get to a society that can match such visions. This is our challenge. Our enemies will tell us not to bother; the first of these, but not the only ones, will be the defenders of the present—those who argue that there is no conceivable alternative to the exploitation of the land and the oppression of the people—to life as it is, life, in effect, always divided into two worlds, one rich, one poor, one white, one brown, one male, one female. This must be rejected but so must the notion that no cookbooks for the future will do, that our best arguments are confined to abstraction plus faith.[6]

It *is* possible to imagine alternatives, of course; we humans are old hands at it, even if our thinking is not always consistent or clear. So the project of a better future may well begin with the imagination, and perhaps our imagination can be nourished by the experiences related here. Morris, again, is helpful.

"I hold that we need not be afraid of scaring our audiences with too brilliant pictures of the Future of Society, nor think ourselves unpractical and utopian for telling them the bare truth, that in destroying monopoly we shall destroy our present civilization... If you tell your audience that you are going to change so little that they will scarcely feel the change, whether you scare anyone or not, you will certainly not interest those who have nothing to hope for in the present society."[7]

---

6   For a stale and unconvincing exposition to the contrary see Terry Eagleton, *Why Marx Was Right* (New Haven: Yale, 2011), 64–106.

7   Quoted in Thompson, *William Morris,* 726.

Contributors

Iain Boal is a social historian of science, technics and the commons, associated with the Retort group, and is one of the coauthors of Retort's *Afflicted Power: Capital and Spectacle in a New Age of War*. He coedited (with James Brook) *Resisting the Virtual Life: The Culture and Politics of Information*, and is the author of *The Green Machine*, a brief history of the bicycle in planetary perspective.

Michael Doyle is associate professor of history and director of the public history program at Ball State University. He is coeditor of *Imagine Nation: The American Counterculture of the 1960s and '70s* and author of the forthcoming *Free Radicals: The Haight-Ashbury Diggers and the American Counterculture*.

Jesse Drew, a young teenage runaway, roamed the United States and thrived thanks to a strong network of urban and rural communes and collectives. He spent many years as a labor activist in traditional smoke-stack industries before becoming involved in grassroots video production and the nascent digital arts movement. He earned his PhD from the University of Texas and is currently Director of Technocultural Studies at the University of California, Davis, where he specializes in digital arts, media archaeology, documentary studies, and the history of labor.

Jeff Lustig is a retired Professor of Government from CSU Sacramento. He has written widely on American and Californian politics and political thought, is former director of the Center for California Studies at CSU Sacramento and was the founding chair of the interdisciplinary California Studies Association. He was a founder of the Northcoast Labor History Project, a state and local leader in the CSU faculty union, and an early member of the Cheeseboard Collective in Berkeley.

Timothy Miller is a professor of Religious Studies at the University of Kansas. He has written three books about American communes/intentional communities, and another on the 1960s counterculture: *The Quest for Utopia in Twentieth-Century America; The 60s Communes; American Communes, 1860–1960: A Bibliography*; and *The Hippies and American Values.*

Ray Raphael is the author of many books, including *Founders: The People Who Brought You a Nation* and the bestselling *A People's History of the American Revolution.* Among his many books on rural Northern California is *Cash Crop: An American Dream.* He lives in Redway, in Southern Humboldt County.

Simon Sadler is Professor of Architectural and Urban History, Chancellor's Fellow and Director of the Art History Program at UC Davis. His publications include *Archigram: Architecture without Architecture* (2005), *The Situationist City* (1998), *Non-Plan: Essays on Freedom, Participation and Change in Modern Architecture and Urbanism* (edited with Jonathan Hughes, 2000), and most recently "An Architecture of the Whole" (in the *Journal of Architectural Education*).

Felicity D. Scott is assistant professor of architecture at the Graduate School of Architecture, Planning and Preservation, Columbia University, and a founding coeditor of *Grey Room*, a quarterly journal of architecture, art, media, and politics published by MIT Press since Fall 2000. In addition to publishing numerous articles in journals and edited anthologies, her book, *Architecture or Techno-Utopia: Politics After Modernism*, was published by MIT Press in 2007, and another book, *Living Archive 7: Ant Farm*, appeared on ACTAR Editorial in May 2008.

Ramón Sender Barayón has lived in various intentional communities, including the Bruderhof (1950s) and its exact opposites, Morning Star and Wheeler's ranches (1960s–'70s). His published books include the online history of both communes (http://badabamama.com/HomeFree. html), a Spanish Civil War family memoir *A Death In Zamora* (2003), collected essays and articles in *A Planetary Sojourn* (2008), *Being of the Sun* coauthored with Alicia Bay Laurel (1973), *The Morning Star Scrapbook* (1976), and the novel *Zero Weather* (1980).

Robyn C. Spencer is an assistant professor of U.S. history at Lehman College who specializes in the history of African American protest in the post–World War II era. She has written on gender and Black Power and is completing a book manuscript on the history of the Black Panther Party in Oakland, California.

Janferie Stone was a sojourner in two communes on the Mendocino coast in the early 1970s. She has taught Native American Studies and anthropology at many levels of the California education system. Her essays have been published in *Sustainable Feminisms (Advances in Gender Research)*, volume 11, edited by Sonita Sarker and *From Rigor to Vigor: Transformations in the Field*, edited by Jean-Guy Goulet and Bruce Miller.

Michael Watts is currently Class of 1963 Professor of Geography and Chair of Development Studies at the University of California, Berkeley, where he has taught for over thirty years. A Guggenheim Fellow in 2003, he served as the director of the Institute of International Studies from 1994 to 2004. Watts's research has addressed a number of development issues especially food and energy security, rural development, and land reform in Africa, South Asia, and Vietnam.

Cal Winslow is a social historian, educated at Antioch College and Warwick University. He is coauthor (with Edward Thompson, Peter Linebaugh, and others) of *Albion's Fatal Tree*. He is the author of *Labor's Civil War in California* and coeditor of *Rebel Rank and File*. He is the director of the Mendocino Institute and is associated with the Retort group. He lives with his family near Caspar on the Mendocino coast.

Lee Worden was born in 1969 and raised in Northern California by a Beat artist and an alternative women's health activist. He is now a mathematician who studies how collectivities behave and change.

Bibliographic Note

The bran tub of topics explored or touched upon in *West of Eden*—from the Black Panthers' Sickle Cell Anemia Foundation and homebrew bioengineers through goat husbandry, early Moog synthesizers, solar-powered hot tubs, and peasant insurgency, to the General Sherman (formerly Karl Marx) sequoia tree, conscious pregnancy, and gleaning in the Central Valley—is far beyond the scope of a brief note. Instead this note is intended simply to orient and offer some landmarks vis à vis the key terms informing *West of Eden* for those new to the territory.

If the literature on communalism is large, on the theme of utopia it is quite simply vast (in 2016 it will be five hundred years since Thomas More coined the word), as can be seen by taking a few steps into the labyrinth at utopia.nypl.org, a collaboration between the Bibliothèque Nationale de France and the New York Public Library. The reader is invited to visit the PM Retort website <www.pmpress.org/retort> and check out the more extensive and detailed bibliographic matter related to the themes and topics in *West of Eden*. Readers are also urged to become actively involved in identifying the documentary evidence surviving from that long pulse of communal energies called "the sixties," whose true history—beyond the stale clichés, ritualized abuse, and hagiography—has hardly begun and whose material traces are permanently threatened with loss, neglect, or destruction. We are especially keen to facilitate the locating and preserving of diaries and photographs or film that record communal lifeways in the city and country. The power of journals and vivid memoir to evoke the texture of lived experience is exemplified by Art Kopecky's stereotype-busting chronicle of his years as a hippie cowherd on a communal ranch in New Mexico, after lighting out from the Bolinas Mesa in a converted day-glo bread van (*New Buffalo: Journals from a Taos Commune*, University of New Mexico Press, 2004).

The fruit of Timothy Miller's research into nineteenth- and twenti-eth-century New World intentional communities—*American Communes, 1860–1960: A Bibliography* (Garland Publishing Company, 1990), *The Hippies and American Values* (University of Tennessee Press, 1991), *The Quest for Utopia in Twentieth-Century America: Volume One, 1900–1960* (Syracuse University Press, 1998), *The 60s Communes: Hippies and Beyond* (Syracuse University Press, 1999), and, with Richard Fairfield and Alan Watts, *The Modern Utopian: Alternative Communities Then and Now* (Process Press, 2010)—is the essential sociological starting point for students of the subject. His immense knowledge of the field informs the conspectus of Californian communalism that opens Part One of *West of Eden*.

The publishing arm of the Fellowship of Intentional Communities—*Communities Directory, Communities* magazine and the FIC website, www.ic.org—offers a portal into the world of ecovillages, cohousing, and contemporary communes (even if the word "commune" these days is anathema, except in Oakland). Laurence Veysey's *The Communal Experience: Anarchist and Mystical Communities in 20th-Century America* (University of Chicago Press, 1978) remains of interest for its moment and place of publication, just as the tide of communalism was on the ebb and the Thatcher-Reagan era was dawning, brutally prefigured by the arrival of the "Chicago boys" in the rubble of Allende's palace, stormy petrels of structural adjustment carrying copies of Garrett Hardin's essay "The Tragedy of the Commons" (*Science* 162, 1968). This fact-free manifesto of market individualism purported to explain why commoning always ends in disaster and environmental degradation, and therefore why enclosure and privative property rights are the *sine qua non* of civilization. As an antidote to Hardin—not to say Ayn Rand and Milton Friedman—John Curl's *For All the People: Uncovering the Hidden History of Cooperation, Cooperative Movements, and Communalism in America* (PM Press, 2012) is an unrivalled survey of such arrangements, and includes a useful ten-page bibliographic essay covering general histories of cooperation and communalism. In 2007 the California Studies Association under Jeff Lustig's inspiring guidance, UC Berkeley's Department of Geography, and Heyday Books (www.heydaybooks.com, whose list is strong on nature and the indigenous cultures of the Bay region in step with the vision of its founder, Malcolm Margolin) collaborated in the organizing of a conference at Berkeley City College entitled "Crisis of the California Commons," that both drew upon, and fed into, research for *West of Eden*. The plenary sessions were recorded, and the audio files can be retrieved via the PM Retort webpage.

At the outset of the "communes project" that became *West of Eden*, and as complement to Miller's wide historical overview, we found *Imagine Nation: The American Counterculture of the 1960s and '70s* (Routledge, 2002), edited by Peter Braunstein and Michael Doyle, to be an indispensible map of the antinomian terrain. It contains richly footnoted, critically informed essays on hallucinogens, feminism, guerrilla theatre, the New Left, the White Panthers, playing at Indians, gay and youth subcultures, countercultural film, alternative technologies, rock music, the politics of race, and underground comics. Berkeley punk zinester Aaron Cometbus took on the topic of hippie communes (*Cometbus* 48 "Back to the Land," now anthologized in *Add Toner: A Cometbus Collection*, Last Gasp Press, 2011) with the ironic, jaundiced fascination of the generation only born in the 1960s. Jentri Anders' *Beyond the Counterculture: The Community of Mateel* (Pullman: Washingon State University Press, 1990) is a social anthropologist's account of one enduring communal experiment in northern California. The underground press which reflected the tone and style of the counterculture—and partly helped constitute it—can be sampled in *On the Ground: An Illustrated Anecdotal History of the Sixties Underground Press in the U.S.* (Sean Stewart, ed., PM Press, 2011). Peter Richardson's *A Bomb in Every Issue: How the Short, Unruly Life of Ramparts Magazine Changed America*, focuses on the Catholic literary quarterly that turned movement muckraker in the mid-1960s (New Press, 2010). *Ten Years that Shook the City: San Francisco 1968–1978* (Chris Carlsson, ed., City Lights Books, 2011) reinforces the clear absurdity of slicing history by standard decades.

The experience of "beloved community" informs the sociological work of ex-communard George Katsiaficas, who theorizes an "eros effect" at play in his analysis of the dynamics of social movements in *The Imagination of the Left: A Global Analysis of 1968* (South End Press, 1987) and *The Subversion of Politics: European Autonomous Social Movements and the Decolonization of Everyday Life* (AK Press, 2006). His time in a political commune in California also leaves its mark in *Liberation, Imagination, and the Black Panther Party: A New Look at the Panthers and Their Legacy* (with Kathleen Cleaver, Routledge, 2001) and *Vietnam Documents: American and Vietnamese Views of the War* (M.E. Sharpe, 1992); compare Roxanne Dunbar-Ortiz's radical feminist perspective in *Outlaw Woman: A Memoir of the War Years, 1960-1975* (City Lights, 2002).

Another former communard, David Kubrin—Newton scholar, Bay Area witch, cofounder of the Liberation School, and associate of Starhawk (*Dreaming the Dark: Magic, Sex, and Politics*, Beacon Press, 1982)—has explored the historical linkages connecting the antinuclear struggles of the sixties to the antiglobalization movements of the 1990s through shared nonviolent horizontal praxis; see "Scaling the Heights to Seattle" in Eddie Yuen et al., *Confronting Capitalism: Dispatches from a Global Movement* (Soft Skull Press, 2004). Kubrin's utopian-communitarian philosophy also deeply informs his *Marxism and Witchcraft: A Marxist Critique of Ecology and an Ecological Critique of Marxism* (Autonomedia, forthcoming).

At the heart of *West of Eden* is a cluster of cognate terms—commune, commons, communication, communal, communard, communing—whose relations and resonances are illuminated, using the method of historical semantics, under the relevant entries in Raymond Williams's *Keywords: A Vocabulary of Culture and Society* (Oxford University Press, 1984). The deep history of "rights of common" and the struggle of commoners everywhere against the extinction of those rights is excavated in the *Magna Carta Manifesto: Liberties and Commons for All* (University of California Press, 2008) by Peter Linebaugh, whose teacher E.P. Thompson wrote a series of classic essays on the topic, collected as *Customs in Common* (Merlin Press, 1993). *The Commoner* (www.commoner.org.uk) is an online theoretical forum publishing contributions by an international network of activists and scholars of enclosures and commons, including Linebaugh, Silvia Federici, George Caffentzis, Richard Pithouse, and Mariarosa dalla Costa. Commonist approaches inform the writings and activities of the Midnight Notes Collective, Retort, Sarai, and Pad.ma. For a pioneering attempt to theorize commons in relation to planetary capitalism, see *The Beginning of History: Value Struggles and Global Capital* (Pluto Press, 2007), a treatise by the Italian farmer, political economist, and convener of *The Commoner*, Massimo De Angelis.

The insightful suggestion by Jeff Lustig that the adjacency of two great commons, the Golden Gate Park and the University of California, Berkeley campus, was a vital feature of the political geography of the counterculture is testament not only to the creative mind of an actor in the drama of those days but to the work of a truckload of critical urbanists drawn into the slipstream of a turbocharged black roadster with an ex-meatcutter from the far periphery of Los Angeles at the wheel. Mike

Davis' urban noir classic, *City of Quartz: Excavating the Future in Los Angeles* (Vintage Books, 1990), was in crucial ways the model for, inter alia, *Imperial San Francisco: Urban Power, Earthly Ruin* (University of California Press, 1999), Gray Brechin's Mumfordian study of the city and its *contado*; and Richard Walker's *The Country in the City: The Greening of the San Francisco Bay Area* (University of Washington Press, 2008). Both books are highly germane in establishing a context for *West of Eden* and the history of the Bay and its hinterland, its bourgeoisie and its bohemia, poignantly glimpsed in *Literary San Francisco: A Pictorial History from its Beginnings to the Present Day* (City Lights, 1980). On the shelves of many communards was Diane di Prima's *Revolutionary Letters* (Last Gasp, 2007). Jack Foley's *Visions & Affiliations: A California Literary Time Line* (Pantograph Press, 2011) is a two-part chrono-encyclopedia of the poetry scene covering more than half a century. Richard Candida Smith traces the genealogies of regional bohemian enclaves in *Utopia and Dissent: Art, Poetry, and Politics in California* (University of California Press, 1996). Bay Area poets of the counterculture are strongly represented in Andrei Codrescu's anthology *American Poetry since 1970: Up Late* (Four Walls Eight Windows, 1987).

Peter Selz surveyed the visual politics of postwar California in *Art of Engagement: Visual Politics in California and Beyond* (University of California Press, 2006). For the moving image Steve Anker, Kathy Geritz, and Steve Seid's *Radical Light: Alternative Film and Video in the San Francisco Bay Area, 1945–2000* (University of California Press, 2010) is now an essential resource. The feisty talents of the Bay Area's current coterie of writers and artists is on parade in *Infinite City: A San Francisco Atlas* (University of California Press, 2011), a many-hued collaboration brilliantly conceived and marshaled by Rebecca Solnit, in which the new tools of critical cartography and countermapping are deployed to reveal the city as palimpsest and power grid.

As for the built world that the communards and cooperators of the 1960s made for themselves and their projects, by comparison with the grand blueprints of nineteenth-century utopian communities, as charted in Dolores Hayden's *Seven American Utopias: The Architecture of Communitarian Socialism, 1790–1975* (MIT Press, 1979), the communal living arrangements of the 1960s and '70s were almost all improvised, ad hoc affairs that haphazardly refunctioned open or built space to new and mostly unauthorized purposes. There is an echo here of a striking statistic in Davis's *Planet of Slums* (Verso, 2006) that 85 percent of urban residents in the global South "occupy property illegally" (Iain Boal, "21st Century Noir," *Mute* 2, no. 3, 2006). Responses to this fact—if such it is— tend to fall along lines of cleavage going back to Bakunin versus Marx. Statists of Left and Right mostly regret the irruption of shacks and shanties disturbing the master plan; anarchists tend to look more leniently on favelas and hippie construction methods, and support the case made in *Housing by People: Towards Autonomy in Building Environments* (Marion Boyars, 1976) by John Turner, the tribune of populist architecture, following an epiphany in the aftermath of the big Peruvian earthquake of 1958, when he watched the results of communal self-help in the *barriadas* of Arequipa. Further ammunition for "architecture without architects" can be found in *Autonomy, Solidarity, Possibility* (Chris Wilbert and Damian F. White, eds., AK Press, 2011) a posthumous collection of the writings of Colin Ward, the English anarchist, town planner, and gentle advocate of informal, incremental human settlements. Informal, however, doesn't begin to describe some of the commoning (read "code violations") on view in Alastair Gordon's riotous *Spaced Out: Radical Environments of the Psychedelic Sixties* (Rizzoli, 2008).

Hippie foodways challenged Cold War cuisine and gave birth to a different kind of counterculture with its epicenter in north Berkeley; a brief history can be found in *The Cheeseboard Collective Works: Bread, Pastry, Cheese, Pizza* (Ten Speed Press, 2003). Mollie Katzen moved west from Ithaca to the East Bay and compiled her collective's recipes into *The Moosewood Cookbook* (Ten Speed Press, 1978) which joined Frances Moore Lappé's mildly Malthusian *Diet for a Small Planet* (Ballantine Books, 1971) as staples in the vegetarian's kitchen. Julie Guthman's *Agrarian Dreams: The Paradox of Organic Farming in California* (University of California Press, 2004) is essential for understanding the ironies at the heart of the culinary revolution now celebrated far beyond the gourmet ghetto around Shattuck and Vine in Berkeley.

Shaping San Francisco (www.shapingsf.org), founded by inveterate citizen-archivist Chris Carlsson, is an image-rich, interactive archive of Bay Area history—especially its lost, neglected, or suppressed history. ShapingSF is complemented by the pioneering Prelinger Archives and Library (www.prelinger.com), a treasure house of materials relevant to the themes of this book. A serendipitous hour spent in the browsable stacks of the appropriation-friendly Prelinger Library on Eighth Street south of

Market will persuade the visitor that Carlsson may be right to insist, as he does in *Nowtopia: How Pirate Programmers, Outlaw Bicyclists, and Vacant-Lot Gardeners Are Inventing the Future Today* (AK Press, 2008) that the better world imagined by dreamers of a new day is already to hand...west of Eden.

IB

18. i. 12

Index

About
PM Press

PM Press was founded at the end of 2007 by a small collection of folks with decades of publishing, media, and organizing experience. PM Press co-conspirators
have published and distributed hundreds of books, pamphlets, CDs, and DVDs.
Members of PM have founded enduring book fairs, spearheaded victorious ten-
ant organizing campaigns, and worked closely with bookstores, academic conferences, and even rock bands to deliver political and challenging ideas to all walks
of life. We're old enough to know what we're doing and young enough to know
what's at stake.

We seek to create radical and stimulating fiction and nonfiction books, pamphlets, t-shirts, visual and audio materials to entertain, educate, and inspire you.
We aim to distribute these through every available channel with every available
technology, whether that means you are seeing anarchist classics at our bookfair
stalls; reading our latest vegan cookbook at the café; downloading geeky fiction
e-books; or digging new music and timely videos from our website.

Contact us for direct ordering and questions about all PM Press releases, as
well as manuscript submissions, review copy requests, foreign rights sales, author
interviews, to book an author for an event, and to have PM Press attend your
bookfair:

PM Press • PO Box 23912 • Oakland, CA 94623
510-658-3906 • info@pmpress.org

Buy books and stay on top of what we are doing at:

www.pmpress.org

MONTHLY SUBSCRIPTION PROGRAM

These are indisputably momentous times—the financial system is melting down globally and the Empire is stumbling. Now more than ever there is a vital need for radical ideas.

In the four years since its founding—and on a mere shoestring—PM Press has risen to the formidable challenge of publishing and distributing knowledge and entertainment for the struggles ahead. With over 175 releases to date, we have published an impressive and stimulating array of literature, art, music, politics, and culture. Using every available medium, we've succeeded in connecting those hungry for ideas and information to those putting them into practice.

Friends of PM allows you to directly help impact, amplify, and revitalize the discourse and actions of radical writers, filmmakers, and artists. It provides us with a stable foundation from which we can build upon our early successes and provides a much-needed subsidy for the materials that can't necessarily pay their own way. You can help make that happen—and receive every new title automatically delivered to your door once a month—by joining as a Friend of PM Press. And, we'll throw in a free T-Shirt when you sign up.

Here are your options:
- $25 a month: Get all books and pamphlets plus 50% discount on all webstore purchases
- $40 a month: Get all PM Press releases (including CDs and DVDs) plus 50% discount on all webstore purchases
- $100 a month: Superstar—Everything plus PM merchandise, free downloads, and 50% discount on all webstore purchases

For those who can't afford $25 or more a month, we're introducing *Sustainer Rates* at $15, $10 and $5. Sustainers get a free PM Press t-shirt and a 50% discount on all purchases from our website.

Your Visa or Mastercard will be billed once a month, until you tell us to stop. Or until our efforts succeed in bringing the revolution around. Or the financial meltdown of Capital makes plastic redundant. Whichever comes first.

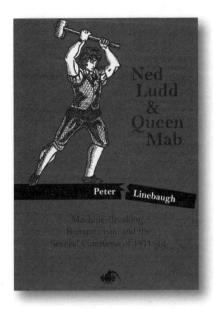

Ned Ludd & Queen Mab

Machine-Breaking, Romanticism, and the Several Commons of 1811–12

Peter Linebaugh

$6.95 • ISBN: 978-1-60486-704-6

Peter Linebaugh, in an extraordinary historical and literary tour de force, enlists the anonymous and scorned 19th century loom-breakers of the English midlands into the front ranks of an international, polyglot, many-colored crew of commoners resisting dispossession in the dawn of capitalist modernity.

"Sneering at the Luddites is still the order of the day. Peter Linebaugh's great act of historical imagination stops the scoffers in their tracks. It takes the cliché of 'globalization' and makes it live: the Yorkshire machine-breakers are put right back in the violent world economy of 1811–12, in touch with the Atlantic slave trade, Mediterranean agribusiness, the Tecumseh rebellion, the brutal racism of London dockland. The local and the global are once again shown to be inseparable—as they are, at present, for the machine-breakers of the new world crisis."
—T.J. Clark, author of *The Absolute Bourgeois* and *Image of the People*

"E.P. Thompson, you may rest now. Linebaugh restores the dignity of the despised luddites with a poetic grace worthy of the master. By a stunning piece of re-casting we see them here not as rebels against the future but among the avant-garde of a planetary resistance movement against capitalist enclosures in the long struggle for a different future. Byron, Shelley, listen up! Peter Linebaugh's *Ned Ludd & Queen Mab* does for 'technology' what his *London Hanged* did for 'crime'. Where was I that day in Bloomsbury when he delivered this commonist manifesto for the 21st century? The Retort Pamphet series is off to a brilliant start."
—Mike Davis, author of *Planet of Slums* and *Buda's Wagon*

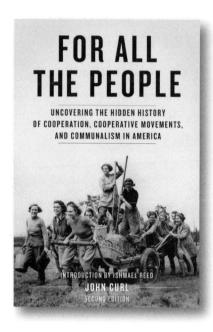

For All the People

Uncovering the Hidden
History of Cooperation,
Cooperative Movements,
and Communalism in
America, 2nd Edition

John Curl
$29.95 • ISBN: 978-1-60486-582-0

Seeking to reclaim a history that has remained largely ignored by most historians, this dramatic and stirring account examines each of the definitive American cooperative movements for social change—farmer, union, consumer, and communalist—that have been all but erased from collective memory.

Focusing far beyond one particular era, organization, leader, or form of cooperation, *For All the People* documents the multigenerational struggle of the American working people for social justice. While the economic system was in its formative years, generation after generation of American working people challenged it by organizing visionary social movements aimed at liberating themselves from what they called wage slavery. Workers substituted a system based on cooperative work and constructed parallel institutions that would supercede the institutions of the wage system.

With an expansive sweep and breathtaking detail, this scholarly yet eminently readable chronicle follows the American worker from the colonial workshop to the modern mass-assembly line, from the family farm to the corporate hierarchy, ultimately painting a vivid panorama of those who built the United States and those who will shape its future.

John Curl, with over forty years of experience as both an active member and scholar of cooperatives, masterfully melds theory, practice, knowledge and analysis, to present the definitive history from below of cooperative America. This second edition contains a new introduction by Ishmael Reed; a new author's preface discussing cooperatives in the Great Recession of 2008 and their future in the 21st century; and a new chapter on the role co-ops played in the Food Revolution of the 1970s.

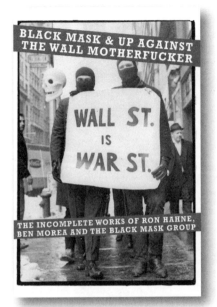

Black Mask & Up Against the Wall Motherfucker

The Incomplete Works of Ron Hahne, Ben Morea, and the Black Mask Group

Ben Morea and Ron Hahne
$15.95 • ISBN: 978-1-60486-021-4

Founded in New York City in the mid-1960s by self-educated ghetto kid and painter Ben Morea, the Black Mask group melded the ideas and inspiration of Dada and the Surrealists, with the anarchism of the Durruti Column from the Spanish Revolution. With a theory and practice that had much in common with their contemporaries the San Francisco Diggers, Dutch Provos, and the French Situationists—who famously excommunicated 3 of the 4 members of the British section of the Situationist International for associating too closely with Black Mask—the group intervened spectacularly in the art, politics and culture of their times. From shutting down the Museum of Modern Art to protesting Wall Street's bankrolling of war, from battling with Maoists at SDS conferences to defending the Valerie Solanas shooting of Andy Warhol, Black Mask successfully straddled the counterculture and politics of the '60s, and remained the Joker in the pack of both sides of "The Movement."

By 1968 Black Mask dissolved into "The Family" (popularly known as Up Against The Wall Motherfucker—the name to which they signed their first leaflet), which combined the confrontational theater and tactics of Black Mask with a much more aggressively "street" approach in dealing with the police, and authorities. Dubbed a "street gang with analysis" they were reputedly the only white grouping taken seriously by the Black Panther Party, and influenced everyone from the Weathermen to the "hippy" communal movements.

This volume collects the complete ten issues of the paper *Black Mask* (produced from 1966–1967 by Ben Morea and Ron Hahne), together with a generous collection of the leaflets, articles, and flyers generated by Black Mask, and UATW/MF, the *UATW/MF* Magazine, and both the *Free Press* and *Rolling Stone* reports on UATW/MF. A lengthy interview with founder Ben Morea provides context and color to this fascinating documentary legacy of NYC's now legendary provocateurs.

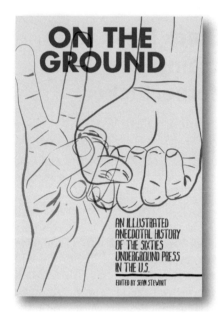

On the Ground

An Illustrated Anecdotal
History of the Sixties
Underground Press in the U.S.

Edited by Sean Stewart
$20.00 • ISBN: 978-1-60486-455-7

In four short years (1965–1969), the
underground press grew from five small
newspapers in as many cities in the U.S.
to over 500 newspapers—with millions of readers—all over the world.
Completely circumventing (and subverting) establishment media by utiliz-
ing their own news service and freely
sharing content amongst each other, the
underground press, at its height, became the unifying institution for the counterculture of the 1960s.

Frustrated with the lack of any mainstream media criticism of the Vietnam War,
empowered by the victories of the civil rights era, emboldened by the anti-co-
lonial movements in the third world and with heads full of acid, a generation
set out to change the world. The underground press was there documenting,
participating in, and providing the resources that would guarantee the growth
of this emergent youth culture. Combining bold visuals, innovative layouts, and
eschewing any pretense toward objectivity, the newspapers were wildly diverse
and wonderfully vibrant.

Neither meant to be an official nor comprehensive history, *On the Ground* focuses
on the anecdotal detail that brings the history alive. Comprised of stories told by
the people involved with the production and distribution of the newspapers—
John Sinclair, Art Kunkin, Paul Krassner, Emory Douglas, John Wilcock, Bill
Ayers, Spain Rodriguez, Trina Robbins, Al Goldstein, Harvey Wasserman and
more—and featuring over 50 full-color scans taken from a broad range of newspapers—*Basta Ya, Berkeley Barb, Berkeley Tribe, Chicago Seed, Helix, It Ain't Me
Babe, Los Angeles Free Press, Osawatomie, Rat Subterranean News, San Francisco
Express Times, San Francisco Oracle, Screw: The Sex Review, The Black Panther,
The East Village Other, The Realist*, and many more—the book provides a true
window into the spirit of the times, giving the reader a feeling for the energy on
the ground.

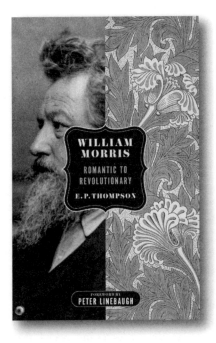

William Morris

Romantic to Revolutionary

E.P. Thompson
$32.95 • ISBN: 978-1-60486-243-0

William Morris—the great nineteenth century craftsman, designer, poet and writer—remains a monumental figure whose influence resonates powerfully today. As an intellectual (and author of the seminal utopian *News From Nowhere*), his concern with artistic and human values led him to cross what he called the 'river of fire' and become a committed socialist—committed not to some theoretical formula but to the day by day struggle of working women and men in Britain and to the evolution of his ideas about art, about work and about how life should be lived.

Many of his ideas accorded none too well with the reforming tendencies dominant in the Labour movement, nor with those of 'orthodox' Marxism, which has looked elsewhere for inspiration. Both sides have been inclined to venerate Morris rather than to pay attention to what he said.

Originally written less than a decade before his groundbreaking *The Making of the English Working Class*, E.P. Thompson brought to this biography his now trademark historical mastery, passion, wit, and essential sympathy. It remains unsurpassed as the definitive work on this remarkable figure, by the major British historian of the twentieth century.

> "Thompson's is the first biography to do justice to Morris's political thought and so assemble the man whole… It is not only the standard biography of Morris; it makes us realize, as no other writer has done, how completely admirable a man this Victorian was—how consistent and honest to himself and others, how incapable of cruelty or jargon and, above all, how free."
>
> —Robert Hughes, *Time Magazine*

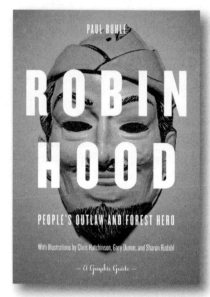

Robin Hood

People's Outlaw and Forest
Hero, A Graphic Guide

Paul Buhle • Illustrated by Chris
Hutchinson, Gary Dumm, and Sharon
Rudahl
$15.00 • ISBN: 978-1-60486-318-5

Where and what was Robin Hood? Why
is an outlaw from fourteenth century
England still a hero today, with films,
festivals and songs dedicated to his living
memory?

This book explores the mysteries, the historical evidence, and the trajectory that led to centuries of village festivals around Mayday and the green space of nature unconquered by the forces in power. Great revolutionaries including William Morris adopted Robin as hero, children's books offered many versions, and Robin entered modern popular culture with cheap novels, silent films and comics.

There, in the world of popular culture, Robin Hood continues to holds unique and secure place. The "bad-good" hero of pulp urban fiction of the 1840s–50s, and more important, the Western outlaw who thwarts the bankers in pulps, films, and comics, is essentially Robin Hood. So are Zorro, the Cisco Kid, and countless Robin Hood knockoff characters in various media.

Robin Hood has a special resonance for leftwing influences on American popular culture in Hollywood, film and television. During the 1930s–50s, future blacklist victims devised radical plots of "people's outlaws," including anti-fascist guerilla fighters, climaxing in *The Adventures of Robin Hood*, network television 1955–58, written under cover by victims of the Blacklist, seen by more viewers than any other version of Robin Hood.

Robin Hood: People's Outlaw and Forest Hero also features 30 pages of collages and comic art, recuperating the artistic interpretations of Robin from seven centuries, and offering new comic art as a comic-within-a book.

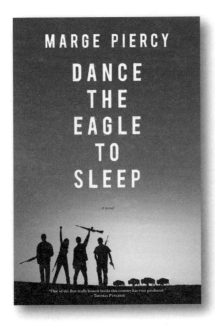

Dance the Eagle to Sleep

A Novel

Marge Piercy
$20.00 • ISBN: 978-1-60486-456-4

Originally published in 1970, Marge Piercy's second novel follows the lives of four teenagers, in a near future society, as they rebel against a military draft and "the system." The occupation of Franklin High School begins, and with it, the open rebellion of America's youth against their channeled, unrewarding lives and the self-serving, plastic society that directs them.

From the disillusionment and alienation of the young at the center of the revolt, to their attempts to build a visionary new society, the nationwide following they gain and the brutally complete repression that inevitably follows, this is a future fiction without a drop of fantasy. As driving, violent, and nuanced today as it was 40 years ago, this anniversary edition includes a new introduction by the author reflecting unapologetically on the novel and the times from which it emerged.

> "*Dance the Eagle to Sleep* is a vision, not an argument… It is brilliant. Miss Piercy was a published poet before she resorted to the novel, exploiting its didactic aspect, and her prose crackles, depolarizes, sends shivers leaping across the synaptic cleft. The 'eagle' is America, bald and all but extinct. The 'dance' is performed by the tribal young, the self-designated 'Indians,' after their council meetings, to celebrate their bodies and their escape from the cannibalizing 'system.' The eagle isn't danced to sleep; it sends bombers to devastate the communes of the young… What a frightening, marvelous book!"
>
> —*New York Times*

> "*Dance the Eagle to Sleep* is a cautionary tale, but it is more than that. It is an important political document. I hope the book is read."
>
> —*The Nation*

Vida

Marge Piercy

$20.00 • ISBN: 978-1-60486-487-8

Originally published in 1979, *Vida* is Marge Piercy's classic bookend to the '60s. *Vida* is full of the pleasures and pains, the experiments, disasters, and victories of an extraordinary band of people. At the center of the novel stands Vida Asch. She has lived underground for almost a decade. Back in the '60s she was a political star of the exuberant antiwar movement—a red-haired beauty photographed for the pages of *Life* magazine—charismatic, passionate, and totally sure she would prevail. Now, a decade later, Vida is on the run, her star-quality replaced by stubborn courage. She comes briefly to rest in a safe house on Cape Cod. To her surprise and annoyance, she finds another person in the house, a fugitive, Joel, ten years younger than she, a kid who dropped into the underground out of the army. As they spend the next days together, Vida finds herself warming toward a man for the first time in years, knowing all too well the dangers.

As counterpoint to the underground '70s, Marge Piercy tells the extraordinary tale of the optimistic '60s, the thousands of people who were members of SAW (Students Against the War) and of the handful who formed a fierce group called the Little Red Wagon. Piercy's characters make vivid and comprehensible the desperation, the courage, and the blind rage of a time when "action" could appear to some to be a more rational choice than the vote.

A new introduction by Marge Piercy situates the book, and the author, in the times from which they emerged.

> "A fully controlled, tightly structured dramatic narrative of such artful intensity that it leads the reader on at almost every page."
> —*New York Times Book Review*

> "Very exciting. Marge Piercy's characters are complex and very human."
> —Margaret Atwood

The Wild Girls

Ursula K. Le Guin

$12.00 • ISBN: 978-1-60486-403-8

Ursula K. Le Guin is the one modern science fiction author who truly needs no introduction. In the forty years since *The Left Hand of Darkness*, her works have changed not only the face but the tone and the agenda of SF, introducing themes of gender, race, socialism and anarchism, all the while thrilling readers with trips to strange (and strangely familiar) new worlds. She is our exemplar of what fantastic literature can and should be about.

Her Nebula winner *The Wild Girls*, newly revised and presented here in book form for the first time, tells of two captive "dirt children" in a society of sword and silk, whose determination to enter "that possible even when unattainable space in which there is room for justice" leads to a violent and loving end.

Plus: Le Guin's scandalous and scorching *Harper's* essay, "Staying Awake While We Read", (also collected here for the first time) which demolishes the pretensions of corporate publishing and the basic assumptions of capitalism as well. And of course our Outspoken Interview which promises to reveal the hidden dimensions of America's best-known SF author. And delivers.

> "She wields her pen with a moral and psychological sophistication rarely seen. What she really does is write fables: splendidly intricate and hugely imaginative tales about such mundane concerns as life, death, love, and sex."
>
> —*Newsweek*

> "Idiosyncratic and convincing, Le Guin's characters have a long afterlife."
> —*Publishers Weekly*

THE

PAUL GOODMAN

READER

Edited by Taylor Stoehr

"His ability to combine linguistic criticism, politics, a version of the nature of man, anthropology, the history of philosophy, and autobiographical testament with literary analysis, and to make a closely woven fabric of argument, seems magical."
—ROBERT MEREDITH, *The Nation*

The Paul Goodman Reader

Paul Goodman • Edited by Taylor Stoehr
$28.95 • ISBN: 978-1-60486-058-0

A one-man think-tank for the New Left, Paul Goodman wrote over thirty books, most of them before his decade of fame as a social critic in the '60s. *The Paul Goodman Reader* that does him justice must be a compendious volume, with excerpts not only from best-sellers like *Growing Up Absurd*, but also from his landmark books on education, community planning, anarchism, psychotherapy, language theory, and poetics. Samples as well from *The Empire City*, a comic novel reviewers compared to Don Quixote, prize-winning short stories, and scores of poems that led America's most respected poetry reviewer, Hayden Carruth, to exclaim, "Not one dull page. It's almost unbelievable."

Goodman called himself as an old-fashioned man of letters, which meant that all these various disciplines and occasions added up to a single abiding concern for the human plight in perilous times, and for human promise and achieved grandeur, love and hope.

> "It was that voice of his that seduced me—that direct, cranky, egotistical, generous American voice... Paul Goodman's voice touched everything he wrote about with intensity, interest, and his own terribly appealing sureness and awkwardness... It was his voice, that is to say, his intelligence and the poetry of his intelligence incarnated, which kept me a loyal and passionate fan."
>
> —Susan Sontag, novelist and public intellectual

Rebel Voices

An IWW Anthology

Edited by Joyce L. Kornbluh •
Preface by Daniel Gross •
Contributions by Franklin
Rosemont • Introduction by Fred
Thompson
$27.95 • ISBN:
978-1-60486-483-0

Welcoming women, Blacks, and immigrants long before most other unions, the Wobblies from the start were labor's outstanding pioneers and innovators, unionizing hundreds of thousands of workers previously regarded as "unorganizable." Wobblies organized the first sit-down strike (at General Electric, Schenectady, 1906), the first major auto strike (6,000 Studebaker workers, Detroit, 1911), the first strike to shut down all three coalfields in Colorado (1927), and the first "no-fare" transit-workers' job-action (Cleveland, 1944). With their imaginative, colorful, and world-famous strikes and free-speech fights, the IWW wrote many of the brightest pages in the annals of working class emancipation.

Wobblies also made immense and invaluable contributions to workers' culture. All but a few of America's most popular labor songs are Wobbly songs. IWW cartoons have long been recognized as labor's finest and funniest.

The impact of the IWW has reverberated far beyond the ranks of organized labor. An important influence on the 1960s New Left, the Wobbly theory and practice of direct action, solidarity, and "class-war" humor have inspired several generations of civil rights and antiwar activists, and are a major source of ideas and inspiration for today's radicals. Indeed, virtually every movement seeking to "make this planet a good place to live" (to quote an old Wobbly slogan), has drawn on the IWW's incomparable experience.

Originally published in 1964 and long out of print, *Rebel Voices* remains by far the biggest and best source on IWW history, fiction, songs, art, and lore. This new edition includes 40 pages of additional material from the 1998 Charles H. Kerr edition from Fred Thompson and Franklin Rosemont, and a new preface by Wobbly organizer Daniel Gross.

Labor's Civil War in California

The NUHW Healthcare Workers' Rebellion

Cal Winslow

$14.00 • ISBN: 978-1-60486-327-7

This book examines one of the most important labor conflicts in the United States today. In 2006 and 2007, disputes developed concerning the practice and direction of the 150,000 member healthcare workers union in California, United Healthcare Workers-West (UHW), with its "parent" organization, the Service Employees International Union (SEIU).

SEIU is the second largest union in the U.S., the fastest growing in recent years. It is a well-organized, well-financed organization, with an ambitious agenda. SEIU perspectives, while packaged as progressive, reject traditional union traditions and practices—union democracy and the idea of "class struggle" are replaced with class collaboration, and the union frequently "wheels and deals" directly with top management and politicians. In 2007 UHW rejected these perspectives and contested them within the union.

The SEIU international leadership retaliated by placing UHW in trusteeship, firing its officers, seizing its assets, and taking control of all union's activities. UHW leaders and members responded by forming a new union, the National Union of Healthcare Workers (NUHW) and challenging the SEIU in virtually every unionized site in the state.

This California conflict is no local brawl; it is not about personalities, it is not about West Coast eccentricities. Its significance is not confined to the fortunes of just one particular union. The truth is that labor has always been divided, comprised of many currents. These are sharply on display today in this dispute—the one authoritarian, top-down, collaborationist, the other bottom-up, rank-and-file, class conscious.

> "The civil war inside the SEIU is a tragic story, yet as Cal Winslow emphasizes in this urgent and dramatic account, it may contain the seeds of authentic renewal in the American labor movement."
> —Mike Davis, author of *City of Quartz*

Anarchist Seeds beneath the Snow

Left-Libertarian Thought and British Writers from William Morris to Colin Ward

David Goodway

$24.95 • ISBN: 978-1-60486-221-8

From William Morris to Oscar Wilde to George Orwell, left-libertarian thought has long been an important but neglected part of British cultural and political history. In *Anarchist Seeds beneath the Snow*, David Goodway seeks to recover and revitalize that indigenous anarchist tradition. This book succeeds as simultaneously a cultural history of left-libertarian thought in Britain and a demonstration of the applicability of that history to current politics. Goodway argues that a recovered anarchist tradition could—and should—be a touchstone for contemporary political radicals. Moving seamlessly from Aldous Huxley and Colin Ward to the war in Iraq, this challenging volume will energize leftist movements throughout the world.

"Goodway outlines with admirable clarity the many variations in anarchist thought. By extending outwards to left-libertarians he takes on even greater diversity."
—Sheila Rowbotham, *Red Pepper*

"A splendid survey of 'left-libertarian thought' in this country, it has given me hours of delight and interest. Though it is very learned, it isn't dry. Goodway's friends in the awkward squad (especially William Blake) are both stimulating and comforting companions in today's political climate."
—A.N. Wilson, *Daily Telegraph*

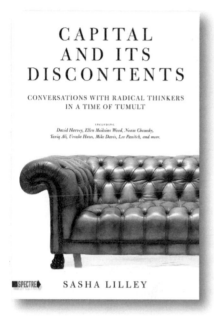

Capital and Its Discontents

Conversations with Radical
Thinkers in a Time of Tumult

Edited by Sasha Lilley
$20.00 • ISBN: 978-1-60486-334-5

Capitalism is stumbling, empire is falter-
ing, and the planet is thawing. Yet many
people are still grasping to understand
these multiple crises and to find a way
forward to a just future. Into the breach
come the essential insights of *Capital and
Its Discontents*, which cut through the
gristle to get to the heart of the matter
about the nature of capitalism and impe-
rialism, capitalism's vulnerabilities at this conjuncture—and what can we do to
hasten its demise.

Through a series of incisive conversations with some of the most eminent thinkers
and political economists on the Left—including David Harvey, Ellen Meiksins
Wood, Mike Davis, Leo Panitch, Tariq Ali, and Noam Chomsky—*Capital and Its
Discontents* illuminates the dynamic contradictions undergirding capitalism and
the potential for its dethroning. The book challenges conventional wisdom on
the Left about the nature of globalization, neoliberalism and imperialism, as well
as the agrarian question in the Global South. It probes deeply into the roots of
the global economic meltdown, the role of debt and privatization in dampening
social revolt, and considers capitalism's dynamic ability to find ever new sources
of accumulation—whether through imperial or ecological plunder or the commodification of previously unpaid female labor.

The Left luminaries in *Capital and Its Discontents* look at potential avenues out
of the mess—as well as wrong turns and needless detours—drawing lessons from
the history of post-colonial states in the Global South, struggles against imperialism past and present, the eternal pendulum swing of radicalism, the corrosive
legacy of postmodernism, and the potentialities of the radical humanist tradition.
At a moment when capitalism as a system is more reviled than ever, here is an
indispensable toolbox of ideas for action by some of the most brilliant thinkers
of our times.